PRINCE: THE MAKING O
PHENOMEN

Prince: The Making of a Pop Music Phenomenon

STAN HAWKINS
University of Oslo, Norway
and
SARAH NIBLOCK
Brunel University, UK

ASHGATE

© Stan Hawkins and Sarah Niblock 2011

All rights reserved. No part of this publication may be reproduced, stored in a retrieval system or transmitted in any form or by any means, electronic, mechanical, photocopying, recording or otherwise without the prior permission of the publisher.

Stan Hawkins and Sarah Niblock have asserted their right under the Copyright, Designs and Patents Act, 1988, to be identified as the authors of this work.

Published by
Ashgate Publishing Limited
Wey Court East
Union Road
Farnham
Surrey, GU9 7PT
England

Ashgate Publishing Company
110 Cherry Street
Suite 3-1
Burlington, VT 05401-3818
USA

www.ashgate.com

British Library Cataloguing in Publication Data
Hawkins, Stan. Prince : the making of a pop music phenomenon. – (Ashgate popular and folk music series)
  1. Prince – Criticism and interpretation. 2. Popular music – Social aspects.
  I. Title II. Series III. Niblock, Sarah.
  782.4'2166'092–dc22

Library of Congress Cataloging-in-Publication Data
Hawkins, Stan.
  Prince : the making of a pop music phenomenon / Stan Hawkins and Sarah Niblock.
     p. cm. – (Ashgate popular and folk music series)
  Includes bibliographical references and index.
  ISBN 978-0-7546-6876-3 (hardcover : alk. paper) – ISBN 978-1-4094-3439-9 (ebook) 1. Prince – Criticism and interpretation. 2. Rock music – United States – History and criticism. I. Niblock, Sarah. II. Title.
  ML420.P974H39 2011
  781.66092–dc22
                                                                              2011014193

ISBN 9780754668763 (hbk)
ISBB 9781472413284 (pbk)
ISBN 9781409434399 (ebk – PDF)
ISBN 9781409494799 (ebk – ePUB)

Bach musicological font developed by © Yo Tomita.

MIX
Paper from responsible sources
FSC® C013985

Printed in the United Kingdom by Henry Ling Limited, at the Dorset Press, Dorchester, DT1 1HD

Contents

List of Music Examples   *vii*
General Editor's Preface   *ix*
Preface   *xi*

Introduction   1

1   The Making of the Authentic Pop Icon   15

2   Inscriptions of Otherness: Dandyism, Style and Queer Sensibility   35

3   A God of Earthly Pleasures   55

4   Voicing the Erotic and the Sublime   75

5   'Take Me with U, Prince': Female Identifications with a Male Pop Icon   95

6   The Princian Sonic Universe: Matters of Compositional and Performative Proficiency   123

7   The Live Experience: Performance and Performativity at the O2 Arena   151

Selected Discography/Filmography   *175*
Bibliography   *179*
Index   *189*

List of Music Examples

4.1	Speech forms in musical dialogue in 'Purple Rain' (Prince and The Revolution, 'Purple Rain', *Purple Rain*, Warner, 1984)	79
4.2	The melodic hook of 'Purple Rain' (Prince and The Revolution, 'Purple Rain', *Purple Rain*, Warner, 1984)	80
4.3	Main riff in section B of 'Raspberry Beret' (Prince and The Revolution, 'Raspberry Beret', *Around the World in a Day*, Paisley Park, 1985)	84
4.4	Groove from 'When Doves Cry' (Prince and The Revolution, 'When Doves Cry', *Purple Rain*, Warner, 1984)	88
4.5	Four-chord synth riff in '1999' (Prince, '1999', *1999*, Warner, 1982)	91
4.6	'Party' in '1999' (Prince, '1999', *1999*, Warner, 1982)	92
6.1	Bass line from 'Tramp' (Otis Redding and Carla Thomas, 'Tramp', *The Dock of the Bay*, Rhino Stax/Atlantic Records, 1967)	135
6.2	'7' – 'and we will watch them fall' (Prince and the New Power Generation, '7', the *Love Symbol* album, Paisley Park/Warner, 1992)	135
6.3	Lyrical articulation in '7' (Prince and the New Power Generation, '7', the *Love Symbol* album, Paisley Park/Warner, 1992)	140
6.4	Bass riffs from *Planet Earth* (Prince, 'Planet Earth', 'Guitar', 'Somewhere Here on Earth', 'All the Midnights in the World', 'Chelsea Rodgers', 'Lions of Judah', Planet Earth, NPG/Columbia, 2007)	143
6.5	Selected riffs from *Planet Earth* (Prince, 'Planet Earth', 'Guitar', 'The One U Wanna C', 'Future Baby Mama', 'Mr. Goodnight', 'Resolution', Planet Earth, NPG/Columbia, 2007)	147

General Editor's Preface

The upheaval that occurred in musicology during the last two decades of the twentieth century has created a new urgency for the study of popular music alongside the development of new critical and theoretical models. A relativistic outlook has replaced the universal perspective of modernism (the international ambitions of the 12-note style); the grand narrative of the evolution and dissolution of tonality has been challenged, and emphasis has shifted to cultural context, reception and subject position. Together, these have conspired to eat away at the status of canonical composers and categories of high and low in music. A need has arisen, also, to recognize and address the emergence of crossovers, mixed and new genres, to engage in debates concerning the vexed problem of what constitutes authenticity in music and to offer a critique of musical practice as the product of free, individual expression.

Popular musicology is now a vital and exciting area of scholarship, and the *Ashgate Popular and Folk Music Series* presents some of the best research in the field. Authors are concerned with locating musical practices, values and meanings in cultural context, and draw upon methodologies and theories developed in cultural studies, semiotics, poststructuralism, psychology and sociology. The series focuses on popular musics of the twentieth and twenty-first centuries. It is designed to embrace the world's popular musics from Acid Jazz to Zydeco, whether high tech or low tech, commercial or non-commercial, contemporary or traditional.

Professor Derek B. Scott
Professor of Critical Musicology
University of Leeds

Preface

It was about 30 years ago that we first caught a glimpse of an unconventional 19-year-old from Minneapolis making his premier TV appearance on *American Bandstand* before he shot to stardom. His name was Prince Rogers Nelson. There is no telling whether at the time we could possibly have predicted his rise to the heights of pop stardom. However, looking back we now see that it is Prince who epitomized the pop star of the 1980s, an era that both of us recall with regard to our own identities as formative and influential.

The suggestion to write this book jointly came from Ashgate after one of us approached the publisher with their PhD thesis. We arranged to meet at the O2 Arena on the thirteenth night of Prince's marathon *21 Nights in London* concert engagement. Almost instantly, albeit with some trepidation, we made the decision to collaborate on this book, which has taken three years to complete. Our respective backgrounds in popular culture and music would seem on the surface vastly different. Yet, as the book unfolded we discovered more and more the commonalities, intersections and overlaps that reflect a general trend in the Humanities towards interdisciplinary work. Moreover, Prince is a star at the nexus of myriad forces and representations, who demands and truly deserves a rich, multidisciplinary analysis.

Inevitably, a book on Prince can be organized in countless ways, and in this book we have chosen a reflexive marriage of media and journalism studies, psychoanalysis and cultural studies to music sociology, music analysis and musicology. And we have set about asking many questions in different ways. Why does Prince move us? What happens when his music touches us? How do we interpret countless biographical details alongside his stupendous productions?

Prince's identity is not without its difficulties, and the reader will note we have grappled with many interpretations. In the main, our method is interpretive, whereby the interplay of our two voices draws the phenomenon of Prince through a system of references that shed light on the history of pop subjectivity. The common denominator is thus subjectivity in the form of Prince's agency, his performativity and his propensity towards a sonic universe that we have described as Princian. Our critique of Prince unavoidably entails aspects of musical reception that follow different courses. Clearly, the task of interpreting the music of a famous artist circles around the issue of content. The song, the film or the video is never fixed and the theoretical challenges of making sense of a performer semantically will always raise concerns and frustrations. The result of this affirms the ambiguity that is inherent in any reading of a score, a recording, a mix or a visual act. So, our interpretation of Prince is instigated with great humility as we are aware of the magnitude of this subject and person, as much as the limits of description and metaphoric writing in academia.

Gratitude goes to our respective universities and departments, Brunel University, School of Arts, and the University of Oslo, Department of Musicology and all the support we received in terms of research funding, as well as support from colleagues, students and friends. Special thanks are due to Per Elias Drabløs, Susan McClary, Anne Danielsen, Erik Steinskog, Eirik Askerøi, Marita Buanes, Eystein Sandvik, Nigel Everitt, Matt Thorne, Barry Curtis, Kenny Jones and Anne Lucas at the O2. Sarah Niblock wishes to offer particular thanks to Professor Jonathan Rutherford for inspiring and steering her PhD, which set the foundation for this book.

Stan Hawkins and Sarah Niblock

Introduction

Thirty years on in the entertainment business, Prince would produce his second book, *21 Nights*, released almost a year after a sell out stint at the O2 Arena in London. Documenting scenes from the performances, the glossy photo shots also included personal memoirs taken between 2am and 8am each morning. Never before had an artist played 21 sell out concerts to a stadium housing 16,000 spectators; the engagement earned 2007's highest grossing concert revenue. By the time *21 Nights* was published, Prince had turned 50 and held a position as one of the United States' all-time pop legends. Attending the concerts, we were enthralled and decided to write this book jointly, with no regrets.

The London event was a major landmark in Prince's career, offering a stimulus for all his fans to pause and reflect on an artist who has affected our generation in unprecedented ways. At this point in time one of us had written a PhD thesis on Prince, while the other had published numerous articles and a book that dealt in part with his music, identity and style. Curiously, though, we would note that he had been afforded little scholarly attention.[1] Why?

Our purpose in undertaking this study jointly attempts to address this question as we consider the multi-disciplinary perspectives that situate such an extraordinary performer within a rich social setting. From the outset, our task has been to provide an approach that opens up for new avenues in the understanding of Prince's subjectivity, our prime objective being to contextualize him within a socio-cultural framework. We are also keen to provide new insights into his music and performance tactics. It should be stated that our combined scholarly backgrounds in media studies, sociology, musicology, gender studies, psychoanalysis and journalism make this book unique. From the outset it is worth stating that our underlying intentions are to attempt a critical interpretation of the makings of the Prince phenomenon, and, by so doing, to highlight his artistic output as a signifying practice of major historical contingency. It stands to reason that the numerous lines of argument taken up in this book are advanced by the following premise: that the visual and audio imagery of Prince offers a rich space for probing at what makes pop music fun and entertaining. As one of the most enigmatic pop icons of all time, Prince entices us into a sonic universe where his sound, styles, ideals and performance antics fashion a subjectivity that becomes a major point of fascination. Brimming with paradoxes and contradictions, Prince epitomizes the postmodern pop icon – it is his own awareness of his very construction that makes him such a compelling subject.

---

[1] See Suzanne Moore (1988), Dave Hill (1989), Stan Hawkins (1992a, 1992b, 2002), Robert Walser (1994), Ellis Cashmore (1997), Anne Danielsen (1998), Susan McClary (2000), Sarah Niblock (2005), James E. Perone (2008).

Drawing on the interdisciplinary field of popular music studies, the focus of this book falls on the persona of a major pop star. We are acutely aware that the field cries out for more work on individual pop artists and close readings of their work that is critically informed with respect to style, music and performance.[2] In order to address this we endeavour to excavate the circumstances that go into the making of a performer of such astonishing proportions. Through a range of categories, we consider performance alongside subjectivity, and probe at how this converges and diverges according to the concepts we promote through the seven chapters. The benefits of co-authoring a book lie in collaborative work that is informed by our vastly different scholarly backgrounds, which have been useful in forming our discussions of the Prince experience. Our respective positions have enabled us to pursue the features that characterize Prince in terms of ethnicity, sexuality, social class and gender. That Prince assumes a unique gender role all through his career constitutes a central discursive position that can be best described as all-defining. One might say his look and sound is the result of a forceful conviction: 'I am a performer as the musical, religious, and cultural forces have created me.' Pathologically, the creative *Vorstellungen* Prince exhibits musically are instated by his fans' devotion. As we have noted during the writing of this book, his performativity suggests the multiple self-fashioning of the pop star.

Right from the start it should be stressed that we do not read Prince's self-fashioning merely in queer terms either. Dynamic, creative and self-styling, he is far from being the same postmodern queer stylist as other pop artists. We find substance and consistency to Prince's oeuvre, both musical and visual, that points to the possibility of continuous identification with the star. This is not so much in spite of the changing contextual backdrop for his fans, but actually because of it. When all around has been undergoing transition and transformation, Prince has remained a familiar, constant and reassuring icon.

Inextricably, the pop sensibility is interwoven into biography. When it comes to Prince's subjectivity, technology has not only affected how he sounds, but also who and what he is. Due to technology, as Simon Frith has argued, 'we now hear music in much more detail than ever before' (Frith 1996, p. 240). Developments in music production have meant that the pop artist can approach the fan through the intimacy of the personality, which is shaped by the countless details of the recording process. In this sense, the editing, amplification and other sonic devices that go into production have created new ways of reception. One might say that the recording studio is not merely the musician's *atelier*, but moreover the site for creating the persona. Obviously, this leads to questions of authorship – undoubtedly complex ones – which cannot be reduced to simple or generalized explanations. What lies behind any pop production is a team of experts: the composer, the producer, the mixer, the engineer and the musicians. By and large, what makes Prince matchless

---

[2] See Hawkins (2011) for an extensive debate that accounts for this lack of research within pop music analysis.

is that he is all of these, and this point alone speaks volumes when it comes to understanding how his subjectivity is immersed in the mix.

We are eager to underline that this book does not claim to be an all-encompassing overview of Prince's artistic output to date. Such a venture, we feel, would be near impossible. While we are both avid fans, the study does not compile lengthy lists of chronological facts, journalistic anecdotes, and performance stats. Others have carried out such tasks and are still doing this. Furthermore, details on Prince are in abundance through the internet and web-related sites. Our mission rather is to provide a reflexive account of the Prince experience from a number of vantage points, our goal being to map our findings against the matrix of events, circumstances and subjectivities that inevitably arise when dealing with an artist of such prolific standing. Invariably, we return time and again to what makes our subject so profound. Why does Prince open up a special space for reconfiguring norms and attitudes? And, how might one access a pop artist who transforms sound into such a rich emotional tapestry? The Prince experience, we argue, is about a host of pleasures, a prerequisite for us working out our own responses and desires, albeit in largely diverse ways. That his music can be encountered in countless different ways is a fascinating point alone, and something we acknowledge throughout the book when we take on board the social, political and cultural circumstances surrounding his act. Aesthetics also come into our readings, as Prince escorts us into the emotional domain of recorded sound, where the fans become immersed in its affective charge. The musical side of pop provides us with the means to gain close proximity to an array of feelings, whose source emanates from the performing artist. A critical challenge, then, is to discover how musical expression is felt as something poignant and real. Prince's songs expose the emotional conditions of our everyday lives, and the charge of his songs comes from a sensibility that is wrapped up in self-parody and irony. Clearly, Prince's humour cannot be overlooked. Humour forms a vital part of his subjectivity, located in his cultural voicing, his sexual politics, his music and, of course, his lyrics. His performances designate an element of humility made pleasurable through the ingenuity of his songs and performances. A major constituent here is the ironic disposition that Prince has mastered from the start of his career. This can be linked to a dandified masculinity – arguably, a symbolic assault on conventional thinking – that is integral to his musical expressiveness, whose basis is provocative at the same time as it is entertaining (see Niblock 2005, Hawkins 2009a). Delivered through a high dose of audio virtuosity and visual lavishness, then, his dandification offers up an intimate space for accessing and thrilling his fans. Ultimately, the Princian effect resonates through a finely tuned balance of musical ideas that are socially, politically and culturally coded.

Fathoming out what makes Prince's music commercially successful certainly raises issues of canonization, and throughout this study we ponder over why certain songs and albums are ranked over others. By whom are canons inscribed and for what purpose? At this stage a few words are necessary on the role of musical criticism and qualitative valuation by the media. Undoubtedly, deciding on which songs one delves into in a book on such a prolific songwriter is a tricky process, mainly because of the influences of reception, taste and popularity. Studies of what determines an international hit, and, not least the implicit assumptions that surround its qualitative rating, are surprisingly undeveloped in popular music studies. This gives rise to concerns of the dismissal of a bulk of Prince's music that has not gained sufficient adulation by music critics. Our position, plainly put, is that the ratings of the 'big hit' or 'best hit' should not overshadow the non-hit nor, for that matter, exclude it from the broader picture. Although many of his most popular recordings form part of our debates, the reader will note that our inclusion of some songs might not be that familiar or necessarily considered his best. Our decision along these lines of selection alone underpins a host of issues relating to genre and style in the context of live and recorded performance. The task of critical evaluation, we insist, is relevant to an understanding of Prince's musicianship, his 'musicking', his creative performance style; thus, to do him any justice we have had to trawl through a wide range of texts regardless of commercial success. That said, we are wary of the sets of values that institutionalize pop music, especially when it comes to the artists never written about in textbooks or discussed in university courses. Musicologists of pop music might learn a lesson or two from the canonization of artists and works in jazz, which has been largely constructed by jazz historians. In Gary Tomlinson's view, emphasizing the 'musical appreciation of jazz' has only transferred to 'African-American music the formalist view that remains debilitatingly dominant in Eurocentric musicology', where the weight falls on 'internalist music analysis' (Tomlinson 1992, p. 131). As a result, elevating the 'music itself' is always in danger of overlooking the 'complex dialogues of self and other in which culture is created' (ibid.). Historically, the negative judgments of specific jazz styles by Eurocentric musicologists have circumvented the blackness of jazz, a case in point being Miles Davis's jazz-rock fusion style from the late 1960s to the early 1970s. As with Davis, Prince is regularly condemned for a diluted style that invokes elements of fusion. Frequently, this assertion intersects with a critique of the transgressive aspect of his expression as something commercially superficial (like his look). As with Davis, Prince's musicality is not necessarily picked up or made worth arguing for. Curiosity in an artist, however, should entail a more important drive than just mastery, and, as we intend to demonstrate all the way through this study, the conditions of Prince's musicality are no straightforward matter.

Broadly speaking, musicianship is defined by performing, song writing, dance, acting, and dramatized rituals. Since the 1970s Prince's musicianship has been a result of the sheer brilliance of his theatricality and technical dexterity, with him mediating ideas that are decidedly individualistic. Unavoidably, his ethnicity, gender and musical heritage is crucial to this aspect, and it is an African American discourse that constitutes a major part of his approach to performance and composition. Portia Maultsby has pointed out that the funk songs of the 1980s had 'a different universal message' and managed to bring 'people of different races and background together around a common cause – to celebrate!' (Maultsby 2009, p.

277). Maultsby suggests that much of this was attributable to the new technologies that popularized disco and subsequently transformed musical trends in funk bands. Notably, the fusion of funk, R&B, rock, pop and new wave, pioneered by Prince in the late 1970s, established a distinct hybrid style in the 1980s. Referred to as the Minneapolis Sound, his style was characterized by highly processed drum tracks with less bass than in traditional funk. Dominated by keyboards and rhythm guitar parts, with brash synthesizers substituting for the horn section, the Minneapolis Sound comprised a rhythmic underlay that was less syncopated than funk and clearly influenced by new wave. Of all his albums, *Dirty Mind*, released in 1980, best encapsulates the Minneapolis Sound; in many ways it was the precursor of the twists and turns in pop during the next three decades. In the context of the 1980s, the Minneapolis Sound was Prince's musical signature. Characterizing something original right from the beginning of his career, it was distinguishable by the tightness of rhythmic layers, well-crafted arrangements, and path-breaking studio productions. The Minneapolis Sound was also conjoined to image, rhetoric and attitude, making Prince the unique pop celebrity he is today. Thus, the relevance of his sonic and visual branding is at the core of all of the discussions relating to his output from the late twentieth century up to the present day.

Derek Scott has observed the significance of the shift from the discourse on 'cultural imperialism' at the start of the twenty-first century, where emphasis is now placed on the local and the global. Notwithstanding the move towards a model of transculturation (that deals with new perspectives on consumption), Scott maintains that there are still limits imposed on the listener and consumer 'by the power of the producer – even in such basic matters as what the producer chooses to make available to the listener' (Scott 2009, p. 13). Bearing this in mind, we consider the impact of MTV in 1981, the power structures of the recording industry and, moreover, the 'producers' behind musical performers. On a scale never witnessed before, Prince and Michael Jackson would become the first two MTV African American artists to be beamed across the planet, accessing a hungry, predominantly white market. For both artists, the complex surfaces of the music industry would shape their style and performance over a number of decades. Undoubtedly, the marketable African American body is a problematic site for exploring many of these issues. Our study therefore addresses the aspect of agency and reception especially through ethnicity and gender. As we argue, Prince's contours of gender representation are a key factor when understanding his appeal. For this reason alone, his fan base has always seemed select, with plenty of evidence of the cut-off points for others not liking Prince. Delving into questions of popularity, we have chosen to prioritize the role of the female fan alongside a consideration of Prince's practices of signifying: clothing, make-up, hair, accessories and gestures. Historically, Prince's imagery has collided with mainstream masculine representations as he has gone about subverting gender norms. In other words, it would be a gross understatement to say he went against the flow of conventional masculine representation in the late twentieth century. Our analyses of selected scenes from his films in the 1980s bear this out as we attempt to piece together his complex iconography and, above all, his negotiation of the feminine through the masculine. This, in turn, directs us to the antics of queering, an integral element of Prince's vocal and visual aesthetic, which intensifies his performance and profoundly affects his gendered representation.

One of the advantages of studying pop music lies in the overlapping paradigms of work undertaken in ethnicity, gender and sexuality, which attach music analysis and musicological inquiry to the broader field of popular music studies. Popular musicology, a bourgeoning new field of study, has its strongest affiliations in sociology, psychoanalysis, cultural and media studies.[3] With its terminological first usage as recent as 1994, 'popular musicology' acknowledges the centrality of the recording within compositional practice, with a wealth of techniques and musical elements impinging on the interpretation. A major portion of our study of Prince is therefore guided by an interdisciplinary approach to music research, as we investigate his work's compositional and production properties. One of the principal aims of our approach is to uncover musical elements in the pop recording that reveal not only the phenomenon of his style, but also his performance practice. We have therefore decided to focus on the details of Prince's productions as a gateway to his creative thinking. This brings us to his most distinctive quality, namely his 'produced voice'. How he stages his voice in the mix has to do with an acute understanding of the evocative power of singing. Accordingly, he pays meticulous attention to vocal features and types that have their corollary in his imagery. Certainly, interpreting such a stylized use of vocality is not without its musicological challenges. For instance, vocal style relates to the technical control of the parameters found in the recording studio, which raises the issue of the artist's positioning of himself within a creative audio landscape. Part of our music analytic method, then, is to approach the intrinsic workings behind the sound structures while considering what constitutes the idealized pop sound. Indisputably, the audio recording, and its related production techniques, constitutes a decisive part of the transference of ideas from the studio to the live performance context. For us, this is probably the most salient point when considering how songs are realized. That Prince's musical ideas are first conceived in the studio suggests that the recording itself is the basis for the live performance; and, of course, the recording always constitutes the 'pop score'.[4] In other words, the recording is the manuscript for exploring the compositional and performance activities that underpin the musical creativity; for it is the synthesis of innumerable musical ideas and the act of music making within the recording studio environment that accounts for the success of Prince's song-writing strategies. In effect, Prince's sonic universe is the result of designing, engineering and processing audio signals in a simulated spatial context.

---

[3] For a detailed discussion of 'popular musicology' and its historic alignment to theoretical models and analytical tools, see Derek Scott (ed.) (2009).

[4] For a definition of the 'pop score', see Hawkins (2002), and an analysis of a range of case studies, which include Prince, Madonna, Morrissey, Annie Lennox and the Pet Shop Boys.

The simulated recording, then, makes possible the organizational properties that go into the Princian signature.

With this we inevitably land at Paisley Park. Designed by the architect firm BOTO Design, Paisley Park's state-of-the-art studio and sound-stage complex in Chanhassen, Minnesota, was completed for Prince in 1988. Covering more than 5,000 square metres, the studio derives its name from Prince's record label, Paisley Park Records, launched in 1985. This was the same year the track 'Paisley Park', from the album *Around the World in a Day*, became a hit. The label would fold in 1994, following Prince's feud with Warner, and his decision to end their distribution deal. Prince would however maintain all the masters that had been recorded under the Paisley Park label, as well as the artists' advances, which were held by the company. Although Warner partially financed the studio, much of the investment came from Prince, and Paisley Park remained his home. Paisley Park would thus continue to play a major role in Prince's musical output, as well as that of the numerous artists who had recorded there, such as George Clinton, The Time, Sheila E., Madhouse, Carmen Electra, Mavis Staples, Taja Sevelle and many others.

As we have already asserted, Prince's music owes much to the technological developments of music production over a period of 30 years. One might say his pop aesthetic chronicles decades of innovation in the technology of sound recording. To return to a previous point, Prince's identity is determined by the very technology with which he realizes his musical ideas. So, behind the production of every one of his tracks is a process that underpins the organizational procedures of a musical idea. Consider the preproduction phase of planning, performing and arranging the idea, choosing people one wishes to work with, and then making technological decisions before the performance takes place. During a track's creation, which culminates in the final recording, countless routines, psychological struggles and alterations are part and parcel of the recording. This would imply that any analysis of a track demands a full awareness of the creative processes that mould the aesthetic object into a recording. Forming a central part of our analytic focus in this book, then, it is the recording that informs the methodological objectives: how does recording technology capture the activities of a performance, how is music technology employed to enhance sonic ideas by adding colour and sculpting design, and what techniques and new configurations does Prince turn to that are pioneering in terms of composition and performance? All in all, his creative approach to optimizing his sound through music technology is central to considering his subjectivity. As such, this forms the backdrop to all our debates on his musical ingenuity.

Conceptualizing pop is based upon music in recorded form. Music exists in the form of a 'simulated performance', its sonic design a direct result of recording techniques. Audio production, after all, is a normal part of creativity in pop, forming a crucial step in the process of interpreting Prince's work. Peter Wicke aptly points out that the 'history of music in the twentieth century was, indeed, written in equal measure by musicians and audio technicians' (Wicke 2009, p. 150). The rich array of possibilities that studio technology offers up, however, not only caters for musicians, technicians and songwriters, but also for listeners and fans. As Wicke maintains, the aim of the recording right from its initial conception was 'to offer within the four walls of the home, a listening experience of a live musical performance' that substituted for 'being present at the actual event' (ibid., p. 151). Significantly, though, acknowledging the very restrictions of audio technology – the impossibility of capturing the acoustic reality of an event – led to a new aesthetic paradigm, where emulating a performance also introduced the virtual performance. By this, the imaginary landscape of the recorded performance gradually offered a new way into inscribing the identity of the musician. The perspectives we offer on Prince's music are therefore intended to provide debates around the musician's role within the studio context as we consider technology's critical dimension in musical reception.

Prince's use of technology as a creative tool is closely linked to his performance practice, a deceptively obvious point. Take his love for improvisation and how this dominates the recording as much as the live context. The jam session, we know, has played a significant role in the way Prince works out his material, forming an integral part of his arrangements and recordings. Jamming is a spontaneous act and comes about through an agreed riff, a bass line, a catchy hook, a chord progression, drum part or even vocal lick. In jamming ideas are teased out. Prince goes for 'tightness' and control when jamming, and it is this element that accommodates his improvisatory flair. Consider the song, 'Jam of the Year', from the *Emancipation* album, a quintessential example of Prince's jam style. Hinting at something free and spontaneous it is at the same time rigidly controlled with humour-like zest. In this track, his setting up of an R&B hook, peppered with jazz-funk, conjures up a feel that is cool, in-control and nonchalant. This type of hook ignites countless jam sessions and (in)directly leads to the final mix.

As we have declared so far, the link between music and subjectivity is one of our major preoccupations. Our challenge, to reiterate, is to trace the ways in which music mediates the ideological, social and generic forces of an original personality. We recognize, though, that conceiving the relationships between subjectivity and music is not without its difficulties, as exemplified in the arduous task of attempting to unravel the many signifiers that configure Prince. Close attention is thus paid to the shifts in his representation over the years. One might say that Prince's albums would be less convincing did they not represent a picture that has expanded over 30 years. And, indeed, Prince's story is a convoluted one. We ask then: how do Prince's tracks, albums, videos and films epitomize postmodern pop, and in what ways do they engage his fans on countless levels? Attempts to answer this are located in our reflections throughout.

Prince's act presents a piquant source of curiosity, disclosed by a finely balanced personality that is playfully indulgent. His flaunting of himself, as we read it, is a disruption of the conventional codes of gender, race, sexuality and more. Obvious contradictions and paradoxes arise from such fluid representations. At any rate, the liberating quality of his style recurs in an array of guises, and alongside each look he fashions comes a fractious subjectivity. One central focal point of this study, then, is musical performance and the construction of representations of difference.

We are interested in what ways Prince avoids restrictive categorization. Certainly, the phenomenon of his construction has its locus in an audiovisual presentation that is manifested through videos, live concerts, interviews and documentaries. Intuitively, Prince has grasped what it is to be a pop star; he has seized on the multi-faceted dimension of entertainment and sustained this over a relatively long period of time. Consider the role of ethnicity. As African American, with multi-race heritage and light skin, at least for some critics, denotes a reduction in 'blackness'. And, in the early years of MTV, it is significant that both Michael Jackson and Prince entered this white domain in a manner that catered for an industry hostile towards non-white performers. Conditions for the effacement of blackness are prevalent in pop music, with it taking decades for black artists to gain access into mainstream pop on an equal footing with whites. Our study therefore notes the subtle intersections of ethnicity, social circumstance and commercial gain as we interpret the black artist's position in mainstream pop historically. More than any other black male star to achieve megastar status, Prince has shirked categorization according to ethnicity, gender and sexuality. Like Malcolm X, Prince has embodied a rejection of being pigeonholed, arguably a mechanism of liberation from the chains of white patriarchy. In fact, he is one of the few black pop artists who has dared speak the truth about masculinity and the politics of essentialization. And this he has done by articulating his look as much as his music. Such self-acceptance leads to a consideration of what it is to be 'cool'. In her visionary study of black masculinity, with specific references to hip-hop artists, bell hooks addresses the coolness of being black:

> Even though popular culture has made the black male body and presence stand for the apex of 'cool,' it is a death-dealing coolness, not one that is life-enhancing, for black males or the folks they associate with. Young males embrace a notion of cool that is about getting pussy and getting ready to kill (or a [sic] least to make somebody think you can kill) because as an identity this one is easier to come by than the quest to know the self and to create a life of meaning. (hooks 2004, p. 155)

From the outset, Prince has been aware that patriarchy destroys black males, and there is little doubt that the ambiguity surrounding his construction provides a potent source for reflecting critically on the embattled and endangered male subject. Significantly, his roots are in the black church with a backdrop of gospel and rhythm and blues. Moreover, his music emanates from the political and religious context of the church, its secularized function connecting communities in struggle.[5]

---

[5] See Neal (1999, chapter 3) for a thorough discussion of the commodifying struggle through black power, civil rights and musical hegemony. Neal highlights the political sensibilities of ideological pursuit that were incorporated into the civil rights movement that reflected the music praxis of African Americans.

Inscribing his body into his musical style, Prince has marketed himself as enormously attractive for some while hugely repulsive for others. This is because his representation is no straightforward matter; the hallmarks of his size, race, sexuality and gender signify a vicarious subversion of norms. The body and its overt engagement of sexuality is a crucial element in pop music, functioning metonymically in its political charge. Particularly in the 1980s Prince's performances, through which he subverted presumptions of gender fixity through displays of ambiguous sexuality, shocked the world. And from the beginning his sound would reinforce his transgressive image. In particular, his voice contributes to an unprecedented display of masculinity. By taking such issues into account, our study assesses vocalization as gendered along many lines in a post-1970s socio-cultural sphere.

It is our firm conviction that Prince is the ideal prototype of pop music, and all seven chapters of this book testify to this phenomenon. In Chapter 1 our aim is to provide an account of Prince's most abiding characteristics, arguing the reasons why he makes such an insightful case study. Considering the rise of the pop icon in the late 1970s and 1980s prompts questions dealing with the enigma of Prince's wide appeal and how this is mapped against his musical originality, as we unravel key aspects of behaviour, attitude and representation. Through a comprehensive consideration of his 'branding' and indefatigable collaboration with musicians, bands, producers and engineers on so many different projects, we attempt to trace the emergence of a style that is constructed around image, sound and cultural rhetoric. Certainly, issues of authenticity arise when identifying the structures of power and control in the music industry. We know that the packaging and commodifying processes that establish an international pop artist such as Prince are complicated. This is borne out by the complex relationship he has had to the record industry, especially in the mid 1990s. Not only did Prince expose and disempower his own record label, but he also sought new ways of mediation through the internet (and his own website), a move that was at least one decade ahead of its time. We feel compelled to remind the reader that Prince was a pioneer in the new era of downloading music, an era that ushered in a set of problems for the music industry that at the time of writing still have not been resolved. Another related issue in Chapter 1 concerns Prince's relationship to his fans. His extraordinarily close rapport offers a very special space for all forms of identification, which helps account for his appeal. By excavating the meanings inherent in his visual, lyrical and musical signification, we consider how these intersect with one another socially and historically. An interdisciplinary approach runs through all the chapters that helps us conceptualize notions of uniqueness, (in)authenticity, originality and the 'sublime'. Thus, opening up a wealth of intertexts, we contemplate 'the making of the Prince phenomenon' within the buoyant field of popular music studies, where methods and theory are drawn from musicology, sociology, psychoanalysis, media and cultural studies, and gender theory.

In Chapter 2, we make a case for 'otherness' in its variety of forms as we set out to exam Prince's unique brand of masculinity and how this contributes to a pop aesthetic that was a precursor to MTV. The matter of a dandified sensibility is centralized in this discussion as we draw on a number of theoretical positions we have both addressed, albeit from different perspectives, in our earlier studies.[6] Prince's emergence as a pop dandy is contextualized through his music and iconography as we turn to his individual style, taking into consideration his ethnic, geographical and cultural influences, particularly in his early life. In this part of our study, we argue that a troubled childhood became the impetus for him securing an historic three-album performer/producer deal by the age of 17, and how the first images he used were seen as an assault on public decency and subsequently banned by certain outlets and radio stations. Controversy undoubtedly marked Prince's early career during the time of Reagan's conservative politics, but it was with *Purple Rain*, in 1984, that he succeeded to break into the white mainstream market. Consequently, the socio-political and cultural context of this period had a direct bearing on his later albums and films, forming a backdrop for ambiguity and transgression.

Chapter 3 is a more elaborate account of Prince's sexualized 'branding', this time with specific reference to his faith. By situating Prince in a long line of other faith-infused black and white artists, we seek to discover how he has achieved a synthesis between faith and sexuality all through his career. The 'positivity' of Prince's faith, we argue, is located within a black tradition that underpins his heritage he has in common with artists such as Mavis Staples, Chaka Khan and Larry Graham. Raised in several denominations, such as the Seventh-day Adventists and Baptists, Prince converted to the Jehovah's Witnesses at the beginning of the millennium. We are curious to discover what effect this had on his music.

Prince's voice, we argue, is a sonic signifier of late twentieth-century pop. Why and how? Chapter 4 takes a close look at the voice as a prime determinant of subjectivity, through a consideration of vocal balance and expressivity. While clearly influenced by so many different genres and traditions, his style of singing is rooted in an African American tradition. The central musicological inquiry here is one of theorizing the voice and locating its embodied meaning. This provides a suitable framework for approaching the issue of the 'produced voice' and how this is erotically charged. As a by-product of electronic and digital manipulation, the reproduced voice is implicated within the aesthetics of pop music, and artists such as Prince have had a profound impact on vocal production. In particular, the transition between analogue and digital technology, with the advent of the CD in 1982, and the mp3 revolutionary take over in the 1990s, would have a bearing on how the artist chooses to sound. These historic developments have had ramifications for innovation in recording techniques, such as in the ways of reproducing the voice. The meticulous details involved in mic-ing the voice, in both recordings and live performance, amount to one of the most important channels for creating intimacy in the identification process between Prince and his fans. Above all, how the voice is processed and then staged is what shapes a song's narrative, bringing it alive. Multi-tracking and dubbing have also had a profound effect on the voice,

---

[6] See Niblock (2005) and Hawkins (2009a).

and we consider the techniques of vocal 'drop in', 'riding the fader', compression, sampling and editing as integral processes of production that effect the voice. In turn this raises issues relating to audio presence in music, which ultimately attests to the 'musical experience'. After all, Prince's aesthetic is about studio treatment and the finely regulated airbrushing techniques that go into the final production. As we seek to demonstrate, his voice emerges from an innate sense of performance and song writing that becomes an intimate site for identification.

The identification process in music covers many aspects, and in Chapter 5 our attention shifts to the question of gender and Prince's renowned associations with females, be they fans, collaborators or even his own traits of ambiguous display. Prince's relationships with his female fans are profound. It is also well known that he has worked with numerous female artists, contributing to their success. In this chapter we set out to explore the nature of Prince's complex and often provocative relationship to the 'feminine' – for his visual appearance is generally non-threatening to the female, which raises the matter of the active female gaze. Well aware that this might cast doubt on some of the most abiding accounts of the female spectator when it comes to considering the female as consumer of pop, we make the argument that Prince's female fans respond to his on-screen image as a site of negotiation, a point of access for their own identity. Taking on board numerous theories that deal with female subjectivity, this chapter delves deeper into the work of Melanie Klein, whose emphasis on the power of the mother object has a releasing quality; the aim is to reveal how Prince's younger fans have turned to his on-screen imagery in the formation of their own subjectivity. We ask what messages might young female fans have derived about femininity in a UK context during the mid 1980s, when Prince's first motion picture, *Purple Rain*, was screened. Undoubtedly, the distinctive feature of this film was the emphasis on the pop star as spectacle. How the female spectator is drawn into a diegetic space where Prince's employment of feminine practices (clothes, make-up, shoes, gestures) becomes a major source of contemplation. For their time, the feminine signifiers inherent in Prince's act reversed dominant gender codes, and, as a result, subverted power relations. For those who did not get it, the effect was one of shock, repulsion and condemnation; he went against the grain of the majority of rock artists who denied any possible pleasure or gratification for the female spectator. Selected scenes from *Purple Rain* are used to exemplify this, as we consider the subversion of visual codes and transgressive intent.

The final two chapters deal with questions of proficiency – a main constituent of the Princian sonic universe and the impact of the live experience. Performativity is a common theme linking both chapters, which helps inform our critical approach to evaluating the musician in making. Chapter 6 approaches this through a discussion of musicianship by way of music analysis, where virtuosic endeavour is part and parcel of Prince's instrumental proficiency. Guitar playing, we insist, can be linked to specific historic moments in popular music, and Prince builds upon this tradition in a variety of ways. The influence of Jimi Hendrix's style of guitar playing brings to the fore questions of power and passion alongside masculinity in rock and metal styles. In addition, we consider the acoustic dimension of his studio production in terms of his aesthetics as we turn to questions of technical expertise and Prince's talent in playing a wide range of instruments. In tandem with his instrumental proficiency, we consider the skills invested into the production of his songs, probing at the discursive meanings that arise through musical interpretation. Finally, Chapter 7 concludes with an emphasis on the Prince-in-concert experience, filtered through the production, live spectacle and the visual trickery of videos and films. The setting for this chapter is London's O2 Arena in 2007 during his legendary '21 Nights' residency. We provide a reading of this tumultuous event by drawing together our reflections and experiences of a live event that we attended together. His now well-known mantra that 'real musicians play real music' prompts us to consider why each show was pre-programmed to heighten the impression of live playing. This is an appropriate moment to return to the question of authenticity as we ponder over Prince's self-fashioning as a dazzling array of signifiers. Accordingly, we attempt to synthesize numerous concepts aired in earlier chapters and to revisit questions of subjectivity, attitude, mannerism and musicianship, in a bid to examine how the visual and the audio intersect at the point of reception. In sum, our project with Prince aims to uncover a long-standing fascination with his eccentricity, ambiguity, impudence and, not least, his *laissez-faire* attitude towards those who scorn him.

What we have discovered in this study is that the spectacle of Prince is not as transparent as it might seem; it has to do with shifting layers of address and affinities on many levels. Perhaps it is this that has determined his longevity in the pop branch. Decades after his emergence into the international limelight, Prince's star-studded career seems, as he himself has claimed, like one long soundtrack. Skilfully crafted, meticulously stylized and beautifully executed it tells an intricately charming story of the imaginative forms of human behaviour that occur through the accomplishments of one body in the space of time.

Chapter 1
The Making of the Authentic Pop Icon

> By common consent, Prince Rogers Nelson is one of the few really significant figures in pop music today. He elevates it to a level of intensity and ingenuity that makes the competition look tired and contrived. Nine albums on from his debut in 1978, he has consolidated his position as a leader and innovator who shows no sign of flagging. (Hoskyns 1988, p. 11)

These words were written about Prince back in 1988, in the wake of his phenomenal rise to global stardom, heralded by the hit film and soundtrack album *Purple Rain*. Now, after a career spanning more than four decades, Prince's status has never waned, and he is undoubtedly one of the last enduring auteurs of the pop industry. His '21 Nights' residency at the O2 Arena in London in 2007 ensured the word 'legend' is now inextricably tied to his name in all media references. 'Comeback' has never entered the Princian lexicon. For more than 30 years, Prince has continuously produced copious innovative musical work. Alongside this, he has mastered his own visual iconography to present a charismatic, mysterious and ambiguous pop identity unlike anything or anyone else. To envision Prince's enduring career is to conceive of a dynamic set of shifting signifiers. Yet there is also something constant and grounded in his public persona that enables continual close identification and loyalty on the part of his followers.

Prince has become a worldwide icon, selling millions of albums and performing at countless sell-out concerts since he released his first album as a shy 19-year-old in 1978. In almost every sense he has confronted and contested the appropriate norms of behaviour and representation at the moment of production and reception. As such, interpreting Prince offers a significant challenge to the study of popular music as he defies so many conventions and consensual notions. Commonly, he inspires references to 'genius', a problematic term imbued with elitist approaches to cultural value as much as discourses surrounding authenticity, yet somehow satisfying when applied to a small black man who can so effectively subvert the phallocentricism of Led Zeppelin's 'Whole Lotta Love'. With such enigmas and contradictions at the heart of Prince's inestimable appeal, he is a rich and fascinating subject for consideration.

One of the central terms in popular music studies is 'authenticity', which identifies and defends that which is thought to be 'good', 'great', 'real' and 'original'. It stems from popular notions of value in art and the idealized narratives of late Romanticism. Its binary opposite is 'weak', a term generally directed at anything felt to be 'derivative' or 'fake'. In popular music studies, 'authenticity' has been rigorously problematized and applied often to that which is 'non-commercial' in terms of pure artistry that seeks no accommodation or compromise with commerce or marketing. It doesn't 'sell out'. How then do we as authors attribute the terms 'authentic' and 'original' to a star who has sold millions of albums worldwide, sold out London's O2 arena, inspired rails of fashion in TopShop and given away his albums free with mid-market and tabloid British newspapers?

'Just because I don't like categories, all I can think of is inspirational. Music that comes from the heart falls into that category' (Prince on *Larry King Live*, 10 December 1999). This quote encapsulates a theme at the heart of Prince's work; a defiance of fixity which has undoubtedly secured his longevity as an icon in a fickle cultural context. His very essence is to blur all genres and influences, eliding any singular categorization. This *auteurship* would seem to be the marker of Prince's authenticity as a producer of cultural texts. Being a performer of integrity does not sit comfortably with his role as the figurehead of a massively successful business empire. In the idealized narratives of creative integrity, commercialism is anathema. Though undeniably virtuosic, Prince's musical prowess is not necessarily unique, for he pays overt homage to other artists in his performances and recordings. The authenticity of Prince is located somewhere different, in a place that appropriately evades musicological or cultural studies theorization. This Princian authenticity is situated in the space where the star and his audience interact, which begs us to conceive of popular music and identification in a different way. Prince is, in effect, a set of shifting signifiers of music, ethnicity and gender that permits an active reading of him, opening up many sites of identification and rapport for fans and scholars. In this way, we cannot divorce a musicological analysis of Prince from the context in which his output is produced and received.

Firstly, there is his pioneering acknowledgement of the power of 'branding' – while the star acknowledges his heroes and their direct influence on his remarkable sound, he managed at the outset of his career to create an original signature sound, image and cultural rhetoric that defied comparisons with his contemporaries. This 'brand' will be unpacked and illustrated in relation to Prince and his collaborators including The Time, August Darnell and Ingrid Chavez. It will be shown how many successors have sought to emulate his approach. Characteristic of Prince's authenticity has been his simultaneous acknowledgement and undercutting of consensually agreed practices – be they musical, sexual, gendered, ethnic or faith-based or political.

Secondly, Prince has also been highly provocative in his relation to new technology, seeking to undercut the traditional, industry view of the relationship between producer and consumer. Whilst Prince has been at pains to maintain full control over his output – visual and musical – there is something in his desire to forge a singular, powerful rapport with his audience through live performance and through technology that problematizes the organization of the music industry. In the mid 1990s, Prince sought to expose and remove the record industry from its established position of dominance and exploitation in the production-distribution process. He sought a new mechanism of direct access through his website, whereby communication between the musician and the listener is considered a pure and valuable relationship. He did this at a time when the consumer who downloaded music was considered an enemy of the music industry.

Thirdly, Prince's assault on the music industry coincided with his encouragement of a close rapport with his fans. The combination of his musical virtuosity, visual ambiguity and his rebuttal of any fixed meanings in his visual and lyrical signification, has meant that anyone can find something appealing in him. Analysing Prince also demands consideration of the audience as an active agent in the creation of that Princian authenticity.

We will therefore explore Prince in an interdisciplinary way that reflexively responds to his output and articulates how Prince as a dynamic site of signification and identification manages to intersect successfully with our own histories and feelings. The uniqueness of each of our own experiences when listening to music or viewing a video, and indeed the whole notion of 'fandom', has been problematic for popular music studies and Prince offers and interesting place to unpack these ideas. In order to consider these ideas in more detail, we will start by exploring Prince's emergence into mainstream culture in the late 1970s and early 1980s.

Hyperreality, Authenticity and the Pop Industry

Philosopher Jean Baudrillard (1994) describes hyperreality as the condition in which culture must continually replicate 'the real' in order to stave off a cultural schizophrenia, when we realize that nothing we are is authentic. Our cultural artefacts, such as pop music, are mass-produced, disposable and replaceable. Yet we must pretend they have meaning to ensure their value and reproduction. In other words, 'authenticity' is just another commodity, something easily marketed and purchased. This is a seductive thought in the context of mass produced pop, but perhaps it is premature to dismiss the notion of authenticity out of hand when considering Prince. Despite his continuous stream of song writing, producing and releasing his own records, Prince constantly re-invents himself. He always plays live, experiments with his catalogue, tries out new band set-ups, involves a variety of different musicians and imbues his output with whatever faith-based philosophy he is attached to at any given moment. By doing this, he has authority second to none and might be seen as a truly unique operator. Since ending his contract with Warner Bros. Records in the mid 1990s, his work is no longer scheduled or determined by the usual release policies and routines dictated by a record company, but simply out of his own desire to create and perform. It is this very centred-ness and consistency in Prince's approach that distinguishes his output from transitory entertainment. Allan Moore helpfully detaches the concept of authenticity from the perceived quality or uniqueness of the music, stating rather that authenticity is 'a matter of interpretation which is made and fought for from within a cultural and, thus, historicised position. It is ascribed, not inscribed' (2002, p. 210). Whether a performer is perceived as authentic, then, depends as much on the receiver, and what they bring to the listening moment. In later chapters, we intend to take this useful conceptualization further in order to explore how Prince's authority over his visual signification, including his still images, promotional videos and performances, collaborates with his sonic design to reinforce his uniqueness and integrity.

It is possible to see how the seeds of this autonomous pop identity were laid in Prince's early years, as his inauspicious upbringing in an ethnically ambiguous environment ensured he was exposed to many cultural and musical influences which can be seen in his work today. Prince was born Prince Rogers Nelson on 7 June 1958, in Minneapolis, Minnesota, to John L. Nelson, a jazz piano player, and his second wife, Mattie Shaw, a singer with Prince's father's band. Prince had three older half-siblings from his father's previous marriage, and a younger full-sibling, Tyka. He grew up in a black, lower middle-class neighbourhood in a city with a mainly white population of Swedish origin. This white culture was reflected in the musical output of local radio stations and clubs visited by Prince when growing up. Prince's negotiation of his own ethnic origins through his father's musical tastes, coupled with his exposure to white, middle-of-the-road rock, may help to explain why Prince fuses many visual and musical styles with ease in his own creative output. One of the first distinguishing characteristics of Prince's sound is his conflation of the hallowed genres of pop and rock. In rock discourse, performers are imbued within authenticity for adhering to their roots and origins; they are raw, honest and untainted by marketing, artifice and image. Rock also has connotations of masculinity and heteronormativity. In sharp contrast, pop has been distinguished as being entertainment, superficial, disposable and primarily targeted at young female consumers who, within some cultural studies theorizations, are more prone to being 'duped' by marketers.

If the terms 'authentic' and 'entertainment' are at opposite ends of the spectrum, then Prince's identity as a performer is ambiguous. Is he a 'rock' performer with the associated responsibility to his art, his public and without any pretence? Or does his commitment to pop and entertainment represent a commercial sell-out? Prince's ambiguity points to a problem inherent in musical studies. Lawrence Grossberg (1992) identifies how the distinction between 'authentic' as opposed to 'entertainment' or 'commercial' underpins notions of value leading to disagreements between 'official' critics and 'unofficial' fans as to which genres fall within each category. As Roy Shuker (1994, p. 8) points out, these distinctions serve an important ideological function rather than any basis in proven fact.

However, it is interesting and not least arguable that Prince possesses enough 'serious rock' credentials to anchor his integrity as a musician performing 'from the heart'. When John L. Nelson left the family home, Prince was seven years old. He left behind a grand piano, which Prince had previously not been allowed to play. By the age of eight, Prince had taught himself the basics of the instrument and progressed to mastery without any formal tuition. Hoskyns quotes him as saying: 'I don't even like the idea of training. I don't feel anybody can teach you an art. I don't think the basics can be taught either. Maybe that's naive and mental, but that's my way' (Hoskyns 1988, p.17).

While Prince has explored his ethnic and gender identity in many ways through his creative output, his most abiding and constant characteristic is his control over his output. Identified as musically prodigious at high school, Prince secured his first multiple-album recording contract at the age of 17, from Warner Bros., unprecedented given his youth, but also in the full control it gave him to write, perform and produce his albums. Subsequently, he became one of the most prolific artists of his generation.

'Before He Wrote the Songs, He Lived Them'

Prince's early sense of autonomy maps onto another characteristic of authenticity, which is an attachment to or constant referencing of one's own origins in order to validate the 'truth' of the artistic expression. For Richard Middleton, 'honesty (truth to cultural experience) becomes the validating criterion of musical value' (Middleton 1990, p. 127). In rock discourse, as Allan Moore has insisted, this validating criterion is reinterpreted as 'unmediated expression', by which is assumed the possibility of the communication of emotional content (inherent possibly in the music itself, but certainly at least in the performance) untrammelled by the difficulties attendant on the encoding of meaning in verbal discourse (Moore 2001, pp. 73–5; 181–4). Prince evokes his past in the earlier part of his career in his first feature film *Purple Rain*, which was surrounded by autobiographical mythology relating to his upbringing.

Our assumption here is that Prince's listeners believe personal experience gives rise to his passionate vocal and musical embellishments. These features can convey to his audience their perception of 'real emotion'. This is backed up by his instrumentation – originally a multi-gendered, multi-ethnic rock line-up that recalls the early 1970s, and more recently a jazz funk combo of, as he puts it, 'real musicians playing real music'. Hence Prince's musical expression has always been presented as 'unmediated' because there is minimal distance between its origins and its reception by the audience.

While Prince alludes to his past in his pop style, he still evades any direct response to questions about his ethnicity, sexual orientation or the nature of his upbringing and family context, as if not wishing to be pinned down and categorized. His promotion of his global identity, his 'New Power Generation' mantra, over and above the specificities of his individual history, subverts the globalized music industry's manufacture of authenticity. Ronald Radano and Philip Bohlman (2000) express concern that 'world music' is about preserving a 'neomythology of musical and racial origins' (p. 30). They argue for a deeper interrogation of the conditions and contexts of music production to illuminate real rather than imagined relationships between race and musical authenticity. They question whether 'the postmodern search for authenticity is fundamentally distinct from earlier attempts to racialise music by insisting on the naturalness of its origins' (ibid.). Prince's physicality, gender ambiguity and ethnicity similarly enable him to evade categorization simply as a black R&B or 'soul' star.

Furthermore, at around 5ft 2ins in height, Prince's stature and physical delicacy defy the stereotype of the sexually charged black superstud. According to a 1983 *Rolling Stone* magazine article, the pop singer's father was of African American ethnicity and his mother was of Italian American ancestry. However his ethnicity is under much debate. Another website states that his mother, Mattie Shaw, was of African American, Native American and White heritage, while his father, John Nelson, is of Black and Italian ancestry.

On the cover of his first album, *For You* (1978), Prince sports an Afro and no make-up, befitting a young soul star attempting to enter the market. But once he gained some critical success, he started to play with his visual representation. On the front cover of his second album, *Prince* (1979), his curls are longer and more relaxed, and on the reverse Prince sits naked, his body concealed by his acoustic guitar. Certain instruments have been identified by musicologists as carrying more authenticity, and the acoustic guitar is one such item. By his third album, *Dirty Mind*, Prince pastiches an array of signs appertaining to ethnicity, gender, sexuality and profanity.

The Pleasure Principle

By the mid 1980s, Prince's oeuvre comprised something more nuanced and complex than even music and image. With the release of *Dirty Mind* Prince was advocating a lifestyle philosophy, melding sexuality and spirituality as a means to access one's inner essence. He achieved this musically by mixing up his genres; unlike the synth soul-disco of his previous studio offerings, *Dirty Mind* was more stripped down, raw and new wave-like with a strong infusion of rock guitar and raw lyrics. This, coupled with rallying lyrics, helped Prince come so much closer to his listener than on his previous albums. For the first time we would hear Prince squealing, imploring, screaming and groaning in close aural proximity, his guitar an extension of his near-tangible physicality as he starts to tout his maxims of hedonism and pleasure.

According to Allan Moore (2002), audiences become engaged not so much with 'authentic' musical acts and gestures, but directly with the originator of those acts and gestures. Prince is a prime example of the originator whose utilized sonic gestures and ambiguity offer a point of access and identification for fans. This point is especially pertinent if we consider the moment of Prince's emergence as a popular artist. While there were economic differences between young people from different classes in the early to mid 1980s, these seemed less important to young people than what they shared – aspirational values and a strong sense of wishing to transcend their situation, if not physically then through music. This meant that youth culture found itself turning its back on the rest of society, rather than addressing the structural contradiction in the way cultural theorists would have liked. Building on Gramsci's model of hegemony and counter hegemony, cultural studies analysed hegemonic, or ruling, social and cultural forms of domination, and sought counter-hegemonic forces of resistance and struggle.[1] But young people, middle-class and working-class alike, resorted to a 'politics of pleasure, a hedonism (in hard times) – a pleasure for its own sake in times when moral regulation of youth is pervasive and deep economic recession is rife' (Redhead 1993, p. 7).

Indeed, pleasure became a key word in cultural studies in the 1980s, as a reaction to the ostensible moralizing of discourses such as feminism, which had denounced fashion and beauty culture throughout the 1970s (Winship 1986). However, much of cultural studies viewed a politics of pleasure as not political enough, because consuming cultural products means to support an economic system that thrives on patriarchal social relations. Consumption of popular culture by the general population, especially by young females, has to some extent always been problematic in the opinion of intellectuals, politicians and moral and social reformers (Strinati 1995, p. 41).

> Pleasures are often ... a conditioned response to certain stimuli and should thus be problematized, along with other forms of experience and behavior and interrogated as to whether they contribute to the production of a better life and society, or help trap us into modes of everyday life that ultimately oppress and degrade us. Resistance and pleasure cannot therefore be valorized per se as progressive elements of the appropriation of cultural texts, rather one needs to describe the specific conditions that give rise to the resistance or pleasure at stake and their specific effects. (Kellner 1995, p. 39)

The two main reasons underlying concerns about the negative consequences of consumption stem, firstly, from the work of F.R. Leavis (1930), who asserted that 'low' culture, such as popular music, had a deadening effect on the intellectual life of its consumers and culture at large, and secondly, from the work of media researchers in the 1970s, such as James D. Halloran (1970), who suggested certain popular cultural forms may have negative effects on their audiences. Mass culture theories such as these have tended to see the audience as passive, vulnerable and manipulable, subject to the forces of consumerism that characterized the development of modern, capitalist culture. This critique of popular culture was based upon the argument that its consumers necessarily had only a limited understanding of the wider social forces and power relationships that were felt to shape their thoughts and actions.[2] Critics of the mass culture theorists, who include Ang (1986) and, from a feminist perspective, Modleski (1982) and Radway (1987), questioned the view that the audience for popular culture could be so undifferentiated and passive, and asserted the need to acknowledge consumers may be more knowing, more active and more discriminating in their consumption of popular culture than had been conceded.

---

[1] See Gramsci (1971) and Hall and Jefferson (1976).
[2] See Bourdieu (1983) and McGuigan (1992).

There is certainly no doubt that the early to mid 1980s heralded a new context for youth culture and consumption, and Prince's emergence against that backdrop was significant. Journalist Jon Savage wrote in *The Face* magazine in June 1983 that youth culture, particularly the New Romantic movement that originated at The Blitz club in London, used femininity to react against the strong, rigidly masculine government of Margaret Thatcher:

> The Blitz obsession with the 'feminine', a fast-moving, sharply-defined exotic surface image with a total lack of any commitment, has defined the terms under which most modern pop groups operate – whether Duran Duran swapping countries with each video or Boy George wearing a dress and not being thought ludicrous. Blitz took up the gauntlet thrown down by the punks and turned it into an all-pervasive camp – whether as a way of looking at things or a way of wearing your clothes. The result has not been without humour, and complete confusion. (Savage 1997, p. 161)

There can be little doubt that Prince was acutely aware of the extent to which his gendered representation could utilize his ambiguity to gain mass appeal. His appearance was counter-cultural and celebrated all the things that were anathema to the status quo – sexual promiscuity and freedom from any moral boundaries, yet infused with a deep conviction that breaking out from moral constraints enables people to access their 'true' selves. Monogamy, gender fixity, adherence to religious doctrines and being defined by ethnicity – all these societal mores which were being promoted heavily during the neo-conservative Reagan/Thatcher period had to be broken for the sake of inner integrity.

From a musicological perspective, scholars such as Brackett, Fast, Hawkins, McClary, Middleton, Moore, Tagg, Walser and others have focused on the shared experience that music offers, the sense of belonging and identity as the root of authenticity rather than the intrinsic quality of the sound itself, as if the moment of consumption brings fixity in an uncertain world. Unlike Madonna, who constantly deconstructed identity as anything pre-ordained, Prince was telling us that we are all the originators of our own destinies as long as we access our inner essence. In a society that was marked by high unemployment and the very real prospect of nuclear war, Prince was offering a safe space for his fans to explore the meanings of their own identities and their place within a confusing socio-cultural context.

Unsurprisingly, few cultural theorists saw pop's musical messages and identities as a positive intervention. One of the reasons for this was the general view at the time that pop marketed to girls – as Prince was at that time – had no purpose but to exploit their new spending power. But girls who had grown up in the context of feminism in the 1960s and 1970s, no longer found themselves situated primarily in the home, a fact largely overlooked by cultural studies until much later. A new female youth culture had grown, and they found themselves very drawn to Prince.

'I'm Not a Woman, I'm Not a Man': Ambiguous Prince Takes Centre Stage

To young women in the mid 1980s it looked as if they could really have it all: 'our unpleasant confusions about our identities (what it means to be black, white, gay or straight, male or female) melted into a pleasurable, seductive ambiguity' (Stuart 1990, p. 31). Educated girls and young women were driven by a combination of fantasy and entrepreneurial zeal. The barrage of messages emanating from popular culture, the media and other institutions, such as the family and schools, meant that teenage girls would not be satisfied with taking a traditional route through female adulthood. The lack of reference to feminism by name was acknowledgement that young women were in the process of integrating feminism into their lives and identities, because they had grown up with it. It was no longer an ideal but a lived reality, it seemed, which vindicated pleasurable heterosexual sex, consumption and aspiration. Sexuality was reclaimed as a symbol of female emancipation, following a path set by a previous generation of women: '... for girls in and around a male-focussed subculture, sexual confidence is calculated to have an impact on social and cultural confidence' (McRobbie and Garber 1991). For young women growing up in this context of cultural and economic shift, consumption of popular cultural texts including music seemed to serve as an important part of the struggle to make sense of this shifting context. More specifically, for girls and young women who were being confronted with a barrage of identity signals, pop music icons may have offered a space for fantasy and reflection on the possibilities available to them. Female practices, such as consuming output by the ambiguous Prince, articulated how female identity could be more than a fore-closed and agreed-upon fixed notion, and could rather be a place of negotiation and of agency.

This is borne out by countless videos and live performances, where Prince addresses the female subject. For instance, 'Cream', one of Prince's raunchiest songs, lends itself well to the music video that came out in 1991.[3] 'Cream' was one of the first songs Prince produced for the *Diamonds and Pearls* album, and it came about as he looked at himself, adoringly, in the mirror (Brown 1995). The fun-filled narrative of the song is definitely directed towards the female onlooker: 'U're so fine, U're filthy cute and baby u know it'. Certainly, Prince went out of his way to make the video as sexy as possible, and, musically, this is achieved by him employing an, if you will, ever-so-dirty sound. The style he appropriates is T. Rex glam rock, and in one sense this song is a tribute to his predecessors, Marc Bolan, David Bowie and not least the New York Dolls. James Perone also identifies this lineage, claiming that 'Cream's' 'tempo, minimalistic instrumental setting, and melody clearly pay tribute to the 1972 glam-rock classic', namely, T. Rex's 'Bang a Gong (Get It On)' (Perone 2008, p. 65). Coupled with his vocal parts are intricate guitar licks that complement the groove's raunchy feel. In particular, the boogie bass provides the impetus for the smooth, sleazy movements of Prince and his troupe of female dancers. In the song's arrangement and video

---

[3] A truncated analysis of this can be found in Hawkins (2002), chapter 6.

there is a sense of cream rising to the top in terms of the synergy between visual object and sonic signifier. The highlight in the video comes when Prince lifts the guitar above his head, pointing it to the heavens, with clipped melodic figures shaping his luring solo passage. Most of all, it is Prince's choreography with a troupe of girl dancers that distinguishes him from 1970s artists, such as Bolan, that in the end makes him one of them. The video can be read as an inscription of his solidarity with the female through the politics of the carnivalesque. Evidence of the Other's gaze, a frequent signifier in Prince's work, designates *his* desire as objectified and unthreatening to the female spectator. Close shots reveal an upward gaze through long black eyelashes, an outstretched beckoning hand to the camera, and then long shots of camp, non-macho dancing. Instantly this gives him an impish humour that dashes any predatory element to the hyper-sexualized *double entendres* of the lyrics. Indeed, his use of self-parody entices the spectator with her point-of-view visual positioning. It is interesting how in this tribute song, with its suggestive video, Prince gets away with the suspender-clad, fetishized images of women in the video, lip-sticked and short-skirted in a similar vein to the four backing musicians in Robert Palmer's 'Addicted to Love' promotional video (see Hawkins 2009a). In the latter case, women were displayed specifically for male stimulation, licking their lips and bouncing bra-lessly as they pretend to (ahem) strum. Palmer's women are metonymic and dehumanized. In contrast to the robotic desensitized female, the 'Cream' video plays on the opposite. For a full ten minutes the main radio edit of the track is preceded by a fantasy sequence in a railway station. Prince and his two main dancers, the Diamond and Pearl, are dressed in black and white in a style that harks back to the 1930s and '40s. They are pursued avidly by camera-wielding journalists dressed in the traditional pin-stripe suit and trilby as in Howard Hawks' *His Girl Friday* (1940). Prince is visually set apart from these stereotypical images of the predatory male by wearing his hair highly bouffanted and dressed in a long light flowing robe. The entire effect is that of the effete dandy. Prince's iconography thus prepares the viewer for a different set of power relations in the main sequence where the backing dancers are a reminder of a bygone era, in their black-and-white costumes, rather than sex objects. The camera does not linger on their physicality as they are very much in the background. Instead, the main female protagonist in the video is Prince's spectacular backing vocalist Rosie Gaines, a mature woman with a strong presence and standard build who reminds the normal female spectator of herself. In contrast to the monochrome-clad Prince and his backing dancers, Gaines is dressed in a rich purple suit. She invites us to look on as Prince plays to her, wriggling supine on his back on the piano as he gazes longingly at her. Gaines returns our gaze as we look at her standing over him. Prince overdoes his self-preening mannerisms as he delivers the aforementioned line, 'U're filthy cute and baby u know it', screaming at us to laugh at him – after all, he is talking about himself. Overall the song and its promotional video can be read as Prince self-parodically paying tribute to the sexiness of assertive women, but most of all as a send-up of his own narcissism, not to mention the entire representation of male heteronormativity. In the end, the tightest and filthiest of grooves drives this song, thanks to the support of the New Power Generation, who are paid full credit for having contributed to everything from the production and arrangement to the composition of each track. When coupled with the provocative allure of the video, the song 'Cream' gives the impression of the cream really rising to the top.

'Prince' the sign would become a space for women fans to evaluate and reconfigure their attitudes towards their own feminine identities, and towards masculinity and their position as subjects within the socio-cultural sphere. The star first appeared in Britain in 1982 as a support act for the Rolling Stones. He performed the electronic funk-rock title track to *Dirty Mind* wearing a G-string, an open flasher-mac, stockings, high-heeled boots and make-up. Backed by his multi-racial band, which featured women prominently, Prince spun and gesticulated boldly and campy, in a style more reminiscent of Mick Jagger, lead singer with the legendary main act, than of the black soul stars who had opened the space for his emergence. While it was possible to identify Prince's historical musical and style influences from his records and his visual signification, his female fans found in him a new and original space for identification. It was his heterosexually-charged yet excessively feminized and dandy appearance and gestures that allowed his female fans to simultaneously desire him and identify with him. Furthermore, it became evident that by the mid 1980s Prince was an artist who displayed full agency in his sophisticated manufacture of signs aimed at female followers. Female consumers of popular culture were made conscious of the manufacture and styling of their pop icons by their record companies through the burgeoning music press aimed at them, such as *Smash Hits*. But Prince's teasing play on his gender, sexuality and ethnicity suggested a star, who wished to communicate with his audience on a level other than marketability. His popular cultural intervention raised many questions around female subjectivity. This young male star seemed to challenge some definitive psychoanalytical notions and cultural studies approaches to the nature of female subjective development.

The importance of women in Prince's upbringing may help explain his promotion of black and white women musical artists, and indeed his rapport with the lives of female fans. In 1972 and following his parents' divorce and remarriages, the 14-year-old Prince found his family life in turmoil. His best friend was another black youth, Andre Anderson, who lived with his mother, Bernadette, and five siblings. Bernadette, a single parent studying for a degree, welcomed Prince into her busy home and gave him his own space in her basement. Biographies of the star have alluded to the large number of strong and emancipated female figures in Prince's early life, which may have had a positive and formative effect on his identity and on his ease in relating to women through his cultural products. His visual appearance in the mid 1980s suggested that he may have looked more to female sources for the origins of his look and gestures. Prince's famcy hair-dos, clothes and make-up did not follow contemporary fashion styles in the mid 1980s, and were quite unlike those of his young male contemporaries such as Michael Jackson or Duran Duran. He styled his hair like Donna Summer, wore make-up like Liza Minnelli, clothes like a regency dandy and gesticulated like Shirley Bassey. As such, his appearance and mannerisms spanned gender, ethnic and geo-cultural boundaries, and girls could emulate his style quite easily.

It is possible to understand the power of Prince's visual signification for the young female spectator in the context of the mid 1980s by seeing how he projected a different type of narcissistic image of masculinity into wider culture. This is most evident in the stark contrast of his visual imagery to the images of masculinity, including gay masculinity, that were widely in circulation at the time. When it comes to the male viewer, Prince's address is equally fascinating. His blurring of binary distinctions is evident in all his work, where the assumptions surrounding homophobia are fully imploded. Lest we forget, many considered Prince the gayest and queerest performer ever to hit mainstream pop. The spectacle of this male queering in his performances of the early 1980s was startling and freakish; it positioned the male fan/viewer in a precarious situation. As Robert Walser insisted in 1994, Prince 'invites men to imagine different modes of eroticism and relations, and invites women to imagine men who can imagine such things' (Walser 1994, p. 85). Most of all, the de-territorialization of his act would transcend the categories of constraint placed upon men in relation to gender and sex. Walser puts it this way: 'he invites everyone to be interpelated into structures of desire that are not territorialized by rigid patriarchal distinctions' (ibid., p. 85). One might argue that Prince's strategy all along has been to valorize the restrictions of male representation by negotiating his gender and sexuality through a body that is displayed as androgynous and dangerously promiscuous.

Feminist academics, such as Laura Mulvey (1975), and popular music scholars, such as Simon Frith and Angela McRobbie (1978), would have found it near impossible to envisage male performance, with its inherently patriarchal under and overtones, as offering a point of access for women at that time. But Prince could be read as a sign that was open to non-traditional interpretation. Arriving as he did against a backdrop of cultural and gender disturbance, Prince beckoned a positive reception from female fans. He achieved this radically subversive position by embodying a catalogue of binary oppositions. Ethnically, he looked neither black nor white. Physically, he combined oddness with sublime beauty. He exaggerated his femininity through the use of dandyism as a visual stylistic signifier. Consciously or unconsciously Prince, who in later years temporarily abandoned his name in favour of a symbol (Jones 1997, p. 167), situated himself on a border that left him indescribable.

There were two key defining moments in the public construction of Prince in relation to female fans in the mid 1980s, which inspire our assertion that Prince beckoned a unique relationship with fans. The first is the media's consistent negative portrayal of the star, as if to mitigate his perceived 'threat' to appropriate norms of gender identity and desire, continuously abstracting Prince-the-man from his creative output. As biographer Dave Hill (1989) wrote of the tabloids, 'it is as though they simply cannot contemplate the notion of a short, slight man who dresses and moves like a popular (mis)conception of a homosexual being attractive to millions of women' (Hill 1989, p. 165). Barthes (1977) has explained how press photographs serve to reinforce dominant ideological messages by concealing the context of the event depicted and through subtle connotation:

> ... on the one hand, the press photograph is an object that has been worked on, chosen, composed, constructed, treated according to professional aesthetic or ideological norms which are so many factors of connotation; while on the other, this same photograph is not only perceived, received, it is *read*, connected more or less consciously by the public that consumes it to a traditional stock of signs. (Barthes 1977, p. 19)

On 9 August 1986, *The Sun*, *The Daily Star*, *The Daily Mirror* and *The Daily Express* showed Prince's topless body. The image that was used repeatedly afterwards showed his arms outstretched, muscles flexed, a fleeting moment from a concert that one of the authors attended, where he was deliberately sending up his mythical media portrayal as a sexual predator. He could be playful and simultaneously contesting at any given moment, using pastiche to subvert male and female gender behaviour. For example, in his on-stage parody of masculinity during this concert at Wembley Arena, he grinned at the audience while seducing his microphone, as if it was a woman, in an excessive manner, and said: 'If you believe any of this you're a bigger fool than I am', ironically sending up commonly-held conceptions perpetuated by tabloid newspapers about his predatory sexual appetite.

Accompanying headlines similarly focused on rumours of his sexuality, for example 'Prince's Creature Comforts' (*The Sun*, 13 August 1986), which referred to his 'disgustingly raunchy stage act' in paragraph two and his alleged night of passion with six young women while performing in London. Prince himself is described in animalistic terms, as a 'strange creature'. *The Star* headlined him as 'Prince of Passion!' (14 August 1986), comparing his zoot-suited acceptability with earlier styles:

> What a fashion transformation from when Prince first burst onto the international scene in 1978. In those days he pranced around the stage in tiger-skin knickers, a black suspender belt and silk stockings. And ex-girlfriend [sic] Apollonia once confided: 'I had a terrible job stopping him wearing my best lingerie and lacy bits!'

The Star wrote that Prince's style was now 'strictly for the boys', in an attempt to reduce his threat to their implied male readership. Ultimately, Prince's body in the mid 1980s was coded, to cite Mulvey, for its 'to-be-looked-at-ness' (indicating that Mulvey's rigid account of spectator positions does not accommodate cultural shift). What had happened in the mainstream context, as Suzanne Moore pointed out, is that 'the usual mechanisms that signal erotic spectacle had crossed gender boundaries' (Moore 1988, p. 47).

Secondly, Prince continued to transcend the boundaries of conventional practices of masculinity in his promotional videos through spectacular dance routines. Yet the positive critical reception of Prince's single 'Kiss' (1986) was interpreted by press reviewers as an apology to women for the misogyny allegedly contained within the *Purple Rain* film (see Chapter 5). In the song, which is upbeat, stripped down and simple in comparison to the multi-layered excess and broodiness of the soundtrack to *Purple Rain*, Prince declares that 'women and girls rule my world', stressing that 'you don't have to be beautiful to turn me on'.

The point we are making here is that Prince was aligned in the public domain specifically in relation to gender relations and femininity in a way not previously seen since Elvis's on-stage sexual gyrations were banned from television screens. Prior to those moments, Prince had indeed been controversial due to the overt sexual content and expletives on his albums, though his lyrics and performances had not been debated specifically in relation to women in the media. The positive critical reception of 'Kiss' opened a space thereafter for Prince to continuously explore female identity and gender relations through his lyrics and visuals.[4]

To go deeper into this argument: if Prince was an innovative symbol of agency and desire in the mid 1980s, we need to map his brand of signification against his contemporary, Madonna, as her influence on fans, particularly females, was immense. In many ways, Prince and Madonna appeared to be the Bonnie and Clyde of 1980s gender disruption. With lace underwear, eyeliner and sex-as-power musical mantras, they waged war on fixed, essentialist ideas about masculine and feminine identities and practices. Indeed, such was their joint allure, that rumours circulated of a relationship between the pair, coinciding with the recording of their duet 'Love Song'[5] for Madonna's *Like A Prayer* album (1989). Sexual expression proved a powerful way to articulate the difference between true feelings and cultural expectation. Madonna appeared to epitomize Judith Butler's notion of 'queer' in her seminal text *Gender Trouble* (1999). The star knowingly parodied and exaggerated female stereotypes, including the virgin and the whore, both of which she tantalizingly subverted, with lashings of blasphemy for good measure. Madonna referenced and promoted historic images of assertive femininity, especially 1930s and '40s screen sirens such as Greta Garbo and Judy Garland. Her continual physical and stylistic play, whether playing a Monroe-esque bombshell or crop-haired dominatrix, chimes with Butler's call for women to reject identity-based politics and instead to expose the productive potential of self-construction so that all 'cultural configurations of sex and gender proliferate' (1999, p. 190). According to this notion, we are no longer restricted to traditional gender identities and might instead favour 'the lesbian heterosexual, a heterosexual lesbian, a male lesbian, a female gay man, or even a feminist sex radical' (Schwichtenberg 1993, p. 141). Madonna's sexual identity experimentation was clearly demonstrated in her book *Sex* (1992), and in the video for 'Justify My Love', which featured

---

[4] See McClary (2000) and Hawkins (2002) for different analyses of the 'Kiss' video, especially with regard to agency and gender-coding.

[5] The song contains three lines of lyrics which were later used in her hit single 'Hung Up' (2005).

homosexuals and transsexuals who typically occupy a space outside the 'imaginable domain of gender' (Schwichtenberg 1993, p. 13).

Like Prince, Madonna asserted full creative control over her output and self-representation, ensuring a sense that this was an authentic artist with little of the male-dominated music industry machinations between her and her fans (see Hawkins 1997, 2004). She beckoned her 'Wannabes' to follow her example and work hard to transcend their material conditions, to realize their 'Material Girl' aspirations. All they had to do was to be performative, to at one and the same time recognize that gender signifiers are empty vessels and to pastiche, parody, imitate myriad identities as means to emancipation and, most importantly, pleasure.

But if Madonna was advocating a Butlerian liberation from any notion of an essential self – and there have been numerous critiques of the star's avocation of these principles – where does that leave the essential self? (see hooks 1992). This was Madonna and Prince's most fundamental difference. While Madonna sought to explode any limitations on self-representation, especially by decoupling sexuality from bodily gender, she simultaneously disavowed the existence of inner identity or individuality. Prince, alternatively, espoused reflexivity rather than performativity as a means to access and negotiate our identity. In Prince's realm, the self is always integral, whether or not that self conforms to societal norms or expectations. Prince's work cuts to the quick of the limiting factor in Butler's premise that there is no such thing as original or authentic (1999, p. 123). For if there is no authenticity then there is surely no such thing as subversion. This premise in effect renders Madonna's exploration of multiple, unfixed identities as compelling, but ultimately unproductive if it devalues the histories and experiences that individuals bring to their gender play. Critics such as Adam Green (2007) have noted that queer theory cannot be a framework for examining selves or subjectivities because it ignores social and cultural contexts. While there is great productive potential in embracing a rich array of marginalized narratives and identities, whether based on gender, sexuality or ethnicity, queer theory has been seen as limited to discussions around discourse.

Prince had more in common with Siouxie Sioux, lead singer with Siouxie and the Banshees and, later, The Creatures. She replaced Johnny Rotten as the new post-punk icon, embodying the suburban dream of transcending the blank uncertainty of a new neo-conservative era. Rather than directly addressing an assault on mainstream femininity and masculinity, Sioux just 'was' herself and went so far as to castigate fans who copied her look. For Sioux, self and individuality were paramount, not playing with surface identities. As Mark Paytress wrote in his biography:

> With a dignity and self-belief that echoed the fights Bette Davies had with Warner Brothers in the '30s, coupled with the fantasy-driven sexuality of Gloria Swanson or David Bowie, Siouxie introduced a new female perspective into a cock-dominated genre that was far less compromising than that suggested by forebears such as Janis Joplin or even Patti Smith. (2003, p. 13)

Of course, a star with the power and media savvy of Prince may have been personally responsible for some of his bizarre headline coverage, knowingly masterminding his self-parody. Steve Jones (2002) has pointed out the symbiotic interdependency of popular music criticism and the industry itself, yet there has been little research into how the relationship works in practice. Whatever Prince's motive, if he was indeed lurking behind his media representation, he has always been acutely aware of his own potency as a singular brand.

The Prince Brand

Prince is unique as an artist, exerting visible and monolithic control over his entire business entity. Throughout the 1980s, Prince produced an album a year and is reputed to possess extensive archives of his unreleased material. He was simultaneously in command of his videos and feature films. His musical development and approach to the music industry form some of the most fascinating dimensions of his biography. According to *NME*, his 2009 tour was the year's second-highest-grossing, 'generating $90.3 million in ticket sales. But thanks to lower production costs, his net take was larger than top grosser Madonna's. Prince took a reported eighty-five percent of the profits from the concerts, which earned an average $910,000 a night'.[6]

His success extends to his influence on other artists and producers. The Minneapolis Sound is attributed to Prince's fusion of synthesizer-led R&B, funk and pop. Countless musicians have sought to emulate Prince's signature brand sound or gain direct artistic or production input from its originator. A diverse list of artists, from young Scottish vocalist Sheena Easton to legendary artists and civil rights campaigner Mavis Staples, travelled to Paisley Park in the 1980s to collaborate with Prince or, alternatively, with his prominent musical associates, Jimmy Jam and Terry Lewis. Jam and Lewis, who had been founder members (with Prince and Morris Day) of The Time, became key exponents of the Minneapolis wall of sound after their success with the SOS Band's 'Just Be Good to Me'. They replaced the Human League's urban new wave metallic rawness with almost baroque emotive embellishment on 'Human'. The Minneapolis sound had its biggest impact in the mid 1980s when Janet Jackson approached Jam and Lewis. Keen to shed her smiley girl-next-door image and secure the same success as her elder brother, Jackson's collaboration with the pair resulted in the multi-platinum album *Control* (1986).

Prince's own work and his collaborations centred on his label Paisley Park, founded in 1985, which was associated with and funded in part by Warner Bros. With the exception of Sheila E. and Prince's own releases, the label never really had commercial success. In 1992, at the height of his career, Prince's relationship

---

[6] See http://www.nme.com/photos/musics-most-gigantic-paydays/168116/10/1 [accessed: 22/6/2011].

with Warner Bros. began to falter. He found the terms and conditions of his new contract with the label delimiting in terms of the number of albums he was allowed to release each year. Gradually, he began to disconnect himself from his company.

This was the year his fourteenth album was released, featuring The New Power Generation. Due to its unpronounceable symbol on the cover, it has been referred to as the *Love Symbol* album. It is noteworthy that Prince changed his name to the symbol shortly after the release of the single, 'My Name Is Prince', the first track on the album, co-written and performed with Tony Mosley. Mosley wrote the rap for the song and his input is significant in that it reflects the current musical trends in the market during the early 1990s. It was only six years after its release that Mosley, having left the NPG, would be filing a lawsuit against Prince, claiming that royalties had not been paid on this song and the other track he co-wrote, 'Sexy MF'.

Stylistically, 'My Name Is Prince' signals a watershed in Prince's output, not only in terms of his use of rap and hip-hop, but also in terms of him venting anger and defiance. At this point in his career, he was aware of the perils of breaking his contract with Warner and doing it alone, and the promo video for the track alone illustrates the issues he had with ownership and identity. Significantly, throughout the video, dressed in a black outfit, and black gloves with gold symbols, he has his face covered by a chain hat as he sings into a microphone in the shape of a revolver. What stands out most in 'My Name Is Prince' is the sheer sentiment of anger that positions Prince at the centre of his own theology. The funk groove, tinged with rock, hip-hop and rap gestures, grinds on the downbeat of each bar, as he exclaims, 'I am funky', with full slam on the first syllable, 'fun'. In each chorus with the incessant repetition of the hook, 'My name is Prince', the singing style is one of shouting as he lambastes the downbeat on the first of each bar with his name. Throughout the emphasis is far more rhythmic than melodic or harmonic, as every utterance comes across as 'in yer face'.[7] As well as harking back to earlier tracks, through samples from 'I Wanna Be Your Lover', 'Partyup' and 'Controversy' (used in the introduction), there is a direct link to the track, 'Gett Off' from his previous album, *Diamonds and Pearls*, which paraphrases the 1969 song 'Mother Popcorn' by James Brown. Boldly defiant, the expression in his singing style extracts the themes of hurt, pride and revenge as he tells the music industry that 'this is a motherfucking party, while u're laying back I'm on the attack paddywack'. The song culminates with eight repetitions of 'My name is Prince'.

Two years later, in 1994, Warner Bros. ended its distribution deal with Paisley Park, effectively closing it down. Prince had already set to work on his musical declaration of independence, which culminated in the triple-CD album, *Emancipation* (1996). Now free of any constraints on his level of output, this was Prince's third release that year, after *Chaos and Disorder* – his final Warner Bros. album, and *Girl 6*. The cover art, depicting hands breaking free from binding

---

[7] Gratitude to Susan McClary for her input in the reading of this song, in one of many pleasurable joint sessions of discussing Prince's music.

chains against a rising sun, could not make his sentiments toward Warner Bros. any plainer. Although many of the tracks were devoted to his wife and unborn child, 'Slave' and 'Face Down' were among several tracks commenting on his former record company.

With no major backing, no supportive hit singles and for a number of years completely out of the industry machinery, Prince still managed to achieve great success and high earnings. He made innovative use of the internet to market and distribute his recordings, along with selling albums such as *Crystal Ball* (1997) though exclusive deals with specific stores. In 2007, he announced that he planned to sue YouTube, eBay and, highly controversially, fan websites for posting music and videos without permission. Walser (1993) insists on two clear types of 'authenticity' that can be observed in rock in general, whereby technological mediation (whether a reliance on signal modifiers, ever more powerful means of amplification, and even technical mastery in many spheres) is equated with artifice, reinstating as authentic/inauthentic the distinction between 'vernacular' and 'trained' or 'pro-fessional'. There is, thus, a relationship here with an alternative category developed by Timothy Taylor, which he terms authenticity of positionality (Taylor 1997, pp. 22–3). Through this, he identifies the authenticity acquired by performers who refuse to 'sell out' to commercial interests. After all, it is the music that says everything, and Prince is a musician's musician. Hardly surprising then that in 2004 he launched an album with a title that suggested music needs to be taken seriously, *Musicology*. Tempting as it might be to read this as some ironic jibe at those of us doing 'serious musicological' work in the academy, it is more likely that he was labouring the well-known point that, 'being a real musician' rules, and in no uncertain terms the electrifying Musicology Tour bore this out.

Conclusion

In marketing terms, the pop artist's identity must be understood as an entity distributed in space and place, contingent on the success of its cultural production. That is, Prince's identity is constituted by the narratives that form a trajectory of authenticating the self. Innovation is a prime ingredient of his identity and made possible by the process of coming up with new and exciting musical material purposefully and creatively. Prince's songs are about the personal and the social, and, most of all, his relationship with his fans. The process of his commodification, then, is grounded in the aesthetics of pop, which is dependent on his fans interpreting his codes. Control over himself and those he works with is manifested in the ambiguous sphere of desperation, inadequacy, elation and triumph, as he confronts the music industry that promotes him at the same time as it disempowers him. A critique of Prince's masculinity, a product of the entertainment world, cannot avoid the issue of consumerism. And in this context, his brand of masculinity becomes an original display of the intrinsic qualities of the 'man in trouble'. Prince's off-stage narratives – those that deal with exploitation by Warner and copyright law suits – present his male identity as admirable, self-worthy and righteous. His tenacity in gaining control over distribution rights and the widespread circulation of his music is unprecedented in the history of popular music, arguably heralding a new era of democracy for the pop star. This process in itself can be best understood through the politics of self-promotion, whereby the production of the self is added to the meaning of the music. Prince's authenticity derives from his discursive construction, rather than from any fixed notion of him as static or 'natural'. His representations of ethnicity, gender and sexuality are proof of his constantly shifting image and circumstance. For instance, Prince gets through to us all that black identity and heterosexuality is not some fixed category that is homogenized or biologically determined. Rather than conforming to stereotypes, Prince explores representations that challenge the power relations of the very binaries, black–white, straight–homo and girl–boy. His authenticity is thus established by a politics of representation that is continuously double-coded.

Under a similar agreement as employed for *Planet Earth*, the *20Ten* album was launched by NPG Records as a free copy with the *Rolling Stone* magazine in Germany, the *Courrier International* in France, the *Het Nieuwsbland* and *De Gentenaar* in Belgium, the *Daily Mirror* in the UK, and the *Daily Record* in Ireland. This was Prince's thirty-third studio album, distributed as a personal diary of what he had considered a very difficult year. Notably, on its release, the album was not available in record stores or as a digital download. As the internet froze with fans trying to get access to the album, Prince stated in an interview with the *Daily Mirror* that 'It's the best way to go … no charts, no internet piracy and no stress. Period.'[8] Despite its mixed reviews, *20Ten*, is a testament to Prince's standing as an extraordinary musician who has survived the perils of the music industry for four decades. In a sense, the album verifies his authenticity through a batch of songs that are stylistically diverse and forward looking. The songs cover almost every idiom he is known for, with a freshness that is inspirational: the spiritual, schmaltzy ballad of 'Sea of Everything', the let's-go-crazy fluffy pop of 'Everybody Loves Me', the party-funk grind of 'Act of God', 'Beginning Endlessly' and 'Sticky Like Glue', the jazz-swing fusion of 'Lavaux', and the soulfulness and Marvin-Gaye-like feel of 'Future Soul Song'. Certainly, Prince has something in common with the all time greats – Elvis Presley, Michael Jackson, James Brown, Jimi Hendrix, The Beatles – in that he has helped define 50 years of pop through the genius of his musicality and inimitable personal expression.

---

[8] http://www.mirror.co.uk/celebs/news/2010/07/10/purple-reign-115875-22402175/ [accessed 10 October 2010].

Chapter 2
Inscriptions of Otherness: Dandyism, Style and Queer Sensibility

It is a characteristic of the visual marketing of Prince that he has integrated a diverse range of genres and styles, including references to various cultures, identities and sexualities. We know in pop music that conventions are smudged in order to create new spaces for defining spectator/listener identities that in turn enable promoters to develop new markets. Consequently, popular music scholars have theorized pop as a constantly shifting social plane where the appropriation of styles and idioms can tell us everything about our culture. In this respect, performativity is implicit in any discussion relating to Prince's own awareness of himself as a performed act. That he communicates through the recording in so many different ways that are socially circumscribed, means that his performances operate in a sphere that is transitory. Furthermore, Prince's creative agency 'can be associated with a profusion of styles that simultaneously articulate the conditions of authenticity and artifice in musical expression' (Hawkins 2002, pp. 160–61). This notion of ambivalence forms part of a discourse on his Otherness, which we intend to illuminate in this chapter.

In the first chapter we introduced how a commercialized, 'authentic' Other can be viewed as a unique and original 'genius'. Following on from that, this chapter will critically interrogate Prince's harnessing and celebration of 'Otherness' through a peculiar brand of masculinity. It is this, we argue, that has contributed to his signature and mass appeal that defines the pop aesthetic primarily shaped by the MTV generation. From the outset, Prince has understood the power of imagery in marketing, self-styling himself as someone ethnically ambiguous and androgynous. In retrospect, this might be seen as a brave step for an up-and-coming star breaking into a carefully delineated pop industry. Prince, however, has also transcended the tried-and-tested approaches to the marketing of black musicians and appealed directly to young people. His identity – subversive, contestational and personally political – slotted well into the ambiguous context in which young people found themselves in the 1980s. And, right from the start, his genderplay underlined an ambiguity that was a disruption of conventional codes of masculinity. On this point, Robert Walser has argued that Prince enticed his fans through structures of desire that were not territorialized by the constraints of patriarchal conformity (Walser 1994, p. 85). This fitted perfectly into a musical idiom that explored the new technologies of production that controlled both a studio and live performance space. As Paul Théberge has insisted, the digitalization of musical instruments and recording engineering in the 1980s became an ideal 'vehicle for a music industry based simultaneously in fashion and nostalgia' (Théberge 1997, p. 213), and, in this sense, the pop artist's link to technological innovation would lead to new aesthetic and formal musical features. With audio technological developments, the boundaries between the pop recording and the live performance became more difficult to distinguish, thus affecting the aesthetics of pop. Moreover, as Tim Warner argues, 'the image of the machine as an object of power and beauty recurs again and again in twentieth-century popular art generally, and pop music in particular' (Warner 2003, p. 12).

Bearing in mind that both the mediation and reception of pop is dependent on technology, we turn to Prince's style to consider the complex surface of ambiguities and contradictions already evident in his early output. As much as his fashioning of an androgynous image, his artwork for his album covers reflect the aspects of his musical style, displaying from early on a penchant for the ludic and the carnivalesque to defy fixed meanings and categorization. We will identify a series of musical moments as landmarks within Prince's early career that best illustrate how Prince intentionally transgressed seemingly foreclosed cultural and musical boundaries. The chapter also singles out themes of ambiguity and transgression that have continued through later albums, nuanced by the socio-political and socio-cultural contexts within which his music was produced and received. As part of our investigation we will use a time-sensitive analysis that looks at the context Prince was working in during the 1970s and early 1980s. Our prime purpose is to reveal the extent of his Otherness and transgression.

David Machin (2010) maintains that we can still learn about the way music works without removing the importance of its effect: 'When linguists describe grammar and the way that lexical and grammatical choices can signify particular broader meanings, we do not see that this somehow reduces what language is or therefore diminishes the way that it has an emotional effect on us (Machin 2010, p.4). He espouses a less semiotic and more discourse-oriented approach to examining the way that sounds, words and, importantly, images can have particular meanings through a mechanism called Critical Discourse Analysis (CDA). In explaining this methodology, Norman Fairclough (1995) writes that social life comprises interconnected networks of social practices of diverse sorts (economic, political, cultural and so on), with individual practices having a semiotic element. All social practices, he maintains, include statements or meanings about social relations, social identities, cultural values and consciousness amongst others. Thus, by applying CDA to the reception of music and its associated cultural forms, we can move beyond thinking about the connotation or denotation of a single gesture or album cover, to thinking about what the wider personal, social or cultural implications of that signification might be. Usefully for a study of the highly visually playful Prince, CDA has moved beyond linguistic codes and has taken on a visual turn thanks to the work of Kress and Van Leeuwen (1996, 2001).[1]

---

[1] Note that these authors argue that our reception of messages is often 'multimodal', connoted linguistically and visually, as opposed to 'monomodal', which usually applies to

Obfuscating Boundaries

As part of our analytic approach, we want to advocate various methodological tools for examining the ways in which Prince encodes his ethnicity in his early album covers. Ethnicity has been but one of a range of ambiguous and often conflicting signs he has exploited to defy simple generic categorization – by both audiences and the music industry he was intending to subvert and transcend. Promotional materials are an important factor in the reception of a star, not least in the way the artist is categorized. Keith Negus, however, has asserted that marketing images such as album covers can be interpreted and appropriated by fans in particular, and 'can enjoy a degree of independence from their specifically commercial function' (Negus 1997, p. 186). As such, extramusical props are commonly remembered by audiences as bringing a star's persona into a closer form of identification.[2] Furthermore, several of the images have sparked off great controversy in the media when it comes to Prince's identity. A comparative analysis can quickly reveal how each image deliberately undercuts conventional representations of black male musical artists in popular circulation at that time. In doing so Prince has systematically obfuscated perceived boundaries between subject (the reader of the image) and object (himself), and in so doing has thoroughly problematized all notions of genre in popular music.

Interestingly, Murali Balaji (2009) has described how the political economy of popular culture often overlooks the ideologies that determine how identities are commodified:

> The commodification of what is reductively known as black music is unique because the commodification routinely intersects with historical constructions of blackness and black gender identities. Therefore, any analysis of the relationships between black musical artists and the cultural industries and the subsequent production of performative identities must take into account America's exploitation of black music genres and black sexuality. (Balaji 2009, p. 225)

To illustrate this point, Laurie Paulik (1998, republished 2007) has examined the paucity of successful black country music artists in the US. African American influences on country music can be traced back to the 1920s, and there is well-documented evidence that successful white artists were greatly influenced by or

---

linguistic coding. In the context of the marketing of Prince, he is decoded multimodally through lyrics, visuals and sonic signification.

[2] In a rare example of female fan criticism (albeit of male stars), Cath Carroll discusses her pleasures in Elton John's record sleeves as a fan in the 1970s. 'Les Gray's Erection' in Sarah Cooper (ed.) (1992) *Girls! Girls! Girls! Essays on Women and Rock* (London: Cassell) pp. 40–47.

worked with black rhythm and blues contemporaries such as Robert Johnson.[3] Paulik asserts that this absence of successful black country music artists is partly due to racism but also due to economics and market segmentation. Segmentation is used by businesses to target products at a particular audience. This direct targeting approach, which requires businesses to research carefully their audience in order to achieve a rapport with their needs, is felt to be more effective and profitable than a mass market 'scatter gun approach'. Markets can be segmented according to characteristics such as geographical, demographic, psychographic and behaviouristic. Demographic characteristics include factors such as ethnicity, while behaviouristic ones include 'brand' loyalty.[4] It appears the country music marketing has not deviated from targeting a highly segmented white sector, despite the very close affiliation of black artists to the genre. One training manual for maximizing profits asserts that 'This selling of the "same jam in a different jar" should not be thought of as an unnecessary extra cost, nor indeed as manipulating customers. If you somehow change the presentation of a core product to give greater appeal to some user groups, and you are able to command a premium for it, then that is good business' (Croft 1994, p. 4). Paulik points out that image is undeniably important in today's country music scene as evidenced by the 'marginally talented, but good-looking, artists who've achieved success. However, in implying that black is an image white country music audiences cannot embrace, the industry has managed not only to misread its audience and lose potential new stars, but to negate its own history' (Paulik 1998).

Prince's marketing followed in the wake of another child prodigy, Stevie Wonder, who was first signed to a contract with Motown Record Corporation in 1961. He made a fair showing in the record charts, but it was not until he supported the Rolling Stones on their 1982 tour that he began to make a significant impact due to his exposure to white audiences. A wave of media articles attested to his cross-racial appeal (Harper 1989, p. 104). Under Berry Gordy's leadership, Motown succeeded in reaching white audiences with black musicians. Arnold Shaw (1986) suggests that Motown represented a '"white synthesis" of traditional black musical forms, facilitating their acceptance by a white market' (p. 223), though Harper (1989) maintains that it was not a simple dichotomy between 'authentically black' music being repackaged as 'unauthentic' outputs for white consumption (p. 106). More significant for Harper is the fact that black-produced music has always been manipulated by market forces, and that Gordy was manipulating one specific black identity amongst many other equally constructed identities to ensure Motown's commercial success (p. 107). In this significant way, Harper differs from other commentators on Motown, such as Nelson George, by playing down racial markers and highlighting other extra-musical techniques employed by Motown to market to wide audiences. One particular technique was the connotation of class-status signifiers through visual marketing in record sleeves and lavish live performances.

[3] See http://www.carlray.com/twang.htm [accessed: June 27, 2011].
[4] See http://www.netmba.com/marketing/market/segmentation/ [accessed: June 27, 2011].

The widespread commercial success of The Supremes, for example, was said to have been dependent on their televisual image, which secured regular influential appearances on the Ed Sullivan Show (p. 109). Harper's assertion is that Motown wanted the question of race to become irrelevant, 'since we "all", "universally", can identify with the "stylish" visual presentation the group offers up' (ibid.).[5]

In a similar way, Prince paid considerable attention to his image creation and marketing so as not to be defined by his ethnicity. A space had been opened up by stars such as Diana Ross and Stevie Wonder for Prince and Michael Jackson to play with their identities. While Jackson utilized many signifiers of high-class status and access to privileged situations, such as his bow tie, Prince utilized a more breathtaking and subversive array of politically-charged signifiers to create a confusing and provocative image.

'For You': Conflating Signifiers

Just before his twentieth birthday, Prince released his debut album *For You*, on 7 April 1978. The cover depicts Prince's head, backlit against a dark background. Prince bears little resemblance to his later styling. He wears no make-up, his skin is un-powdered and even a little darker in shade than his natural olive complexion. Moustachioed and sporting a large Afro hairstyle, Prince epitomizes the styling of popular soul artists in the late 1970s, such as the young Michael Jackson. Like Jackson, Prince broke with the hyper-masculine conventions of the black soul star. While artists such as Teddy Pendergrass and Marvin Gaye were depicted looking bold, manly and often gazing to the side in meaningful contemplation of the material world, Prince stares directly at the viewer, wide-eyed and full-lipped.

It is far easier to find comparable images on album sleeves for female artists such as Donna Summer, Natalie Cole, Gloria Gaynor and Betty Davies. Indeed, Prince's second album, titled *Prince*, released in 1979, almost replicates the cover image for Summer's 1977 album *Once Upon a Time*, even down to the ornate title typeface. This would have to be a deliberate act of pastiche – Prince must have been aware of Summer's album, given her huge profile at the time. The tone of Prince's skin, his looser curled hairstyle, his eye make-up – even the slight twist in his left shoulder – suggest his desire to be positioned in the same space as his female disco contemporary, rather than in those of his male counterparts.

Contrast this with Michael Jackson's simultaneous 1979 release, *Off The Wall*, and the distinctions between Prince and Jackson could not be clearer. In his artwork, Jackson wears a black tuxedo suit over a white shirt and bow tie connoting formality. Smiling broadly, his face is un-made up, and his Afro hair is shorter than Prince's and natural looking as opposed to coiffured. Jackson proffers

---

[5] Motown's most successful artist, Michael Jackson, by his death, was felt somewhat controversially to have 'transcended' his own race. Though conversely, hip-hop's ethnic identity was highly relevant in its marketing.

an uncomplicated image of a young, attractive black cross-over performer with a sharply dressed image suggestive of adherence to formal social codes, albeit with the slight subversion of visible bright white socks. The image is accessible, unthreatening and non-sexual, and could probably have been filed under soul or R&B in a record store. In stark contrast, it would be hard to file 'Prince' under any category but the letter P.

The inner sleeves for both of Prince's earliest albums contain images that further problematize Prince's generic categorization as 'typical' black, male soul artist, and they also allude to his other musical influences. On the inner sleeve of *For You*, Prince is naked but for a carefully-positioned acoustic guitar, sitting on a bed seemingly surfing through outer space. Whilst not stretching the signifiers quite as far as Earth Wind and Fire did (with their Ancient Egyptian/ alien mythology), Prince certainly nods to their extra-terrestrialism, albeit more by portraying himself as a soulful deity. Likewise, his own mythological Otherness is reinforced in the rear sleeve art for 'Prince' as the star is once again naked as if to connote his oneness and purity. Hilariously, and with great dignity, he rides a white Pegasus.

Prince's near nudity – which stretched to performing a stage show in little more than a G-string and stockings – might, on one level, be construed as capitulating to the black/white, body/mind dichotomy. Frith contextualizes the idea that black culture and music are 'earthy' in the Romantic tradition where black people were seen as 'uncorrupted by culture, still close to human essence' (1996, p. 127). On the contrary, Prince showed an active, intellectual agency in constructing his image, far and away from primitive notions of unmediated and 'natural' sensuality. Stuart Hall (1992) has written that African American musicians 'have used the body as if it was, and it often was, the only cultural capital we had. We have worked on ourselves as the canvases of representation' (Hall 1992, p. 27). Here, Hall articulates the dilemma that while the artist's self-representation is inextricably bound to commodity culture and market imperatives, it is no less a space to explore memories, experiences and potential. Likewise, philosopher Mark Johnson (1987) has shown that the culturally mediated body serves as the basis for all human discourses, and the task of coming to understand the embodiedness of all culture remains a crucial endeavour. McClary and Walser, who have commented on Michael Jackson's Otherness as potentially productive, express concern at the perceived misogyny in his videos. About Prince they are more positive:

> ... when Prince blurs the polarized oppositions that still organize notions of race and gender (i.e., white/black, male/female), he destabilizes the signs that bind desire in channels established by white patriarchy, an act that suggests that changing desires is at least as important as changing minds.[6]

---

[6] See http://www.sibetrans.com/trans/a267/theorizing-the-body-in-african-american-music [accessed: June 27, 2011]

Even in the short space of these two early albums, Prince conflated a range of signifiers of ethnicity, gender and genres of music from soul to disco, right through to the excesses of heavy rock. Indeed, at the point of his emergence, Prince's visual work would probe at the essentialism of widely-held notions of 'black music', and attempts to neatly categorize black artists into specific genres.[7] It is the cultural categorization, often market-led, that resulted in Scott Joplin's ragtime music being celebrated while his operatic output was ignored (Machin 2010, p. 21). In other words, the creation of an essentialist view of black identity by the music industry served merely to satisfy market forces. As a young man, Prince, who had grown up in the predominantly white twin-cities of Minneapolis St Paul and had been weaned on a varied diet of musical influences, was best-placed to crash through any attempt at stereotyping him.

At this point we want to consider in more detail the ways in which Prince has continuously obfuscated his differences, and what implications this has had for his branding and marketing strategies. From the outset Prince has defied ideals of heteronormativity by not acting out his masculinity in the 'right way'. Indeed, his ways of queering his masculinity are articulated through forms of behaviour that surface in his musical performances, which are inextricably attached to the politics of gender representation. Attempting to work out how masculinity is performatively instated through heterosexuality raises all sorts of concerns connected to the 'policing of identity'. So what then makes the spectacle of Prince's work, and how does his gendered display function?

In his early years much of his act was parodied by the musical styles he turned to. Lyrics, gestures and mannerisms were theatricalized humorously in tandem with the sound and stylistic referents he turned to. The spectacle of Prince's posturing was important in challenging traditional representations of gender, as he demonstrated the phenomenon of parodying the construction of masculinity. Of course, misogyny has always been lurking in many forms and guises in Prince's act, and references in so many of his songs to the female as a sex object underlie an alternative to macho posturing that is nevertheless ardent in its intentions.[8] Yet, there are many blurred moments in the task of assessing Prince's relationship to females that we need to tread cautiously when it comes to evaluating his motives. For what Prince opens up is the potential for resistance to the norms and conventions of masculinity. In fact in a Butlerian light, he shows us that heterosexuality is not that much more than an institution that struggles to reinforce its idealizations. This is what makes the straight/queer dichotomy so compelling, and, moreover, a relevant marker for considering what establishes Prince's masculine display.

---

[7] Numerous writers have challenged the very idea of 'black music' being a category whatsoever. Tagg (1989) and Negus (1996), for instance, have shown separately how there is no intrinsic quality of 'black' music that does not exist in music emanating from other groups or cultures.

[8] For a full discussion of this, see Hawkins (2002), Chapter 6.

Epitomizing postmodern pop, Prince has consistently based his subjectivity upon the fluidity of identification, destabilizing the rigid constructs of heterosexuality, showing that the fan's spectatorial position is extremely varied. In staging his masculinity, Prince reminds us that he can be the object of many different gazes. Flirting with an eroticism that is so queerly defined, his initial appearances on the international pop stage (especially through MTV) challenged the scopophilic male gaze in ways that were pathologized by hypersexualized performances. Importantly, his own response to the mainstream pop artists around him at the time has been that of upsetting the binarisms of gender, ethnic and sexual categorization. One cannot bypass the startling effect of Prince's image in the early 1980s, which provided a new space for erotic identification and fantasy in pop, quite clearly pushing forward the transgressive aspects of male representation already started by artists such as David Bowie, Mick Jagger, Little Richard and George Clinton. Most remarkably, his outlandish performances were forays into musical events that symbolized the dawning of a new era in pop.

Questions of how masculinity conjoins to musical conventions have become an increasingly important area of musicological research in the wake of Susan McClary's work, with a steady stream of gender-related scholarship during the past decades.[9] Biddle and Gibson (2009) have noted the directions taken by musicologists towards feminism and profeminist scholarship and how these have signalled part of a paradigm shift that is now termed as 'the postmodern moment': 'claims to the kind of authority that were once wielded in the name of the greats are ever more rarely made and where they persist they come to look defensive' (Biddle and Gibson 2009, p. 4). In this context, though, the 'greats' refer to the classical composers, all white and male (and wishfully heterosexual). Inevitably, the strategies of feminist musicology, and the unearthing of hegemonic practices radicalized by McClary would lead to discursive trajectories into masculinity as an object of study and, particularly, the issue of non-heteronormative masculinity as the Other.

Characterizing the majority of studies from the early 1990s onwards, which dealt with the intersubjectivities of the body and the Western canon (based around the male composer), has been a general curiosity for working out how music is gendered and sexualized, and, moreover how the body in performance is inscribed. A critical approach to determining the relationships between musical practices and masculinity has thoughtfully engaged a diverse range of theoretical musicological perspectives that overlap with a wide range of disciplines, such as psychoanalysis, sociology, cultural studies, social anthropology, media studies, critical theory and philosophy. And, as we have so far intimated, this study, while constituting a strong focus on issues dealing with the music, is interdisciplinary in that we engage in an array of approaches that impact on a critical evaluation and account of a male pop artist. Gender-coded musical expression as exemplified by

---

[9] See Susan McClary (1989, 1991, 2000). McClary has also written on Prince in several articles.

Prince, we maintain, is traceable through questions relating to style, preferences, trends and cultural constructions, all of which are subtly bound up in narratives of musical mastery. In the section that follows we will attempt a concise description of how Prince's masculinity can be critiqued through the discourses surrounding dandyism. In this light, then, one of our main objectives is to debate how Prince's masculinity is modelled on an aesthetic that converts musical style into dandyism, where the artist becomes constituted through the idiosyncrasies of his very own visual and sonic spectacle.

Princian Dandification

Prince has not stopped at conflating generic and ethnic signifiers to subvert classification. Just as his audiences have been in thrall of his bodily display, Prince has covered himself from head to toe in richly ornate fabrics and lace. To what end and purpose, one might ask?

Between 1983 and 1988 Prince utilized dandy visual signifiers most notably in a manner that expressly offered him a site for identification along both ethnic and gender lines. His clothes, hair, face and gestures connoted gender ambiguity, opening a space for females to enjoy a non-threatening masculinity and for straight males to admire his style and charisma. Ethnically, he continued a rich trajectory of contestational fashion signifiers that symbolized a sartorial fight against subjugation. The clothes of gentility do not say 'I am a man – and how!' but 'I am a gentleman, and I hope to attract woman not by asserting my masculinity but by demonstrating my membership of a social class' (Laver 1968, p. 112).

Since the earliest days of his career, Prince has not attempted to follow fashion or set trends, but has rather represented himself as singularly unique. It has not been possible to purchase replica Prince 'wannabe' outfits[10] – even his own merchandise outlets and his former shop in Camden steered away from selling anything resembling a Prince costume. It is useful to consider Prince's singularity of identity in the context of the dandy movement. By examining the origins and legacy of these original peacock males in the eighteenth and nineteenth centuries, it can be seen uncontrovertibly how Prince was launching an assault in the mid 1980s on the mainstream practices of white, middle-class, conservative masculinity. From the outset he would exaggerate the business look with sharply cut suits embellished with lace and brocade in the parodic style of the Zazous in France decades earlier.[11] Furthermore, Prince recognized that witty clothes could make powerful and memorable points.

---

[10] A term used by Madonna's young female fans in the mid 1980s, who closely replicated her appearance, and who tried to be self-made stars like her.

[11] The Zazous were a sub-culture of young French during the Second World War who expressed their opposition to German occupation by wearing exaggerated, colourful, oversized suits made with excess drapery in protest at clothing rationing. They celebrated

His exuberant camp-ness, full of visual puns, commented on the banality of white, mainstream, Western masculinity in the mid 1980s. His dandified zoot suit would harness the raw energy and anger of hard-times street fashion coupled with decadence and indifference to aristocratic mores. As such, his theatricality mirrored the New Romantic movement of the early 1980s London fashion scene, with its strong anti-establishment bias:

> Rich brocades, velvet and embroidery, Indian silks and cotton shirts printed with flowers – the effect was part eighteenth century, part Thirties Colonialist and remarkably similar in spirit to the dress of the swinging sixties pop world. (McDowell 1997, p. 201)

Paradoxically, Prince's arch sartorially-symbolic contender in the mid 1980s was not Michael Jackson (they had much in common and were not rivals except as depicted in the media), but rather Bruce Springsteen. He epitomized America's – and simultaneously a lot of Britain's – fashion philosophy based on casual, relaxed clothes, which, to the outsider, appeared to be a negation of status dress.

Prince's dandified ethnic masculinity represented a powerful visual and symbolic assault on the mainstream. His image served as an acknowledgement of the rich heritage of confrontational ethnic dandy subcultures historically, but also suffused with a sense of wishing to represent his own ambiguous personal origins. The dandy is a shifting cultural figure, preceded by and located within a set of political and historical conditions. Historically, the practitioners of dandyism have offered such a space on the visual plane for those on the borders of, say, class, racial and gender identities, to transgress conventional practices. Indeed, clothing has served to set the dandy apart from those around him; Prince wished to occupy a different 'place' to his pop contemporaries, and for his female fans to also envision him differently to other male performers. This possibility, and the fact that he chose to emulate the dandy movement with its long trajectory of political and gender subversion, suggests Prince was intervening directly in contemporary debates about gender representation and relations.

Despite his heterosexual status, Prince's visual coding has alluded to gay references in a wider cultural context, notably advertising, further nuancing his appeal. This part of our study therefore recognizes that Prince's dandyism has not only served as a stylistic device to beckon a wide array of identifications, but also functioned on a political level. In effect, Prince's self-fashioning (and the ambiguity that comes with this) refers directly to historic moments of class, gender and ethnic struggle.

---

hedonism and jazz and were suspicious of the work ethic under Nazi/Vichy rule, which they saw as an attempt to indoctrinate the youth. For more on this movement, see Drane, D. (2001).

'Dandy', as a term, has normally been ascribed to a male who pays impeccable attention to his clothes (Walden 2002, p. 36), which, in turn, was viewed in the eighteenth and nineteenth centuries as a deliberately provocative statement against the monarchy. According to the Victorian cultural commentator, Charles Baudelaire (1863), dandies would appear especially in the transitory periods when democracy was not yet all-powerful. Dandyism arose in France and later in England as a protest against the rule of kings over fashion, just as democracy rose against the divine right of kings in politics. One of the most famous British dandies was George 'Beau' Brummell. According to Laver:

> Without plunging too deeply into the mysteries of psychoanalysis, it is perhaps helpful to consider him a narcissist. The simplest form of narcissism involves the display of the naked or near-naked body; but this original, crude exhibitionist tendency tends to be sublimated by being displaced onto clothes. (Laver 1968, p. 28)

Laver adds that while it might be thought a logical consequence that the very high degree of narcissism characteristic of the dandy correlates with some degree of sexual ambiguity, 'there is no evidence that Brummell ... was a homosexual' (ibid.).

The important legacy of Brummell to Prince was that he symbolized, essentially, a conspiracy against aristocracy, officialdom and patriarchal law. Prince's quasi-aristocratic image embraced Brummell's challenge to patriarchy, while taking the stylistic device one step further and using it to engage with his audience. Brummell identified that the day of aristocracy was over and that attention to clothing meant that all gentlemen were equal: 'Even if one of them is called George, Prince of Wales, and the other is called George Brummell. Indeed there was nothing to distinguish them except that Brummell's cravat was more carefully tied and his coat better fitting' (ibid., p. 34). Similarly, the effect of cravats and the high, ruffled collars worn by Prince on the artwork and promotional images for his albums *Controversy*, *1999* and *Purple Rain*, was to constrict the throat and hold the head rigid, thereby giving the look of blasé indifference which was expected of the perfect eighteenth-century dandy. With Prince, who not only wore Edwardian styles but also diamante jewellery, full make-up and shiny fabrics, the suggestion was that all men and all women were to be seen as equal.

Significantly, Prince's look, as with all dandies, has been very much about social climbing. It has corresponded with the growing presence in Western popular culture of power-dressing – though Prince has eschewed the ubiquitous pin-stripe suit and red braces, as epitomized in the film *Wall Street* (Oliver Stone, 1987), for even bigger shoulder pads and brighter, more luxurious fabrics. Michael Sadler, in *Bulwer: A Panorama* (1931), draws an interesting parallel between the period following the Battle of Waterloo and the time immediately after the First World War. Both involved social upheaval, the break-up of old social categories, a frenzied search for pleasure and the means to pay for it. 'Everything that glittered', wrote Sadler, 'might not be gold; but most things provided they glittered sufficiently, served for currency.' Nothing was 'of importance to the still aspiring elegant beside the conviction that, if he tried hard enough, he too might join the elite ...' (ibid., p. 47). This also finds parallels with the entrepreneurial and capitalist zeal of the 1980s.

Important to remember here is that the dandy, and subsequently Prince, was projecting an image – and a challenge – on the visual plane. The positioning of female viewers, in particular, has been negative, with desirous male pop stars being denounced as dupes in countless accounts. The dandy's impact is visual and gestural, connecting with Lacan's statement that: 'in the so-called waking state, there is an elision of the gaze, and an elision of the fact that not only does it look, it also shows' (Lacan 1977, p. 75). Here Lacan, drawing on Saussure, was speaking of the connotative potential of the visual to impact on the self. The spectator of the dandy Prince was engaged in a symbolic visual exchange, for s/he is at one and the same time looking, and being shown something.

The connection between looking, identity and cultural context is evident in how Prince re-signified dandy visual codes to engage with his spectators. For example, in *The Man of Fashion: Peacock Males and Perfect Gentlemen* (1997), Colin McDowell explains how the semiotics of lace has varied over the centuries. Whereas in the sixteenth century, it represented the status and wealth of the fashionable courtier – chronicler Philip Stubbes wrote of 'great and monstrous ruffs ... some a quarter of a yard deep' – by the seventeenth it was the mark not only of the trendy man but also of the man worthy of respect, be he government official, successful merchant or hereditary peer (McDowell 1997, p. 18). By 1984 and the launch of *Purple Rain*, lace for men represented cross-dressing in a style that juxtaposed purity and perversion. Prince's excess of lace at that time signified his desire to be provocative to patriarchal, white authority. This has much in common with previous fashion movements that had used dandyish clothes as an assault on the mainstream exercise of power.

Consider the Macaronis of the nineteenth century, the first political youth movement to use clothes as a cultural weapon. Their very name was an act of aggression – to choose an Italian food, which had none of the solid associations of roast beef or old England, was guaranteed to insult the Establishment who, unlike most of the population of Britain at the time, actually knew what macaroni was, and could be relied upon to dislike it as slippery, unreliable and unsatisfactory (ibid., p. 44). Italy was also viewed in upper-middle-class British society as the home of unnatural practices. The Macaronis used their elaborate clothing as a way of attacking traditional values: '(...) perfect masculine elegance could be supplied; broad shoulders, narrow waist and immaculately figure-conscious pantaloons. The high collar lent status – and automatically imposed a swanky, arrogant lift to the whole body' (ibid., p. 54).

The Macaroni style was reworked by the Zoot Suiters, young Mexican Americans, in the post-war years. Zoot suit jackets were knee-length and usually double-breasted and wide-shouldered. Trousers were baggy in the thigh and narrowed to 12-inches at the cuff. Ties were either very wide or very narrow and the hat was always a wide-brimmed fedora. The cut of Prince's suits from the *Purple Rain* era onwards very much mirrored that of the zoot suit, which was initially an African American style that developed as part of the jazz craze (ibid., p. 116). McDowell writes: 'It was the first true dandy fashion of the twentieth century in the sense that it was an outsider fashion which became an almost instant thorn in the flesh of the authorities' (ibid.).

Everything about the zoot suit, as with Prince's cloud patterns and ruched trousers with buttons up the sides, seems exaggerated, an affront to established taste. Moreover, Prince has always worn high-heeled boots made from the same fabric as his suits. Lest we forget, the zoot suit was seen as dangerously subversive by the American authorities, and it was declared unpatriotic, since the large amount of material it required contravened wartime rationing regulations. White servicemen physically attacked zoot suit wearers by stripping them of their suits. Indeed, riots spread across the US as battles broke out between marines and young black and Hispanic zoot suit wearers.[12]

The subversive quality of the zoot suit subsequently made it attractive to the Zazous. They wore it in defiance of the clothing regulations established by the German occupiers, for they did not want to wear the grey, unostentatious clothing demanded by their invaders.[13] Therefore, for the Zazous, the zoot suit was a political statement just as it was in the ghettos of America. While there was a gap in the development of men's 'street' fashion from then until the 1950s and 1960s, the zoot suit left a signifier of racial confrontation that became fused with the gender play that would be associated with music and fashion for men in later decades.

Notably, Prince fused the zoot suit jacket shape during *Purple Rain* with the narrower leg cut and effeminate winkle-picker of the Italian look. Italian tailoring signified masculine preening and narcissism as well as financial affluence and decadence. It made fashion a preoccupation amongst men who had previously hidden behind banal middle-class clothing, and it was subversive for its origins amongst streetwise young radicals. By drawing on these styles in the mid 1980s, Prince was launching an assault on dominant representations of masculinity that made him conducive to assimilation by style-conscious women searching for a means of self-representation and subjectivity that was not defined by patriarchy.

Many of these issues concerning dandyism lead onto the state of his queerness. For the particularity of dandifying oneself is about defining oneself as an Other, and, in Prince's case, bending the norms to redefine his straightness makes him queer, very much on his own terms. In late twentieth-century pop, the performance is disseminated through a playful approach to gender-on-display, where the body 'inscribes ideals of gender and sexuality that are part of the process of politicizing style and expression spatially and temporally' (Hawkins 2009a, p. 105). Discernible

---

[12] See Stuart Cosgrove's analysis of the political imperative of the zoot suit at http://invention.smithsonian.org/centerpieces/whole_cloth/u7sf/u7materials/cosgrove.html [accessed: June 27, 2011].

[13] It is significant that the Nazis were also intent on eradicating jazz!

in all Prince's videos are representational politics that function through the stylistic and technical codes of his music production. As a transgressive mediator of gender, his brand of queering is employed to prescribe difference at the same time as supporting dominant values, and the ambiguity we often experience in Prince's act corresponds to the trends of dandyism in the nineteenth and twentieth centuries that paved the way for celebrity culture in pop.

When it comes to working out the intricate intersections between dandyism and queering, we need to bear in mind that queering works on a sliding scale. For instance, the nature of Prince's queering permits his straightness to sidestep the direct questions of his sexual preference. In common with a legacy of British pop artists, Prince has 'successfully negotiated the movement between queer and straight, exhibiting the sensational possibilities of sexual identity as fluid' on *his* terms (Hawkins 2009a, p. 106). This sheds light on how queering forms an integral part of staging dandyism, and, moreover, why contesting stereotypes opens up a space for recreating male subjectivity. Dandyism, after all, is a structuring device that works politically and socially in its bid to theatricalize the body, and rife with a queer sensibility, Prince's subjectivity can be read as a marker of opposition. Also contributing to this is a camp-ness that corresponds to tropes of behaviour and attitude.

Situated within a political context, one should remember that Prince was coding himself camply during the Thatcher/Reagan period, in a way that contrasted directly with his peers and transgressed patriarchal conventions of the moment. Camp, like queerness, is useful in further debating the antics of the dandy. Often perceived as camp, gay men had become a growing and visible presence in British pop culture during the 1980s. Gay comedy acts, such as The Joan Collins Fan Club, along with musical artists such as Pet Shop Boys, Frankie Goes to Hollywood and Boy George, made homosexual culture, including campness, cool. The origins and definitions of the concept of camp have been widely debated in academic circles. Some writers, such as Susan Sontag (1964), draw attention to its exaggeration, artificiality, daring and wittiness. Building on this work, Mark Booth (1983) usefully defines camp thus: 'To be camp is to present oneself as being committed to the marginal with a commitment greater than the marginal merits' (p. 18).

Accordingly, in camp culture, marginal categories such as kitsch, trash and 'cultural slumming' (Hoggart 1958) are favoured and celebrated. But camp is most often characterized as ambiguous and exaggerated sexuality, often associated with homosexuality, something that Booth decries as a popular confusion:

> In camp culture, the popular image of the homosexual, like the popular image of the feminine woman, is mimicked as a type of the marginal. So while it may be true that many homosexuals are camp, only a small proportion of people who exhibit symptoms of camp behaviour are homosexual. (ibid., p. 70)

Fabio Cleto, drawing on Sontag, shares the view, which angered the gay community on publication of Sontag's 'Notes on Camp', that the concept's origins do not lie in homosexual culture, but rather it was adopted there. He suggests that we rethink the many types of camp – low camp and high camp for instance, as a variety of re-presentations and historical re-articulations, which are grounded in the varying characteristics, such as theatricality, irony, sexual deviance and aristocratic-ness. 'The definition of camp may thus well reside, I think, in its modes and reasons of resistance to definition, or in a metaphor of such indefinibility as materially constituted' (Cleto 1999, p. 6). In this regard, one can see the potential for its application in a range of ways in a range of communities and temporal contexts, as elaborated by Andrew Ross in his essay 'Uses of Camp' (1989). For Ross, camp is not essentially masculine or homosexual; and it might, in Prince's case, represent a safe engagement with femininity.

Hyper-feminized, strong female icons, such as Liza Minnelli, Shirley Bassey, Joan Collins and Dusty Springfield, would enjoy a resurgence of popularity through their celebration in the work of musical artists such as Yellow and Pet Shop Boys. These women's old-fashioned glamour and theatricality was ostensibly being celebrated by the gay community. Yet, significantly, and arguably, more revolutionary, Prince's own camp intervention into this growing commercial phenomenon was not to put a diva on his label (though he did write for and produce Mavis Staples), but rather to be one himself, a queer, androgynous, over-the-top male diva!

This is blatantly evident in the promotional video for the song 'Raspberry Beret' (1985). Directed by Prince, this three-minute film encapsulates the most resonant and recurring visual rhetorical signs of the star's work. Pastiching surrealism, counter-culture and the gestures and appearance of female divas, the video crystallizes Prince's authorial and transgressive intervention into mainstream popular culture. The figure of Prince presented in this video provocatively offered a site for identification, objectification and negotiation.

'Raspberry Beret': Re-inscribing the Dandy as Pop Effete

'Raspberry Beret', the first single to be taken from the psychedelic *Around the World in a Day* (1985) album, released after *Purple Rain*, is an innocent adolescent fantasy of boy meets girl, fleeing a dead-end job for an afternoon of romance in the countryside.

The promotional video, which Prince directed himself, is an optimistic and upbeat homage to flower-power counter-culture. Opening with a spinning psychedelic image of the drum, it features the band's name and song title written in 'Sgt Pepper' style script. The scene is a studio, ostensibly in the sky, with The Revolution playing on a series of podia. The *mise-en-scène* is semi-animated so that the backdrop is part live-action and part sketches of a pastoral scene to mirror the song's description of a journey out of the city into the countryside. Brightly-dressed dancers make up the audience for this surreal gig. Girls are dressed principally as boys, in ruffed shirts and colourful satin trouser suits. Balloons and flowers are strewn across the podia and the instruments.

Prince enters from backstage, mincing in from behind a pedestal with camp effete. He is wearing a pale blue suit covered with clouds to match the sky backdrop. Once the singing commences, the blue of his suit disappears so that we only see the clouds. A young female fan hands Prince a white guitar (the one he was presented with by Apollonia in *Purple Rain*). But the first thing he does on stage is to cough, to clear his throat audibly. Prince later told *Rolling Stone* magazine:

> A lot of my peers make remarks about us doing silly things on stage and on records ... the music, the dances, the lyrics. What they fail to realise is that is exactly what we want to do. It's not silliness, it's sickness. Sickness is just slang for doing things somebody else wouldn't do. That's what I'm looking for all the time.[14]

The throat-clearing moment jolts the spectator and sets the stage for the high camp act that is to follow. Hill has commented:

> ... the cleverest thing [sic] about this spinning, pastel-shaded production are Prince's facial stunts for the camera. It is a better piece of acting than anything he did in Purple Rain; just smirking and swooning, pulling faces and fluttering his lashes ... but never actually looking into the lens at all. It is a beautiful spook of an innocence he would struggle to sustain in his work, never mind what kind of chaotic worldliness went on around him. (Hill 1989, p. 73)

The song is then performed, interspersed with animated representations of the narrative projected behind Prince. Throughout the song a range of musical ideas emerge that help frame Prince's imagery, and the actual vocal performance is rich in its timbral shading and phrasing (see Chapter 4 for a more in-depth analysis of the music in this track). Rhythm guitarist Wendy, dressed as Dorothy Parker, joins him at the front of the stage for vocal duets. But her presence and appearance is incomparable to that of Prince, for his dandyism is camped up to the nines. Without a central biological female to fetishize, Prince styled himself accordingly to connote to-be-looked-at-ness. His lack of masculinity, while not quite androgynous, represents an adoption of a female pose, ostensibly putting him in league with E. Ann Kaplan's (1987) critique of rock bands, such as Mötley Crüe, whom she claims 'have incorporated the feminine, as it were, making its actual presence superfluous ... [their] feminised appearance seems rather to mark the absence of women as something desirable' (Kaplan 1987, p. 72).

Prince's facial expressions are hugely exaggerated in the video, which, coupled with his heavily made-up eyes and sculpted hair, means he directly resembles Liza

---

[14] http://princetext.tripod.com/i_stone85.html [accessed: June 27, 2011].

Minnelli in his looks and gestures. His eyeliner, blusher, mascara and lip-gloss, and his repeated checks in the mirror, provide a flamboyant point of identification between star and female fan. Furthermore, he does not display an understated, 'natural' femininity, but rather opts for an exaggerated femininity, which has made him a site of projection for the mass media who, as has been documented, defamed him as an example of the perils of playing with gender conventions. In feminist theory, women's enactment of femininity has routinely been conceptualized as capitulation to oppression.[15] Jackie Stacey (1994) has demonstrated how self-fashioning femininity is not synonymous with passivity. She points to the fact that in the 1930s, hair dyeing could represent an act of transgression by women, suggesting 'sexuality, independence and even prostitution' (Stacey 1994, p. 204). However, Val Wilmer (1989), in writing about his fascination for the glamour or 'feminine excess' embodied by black artists in the 1950s and 1960s, identifies its troubling effect on normative gender divisions, along with the appeal that such forms of femininity might have had:

> [Jimmy Cotton] 'konked' his hair too, and wore it 'high' in a black tradition of personal adornment ... splendid enough to impress English people who had never seen the effect outside publicity photos of Little Richard. With his fingers he moulded Marcel Waves deep in his Vaselined 'process', keeping it in place at night with a head-wrap ... There was something distinctly 'feminine' about these blues-men who preferred the soft-waved look and manicured hands. It puzzled white male writers, who got hung up on theories of sexual ambiguity and were rather embarrassed by this apparently less than macho streak in their idols. Yet I understood it when men talked about 'keeping themselves pretty' for women; it was a reaction against calluses of the field-hand and the grimy, broken nails of the assembly line. (Wilmer 1989, p. 69)

The analyses of rock music as a signifying practice through which particular discourses of masculinity are constituted are yet to be completed. Frith (1988) looks back at the decade of gender-bending in rock, suggesting that Boy George, Marilyn, Annie Lennox and others projected the problem of sexuality onto males: 'Masculinity became a packaging problem' (Frith 1988, p. 166). Frith notes that 'popular culture has always meant putting together 'a people' rather than simply reflecting or expressing them' (ibid., p. 168). And that music is sold on the basis of the pop artist's sound as much as his or her identity raises interesting questions related to reception. In this sense, music helps model identity, bringing people together and shaping subjectivities. Frith's work has retained an explicit focus on this prime role of music, where the tenet of many of his arguments is about understanding music's connectedness and its mediation of subjectivities from a sociological perspective.

---

[15] See, for example, Pamela Robertson (1996).

Fashioning 'Otherness' through Musical Coding

What then about the fashioning of sounds, and the cunning production tricks that go into sampled riffs? And how does such delineation take place? One of the musicological challenges of pursuing the structural processes and devices in the recording and live performance has to do with revealing features as 'auditory events in space and time' (Hawkins 2002, p. 10). A general concept of the code (which is derived from semiotics) can be helpful for identifying auditory events. Primary musical codes can be broadly categorized as stylistic and technical. Stylistic codes relate to 'categories of idiolects, sub-codes, dialects and norms', while technical codes involve the components of composition and production, such as 'pitch, melody, rhythm, chord progressions and texture' (ibid.). It is how the creative process in artists such as Prince convert into stylistic and technical codes that becomes a fascinating aspect of musicological analysis.

Through their interrelationship and organization on multiple levels, stylistic and technical codes offer a way forward to understanding how the creative process of musical composition operates. The make-up of any one track is dependent on the unity of musical codes in a bid to mediate expression 'through invocations of resistance, compliance and pleasure' (ibid., p. 12). Within the average duration of a pop song (3–4 minutes) the inner workings of technical and stylistic codes involve a range of properties, such as form (the song's formal sectional structure), harmonic material (goal-directed or static chordal progression), production techniques (the control of material within the mix), textures and timbres (the heterogeneous profusion of instruments and vocal tracks) and rhythmic syntax (recurring groups and metric patterns that denote beat and groove). A detailed investigation of these musical properties will be undertaken in Chapters 4 and 6.

For the music analyst intent on seeking out primary signification (as outlined above), there is always the matter of discursive assimilation. Perhaps this is mainly down to the fact that pop representations cannot detach the eye from the ear. Secondary signification is therefore a critical aspect of working out meaning in pop, and musical codes need to be constantly correlated with other texts. To enter a track discursively, then, entails a consideration of cultural expression with relation to the musical material and the controlling metaphors that determine its materiality.

All too frequently, gendered and ethnic identities in popular music may appear stable, but this is due to a constant process of reiteration in performance. In rock music, as Frith (1988) and others have shown, the binaries that exist in the performance and marketing of rock identities therefore serve to promote a monolithic masculinity and contain or even exile 'excessive' femininity. Prince's performances do the exact opposite. The video of 'Raspberry Beret' shows how Prince and his female followers subjectively identify in a manner that transcends the boundaries of patriarchy within the music industry, and his dandyness is integral to this subversion in three ways.

First, Prince's self-fashioning with femininity, in relation to his body, his performance and sometimes even his voice, can be interpreted as providing and drawing on a pleasurable array of feminine identifications. Moreover, his visual references to female performers provide a site of identification that problematizes reductive binary oppositions between male and female in circulation at the time in popular culture. His camp, feminized gestures and looks defuse the patriarchal symbolic potential of his status as a performer in order to offer an alternative discourse of gender relations and gender identifications.

Second, Prince's brand of dandy-ness serves to destabilize his corporeal reality within the diegetic space which problematizes any gendered look. Special effects editing using the blue patches of Prince's outfit make his body merge with the animated background. His physicality is removed, except for his head, feminized guitar and white clouds on his suit, blending him in with the pleasurable imagos of his fantasy that flash by. The *mise-en-scène* is dream-like, turning Prince into a literal projection onto a screen. This use of the film within the film turns Prince into a 2D imago by de-signifying his masculinity and ethnicity through the loss of his body other than his camply expressive and cosmeticized face.

Third, the audiovisual representation of a pop artist emphasizes the nuances of temperament that set out to seduce and entertain us. What is at issue here when it comes to Prince is the high visibility of his body on display. Moreover, it is his bodily poise that complements his musicality, drawing in the empathic responses of fans in a wide variety of situational contexts. The profiling of his biography is thus a crucial strategy in marketing his music, and this is mediated through a temperament that is flamboyant yet at the same time coy. Through an air of indifference, he has continuously denounced the gender and ethnic stereotypes that prop up the music industry. In sum, one might say that Prince's brand of dandyism is conveyed by a resistance to the conventions and practices that normalize masculinity. The significance of this is that Prince exhibits a radical form of self-aestheticization that is manifested in the joy of delighting and shocking others, with a sense of pride in never being ruffled himself.

Conclusion

Weird, repulsive, sexy or appealing, the sound and image of Prince in the late 1970s and early 1980s during his rise to fame offered a sensuously different experience. In a sense, he continued David Bowie's mission to reinvent a space for males to inhabit that could map out different forms of representation and subjectivity. A central component of Prince's pop act was that it inscribed genderplay as a risky, if not dirty, alternative for straightness. In this sense, Prince's queering antics can be understood as markers of opposition within a heteronormative framework. Our contention is that it is the desirability in his resistance that becomes a main referent of his aesthetic. Prince's queerness takes a convoluted journey, accentuating ideals that are enhanced through the minute details of his musical expressivity. Mapped against the vigorous representations of white American rock, Prince's preoccupation with gender-bending, the feminine and the effete was startling for its time. And before his breakthrough into the mainstream white market with *Purple Rain*, the intricacies of his troubled identity targeted a very different public. Fascinatingly, over three decades his look, with all the indisputable signifiers of femininity (clothes, make-up, accessories and high-heeled shoes), has helped reconfigure our views around sexuality, race, gender and normalized behaviour. Yet, still today Prince remains one of the most transgressive artists, with his queering working as an agent for prescribing difference and ambiguity. In other words, what makes him the ideal pop dandy is his own unique brand of masculinity that always suggests something out of the ordinary. Let us say he is dandy because he breaks down barriers and subverts the status quo; his fantasmatic fooling around with norms attached to gender and sexuality can be read as a satirization of the constructedness of conventional masculinity. For he knows full well that he can reach his fans through evoking erotic desire by means of a coquettish style that is cultivated by camp. Ultimately, Prince has all the markers of a glamorous pop star, and it is through his crafted performances as singer, writer, multi-instrumentalist and producer, that he articulates the particularity of his musical wisdom through the bliss of entertainment.

Chapter 3
A God of Earthly Pleasures

'I'm Single, Celibate and Sexy, I Feel Free'

When Prince made this declaration to *USA Today* in 2008, in reply to questions about his commitment to the Jehovah's Witness faith, the public response was perhaps unexpected. Instead of prompting concerns that the 50-year-old star was losing his legendary sex appeal, it heralded fervent support that he was now, actually, even sexier than ever. To his fans, it has never been in doubt that sex is at the heart of Prince's oeuvre, even if he says he has given up practising what he preaches. Prince's melding of sexuality with spirituality has been at the forefront of his work since the early 1980s when he felt sufficiently accepted and established to push the boundaries. His alignment of sexual expression with access to higher powers has situated him as a uniquely provocative and confrontational artist. So extreme has this been that Prince's fusion of sexiness and godliness was denounced as blasphemous by the notorious Parents Resource Music Center censorship group in the US. However, his missionary zeal has not dampened the affection and support of his non-believer fans, who enthusiastically sing along to his live renditions of 'The Cross' or 'The Ladder'.

References to faith, spirituality and transcendence have been ever-present in Prince's output, both musically and visually, since he adopted a 'preacher man' appearance on the cover of *Controversy* in 1981 and incanted 'Annie Christian' decrying the murder of John Lennon. Rather than adhering to a specific organized religion, Prince has explored a plethora of faith-based philosophies, embracing Christianity, Buddhism and New Age Humanism. There is nothing novel in religious inflection in popular music; Prince follows a long tradition, evidenced in both black and white secular music, of drawing on religious and spiritual themes. His emotional evocations and cataclysmic spiritual inculcations are reminiscent of his innumerable musical forebears, including Sam Cooke, James Brown and Elvis Presley. However, Prince has not delivered a wholly consistent message about his faith over the decades. In many ways, he displays much in common with his black roots in gospel, while still contradicting those traditions by deliberately blurring the boundaries between 'good' and 'bad'. He also shares facets of representation with white artists, evoking the mystic Eastern spirituality of the Beatles and the anthemic redemption songs of Cliff Richard. Undoubtedly, there is something unique in Prince's 'ministry' that distinguishes him from other artists.

This chapter will analyse the impact of Prince's synthesis of the sacred and the profane as we explore the mechanisms by which faith, as in every other aspect of his output, is distinctively articulated and controlled. We will also consider

Prince's beliefs as portrayed through his musical and visual output, illuminating the political messages that his synthesis of the holy and the profane reveal. We will consider a sample of songs, such as 'Anna Stesia' (from *LoveSexy*), 'Thunder' (from *Diamonds and Pearls*), 'The Holy River' (from *Emancipation*) and others to show that while the content might be overtly theological, the delivery often undercuts and eroticizes the message. Similarly, when analysing the extra-musical references to spirituality on album covers and in his second feature film, *Under the Cherry Moon*, we will point out how Prince's affiliation to faith is ambiguous and verges on self-parody. The contrast between Prince's overall self-representation as a messenger or missionary is quite stark when compared with that of similar artists with 'career longevity', such as Cliff Richard and the late Michael Jackson, who have emphasized their 'Jesus-like' qualities. This will demonstrate ultimately how Prince's inflection of non-denominational faith is but one facet of his overall ministry to reveal and transgress social boundaries.

Origins of the Sacred and the Secular in Prince's Music

Controversy over the juxtaposition of the sacred and the profane in Prince's musical and visual output has similarly been a long-running issue for black music since the early part of the twentieth century. It encapsulates the firmly held division that once existed, and still resonates, between the practices of faith in African American and Western European cultures.[1] Teresa L. Reed's (2003) fascinating account of religion in black popular music argues that black secular music has conveyed the evolving religious consciousness of African Americans since African slaves arrived from the Colonies. 'They did not distinguish between music for secular use and music for scared consumption', she writes (2003, p. 5), using the example of spirituals being sung in the fields as slaves worked. She explains how it was the West European model of worship that actually started the separation of the sacred from the profane, specifically in the way that Western Europeans praised God in churches. Certain practices were judged as appropriate or inappropriate for church (ibid., p. 6). Consequently, black African religious songs were criticized for displaying spontaneity, emotional intensity and dance that, to white observers anyway, were seen as intolerable secular behaviour (ibid., p. 6).

The modern genre of blues emerged from the traditions of early African American slaves based on 'field hollers' or traditional work songs found in slave communities in the south. Although founded in African heritage, the blues served as an accessible form of self-expression in the African American community. Early bluesmen and women included Robert Johnson, Ma Rainy, Blind Lemon Jefferson, Blind Willie McTell, Bessie Smith and Leadbelly, for whom the blues expressed the woes of poverty, homelessness, alienation, alongside the highs and lows of romantic love. Religion was a recurring theme of this musical form, but

---

[1] See, for example, Southern (1997) and Stewart (1998).

it was not the focus. This in itself proved controversial and provoked the older generations of blacks whose most familiar form of song was the Negro spiritual. As Reed notes, 'from the time the larger society recognised it as a distinct genre, the music was associated with moral decadence' (ibid., p. 9).

The emerging music industry's response to this was interesting, and may also have in some way contributed to the perception amongst religious black people that music belonged to either God or the Devil. By the 1920s several black blues musicians, including Blind Lemon Jefferson, who recorded gospel songs under the pseudonym Deacon L.J. Bates, had dual identities to ensure they could appeal to both sacred and secular markets. Market distinction turned to moral panic in the 1950s when rhythm and blues popular music became intertwined with the emerging youth culture. Even the guitar was seen as the Devil's instrument, and myths emerged of the ritual of selling one's soul to Satan in exchange for musical skills. This transition from gospel to secular in 1950s black music occurred against the backdrop of a significant shift in post-war social and political relations, and was mirrored in the resistance teenagers started to exert against older generations.

> While more conservative and middle-aged whites may have been more comfortable with the sanitized sounds of the Platters, white teenagers were receptive to the energy and ethnicity of black artists who retained their black gospel stylings in their musical delivery. These young 'rebels' recognized, appreciated and even imitated unmistakably black sounds with huge doses of charisma from the black church. Ray Charles, Little Richard, and James Brown, for example, wedded church flavour to secular lyrics to such an extent that regardless of a song's message, the gospel ethos essentially remained intact. (Reed 2003, pp. 103–4)

While white producers/entrepreneurs undoubtedly exploited black artists, they also enabled them to cross over into the mainstream white audience.[2] Crossing over symbolized a shift from the segregated past into a future that might be more integrated. Secondly, the transition offered artists – and by identification their fans – some freedom to explore other themes than the purely religious. Musically, the success of key artists and their widespread acceptance signified that perhaps pop, rhythm and blues were not necessarily the realm of the irreligious. 'The irony, of course, was that by the 1950s, blacks who were most successful at 'the Devil's music' were able to access many of the very opportunities for which ordinary blacks had struggled and prayed throughout their history in America' (ibid., p. 96). Some of the grim endings of these black prodigies – Sam Cooke was shot in 1964, Otis Redding died in a plane crash in 1967 and Marvin Gaye was shot by his father

---

[2] It is significant – and not entirely unrelated to the experiences of his gospel forebears – that the 18-year-old Prince refused to hand over any production rights when he signed his first contract with Warner Bros., and has insisted on full control over his output ever since.

in 1984 – led some to believe that, akin to the Robert Johnson legend, the devil had come to collect his dues.

In the 1960s and 1970s a lot of prominent black musical artists, such as Curtis Mayfield, the Staple Singers and Aretha Franklin, did foreground faith-based themes in their music. But their songs and lyrics signified a fusion of secular and sacred identities rather than a return to simple binaries of God and the Devil. The 1970s saw the evolution of the 'message song', from its gospel roots into more global themes. The message song had prominence during the Civil Rights Movement when protestors sang 'We Shall Overcome' as their declaration of solidarity. Message songs were also popularized in white secular music since the 1960s. Artists such as Bob Dylan produced music as a commentary on the world and as part of the protest against the war in Vietnam.

The rise of funk in the 1970s corresponded with a move away from Christianity by black artists who wanted to use music more as a way of exploring and expressing facets of their racial identity:

> As a style of music, funk emphasizes group singing, and imaginative, often percussive bass line, a prominent horn section, and lyrics that direct its participants to party with reckless abandon. It is very difficult, however, to describe funk in strictly musical terms. As salient as the music itself is funk's philosophy. (Reed 2003, p. 137)

Black identity was bound up musically with expressions of one-ness and liberation, a philosophy linked with African cosmology. Its ethos was that people are created in harmony with nature in ways that free expression is tantamount to spiritual and mental health. This funk philosophy, ever-present in Prince's work, is quite different from the traditional God versus Devil dichotomy. Sexual freedom is portrayed as an essential facet of nature and represents liberation. It may be no coincidence that Prince also adopted George Clinton's spiritually infused use of 'The One' to get his band to play on the same beat. Funk was influenced musically and spiritually by the work of Sun Ra, a composer, bandleader and multi-keyboardist who led his own big band, called the Arkestra, for nearly 35 years. Like the black preachers of Christian tradition, Sun Ra attempted to transport his audience from 'here' to 'there', to a higher level of consciousness, though chants, colourful costumes and allusions to Egyptology and alien visitations. In the late 1960s Sun Ra and the Arkestra entered this 'Intergalactic' phase. Performances in this period incorporated dancers, films and light shows. Sun Ra pioneered a Moog synthesizer, which became an important sonic marker of the Arkestra. His influence was seen in the 1970s in the missionary zeal of Maurice White of Earth Wind and Fire. White's interest in Egyptology and mysticism provided a visual platform and again emphasized the need for a unified global consciousness rather than a specifically faith-based approach.

A significant feature of the late 1970s, which greatly influenced Prince, was the crossover of black dance music. In her study of funk grooves, Anne Danielsen has labelled this period as crossover for two reasons: first, there was an urge to cross over which 'affected the core structures of the black music industry', and second, this period was 'an era of crossover at the level of style' (Danielsen 2006, p. 97). Danielsen's point about style is verified by the emergence in the late 1970s of a 'softer sound', which she describes as 'highly danceable funk' that, being lighter, 'lacked the edges of James Brown' (ibid.). That the emergent styles were directly marketed to the commercial mainstream pre-empted 'the formidable mainstream successes of Michael Jackson and Prince' (ibid.). Crossover also had much to do with processes of secularization. As Danielsen claims, a 'secular focus on bodily pleasure' was a critical factor accounting for the success of crossover styles amongst a white population:

> ... it made funk more useful for the identity purposes of the new groups of (white) listeners, who did not immediately relate to, or perhaps even recognize, the spiritual dimension of black musicking. ... the bodily appeal and dance floor experience of funk offered a refuge from this overriding need for control and self-presence. (Danielsen 2006, p. 107)

Jayson Toynbee enters the picture from a different direction connecting musicking to religion and sexuality in popular music in the 1970s through a study of Bob Marley. Marley's faith, Toynbee claims, served as both a driver and a contradiction in Marley's sexuality.

> In the case of his sexual activity we can certainly assess outcomes: he was very successful. But this is a case where practice from another sphere – religion – became an unacknowledged condition of action. As a Rastafarian man he considered women to be of less importance than men (not an exclusively Rastafarian belief of course). This belief provided a rationale for his sexual promiscuity. At the same time his approach to sex and gender contradicted his emancipatory, world-changing politics built in part at least on the tenets of Rastafari. Finally, sex and gender relations figured as a major theme in Marley's song writing, in ways that have complex ramifications. In short, it seems that unintended consequences and unacknowledged conditions of Marley's actions were constantly feeding back into his life and work through the contradictory impact of one sphere of practice upon another. (Toynbee 2007, p. 27)

At this point in the chapter we need to clarify what is meant by Prince's beliefs. Other terms than 'beliefs' that may be applicable that come to mind are 'world-view', 'philosophy', 'ideology', 'religion' and 'ethos', for example. Each of these terms could be applied with some degree of accuracy, yet all are lacking for various reasons. Clifford Geertz (1973) has clarified the terms 'ethos' and 'world-view':

> The moral (and aesthetic) aspects of a given culture, the evaluative elements, have commonly been summed up in the term 'ethos', while the cognitive,

existential aspects have been designated by the term 'world view'. A people's ethos is the tone, character, and quality of their life, its moral and aesthetic style and mood; it is the underlying attitude toward themselves and their world that life reflects. Their worldview is their picture of the way things in sheer actuality are, their concept of nature, of self, of society. It contains their most comprehensive ideas of order. (Geertz 1973, pp. 126–7)

The meaning of 'ideology' is more difficult to assess. Geertz recounts the negative connotations of this term as stated by Werner Stark: ideology is 'psychologically "deformed" ("warped", "contaminated", "falsified", "distorted", "clouded") by the pressure of personal emotions like hate, desire, anxiety, or fear' (ibid., pp. 196–7). Geertz, however, assigns ideology a more positive function:

Ideology names the structure of situations in such a way that the attitude contained toward them is one of commitment. Its style is ornate, vivid, deliberately suggestive; by objectifying moral sentiment through the same devices that science shuns, it seeks to motivate action. (ibid., p. 231)

The word 'philosophy' has been used more than any other to describe musical performers' beliefs. It seems to be the easiest one to apply, as it is a general, all-encompassing term. Manly P. Hall has even described it as something that 'reveals to man his kinship with the All. It shows him that he is a brother to the suns which dot the firmament; it lifts him from a taxpayer on a whirling atom to a citizen of Cosmos' (Hall 1952, p. CCIV).

When examining Prince's beliefs, it becomes apparent that they contain elements of all of the above. Like ethos, they clearly have their own tone and character and are certainly a creative product that to many people appear, if not irrational, at least inscrutable. They also take into account Prince's view of the world, humanity and himself, and so qualify as a world-view. They are ideological in that they have a clear goal and are usually articulated in ways that can easily be described as 'ornate' or 'vivid'. Moreover, Prince's beliefs include goals that clearly coincide with those of Hall's philosophy and, as will be shown in the case of several tracks and albums, even employ the same kind of outer space and mystical imagery.

Prince had a church-going childhood and was raised as a Seventh Day Adventist, a branch of Protestant Christianity founded in the 1860s in the US. The Seventh-day Adventists share most of their beliefs with the mainstream Christian churches, but have some extra beliefs of their own. Adventists believe that the Second Coming of Christ will happen soon. Christ's return 'will be literal, personal, visible, and worldwide'. On that day, the righteous dead will be resurrected and taken with him to Heaven, together with the righteous living. The unrighteous will die. One way Adventists keep fit is by eating a healthy diet, following the food rules laid down in Leviticus 11. A vegetarian diet is recommended but not insisted upon. Adventists do not use alcohol, tobacco or recreational drugs. The religion frowns upon sex outside marriage, displays of sexuality, opulent or showy clothing and jewellery. On this basis it is not hard to surmise that Prince was not a strict adherent!

The story of Prince's conversion to the Jehovah's Witness faith has been linked to his connection with veteran Sly and the Family Stone bass player, Larry Graham, who started touring with Prince in the late 1990s. Prince subsequently released Graham's album *Graham Central Station 2000* on his NPG label. Graham confirmed to *The Times* newspaper in 1998 that stories of the pair knocking on people's doors to proselytize were true. A newspaper in Minneapolis had reported how a couple had answered their front door to find Prince and Graham offering them a copy of the *Watchtower*, the religion's in-house magazine. He stayed to chat for 20 minutes before moving onto the next house. The Jehovah's Witness movement is Christian-based and has nearly seven million active members. They believe that the Bible is the Word of God and consider its 66 books to be divinely inspired and historically accurate, rejecting any subsequent human developments or interpretations such as Christmas and Easter. They believe that mankind's time on Earth is nearing an end; when the 'End' finally comes, only 144,000 people will ascend to Heaven. These 'anointed' individuals will rule the Earth from there with Christ.

Regardless of whichever faith Prince has had allegiances to during his career, he remains – artistically at least – one step removed from strict adherence and, instead, espouses a more philosophical approach to a shared human consciousness. Whether this has anything knowingly to do with maintaining mass appeal is uncertain, but as with ethnicity, sexuality and gender, Prince has never operated within a set of rules or regulations – even divinely inspired. Yet, his faith-based identity cannot be separated from his sexuality and ethnicity any more than he can split off his gender identity from his politics. If, as Geertz says, ideology can serve positively to motivate action, then Prince's public display of spirituality is intertwined with his over-riding emphasis on breaking free of all societal constraints in order to reach a point of self-realization. This all serves to endow Prince with incredible charisma. Political philosopher Max Weber (1947) defines charismatic authority as:

> a certain quality of an individual personality by virtue of which he is set apart from ordinary men and treated as endowed with supernatural, superhuman, or at least specifically exceptional powers or qualities. These as such are not accessible to the ordinary person, but are regarded as of divine origin or as exemplary, and on the basis of them the individual is treated as a leader. (Weber 1947, p. 329)

Prince's charismatic authority operates outside the realm of every-day routine and, as Weber theorizes, 'is sharply opposed to both rational, and particularly bureaucratic authority, and to traditional authority, whether in its patriarchal, patrimonial, or any other form' (1947, p. 332). Chris Rojeck (2007) sheds further light on the powers that celebrities have to mimic the role of the religion in the public consciousness. Firstly, they are elevated to a position that makes them superhuman, and above the status of ordinary member of the public (ibid., p. 176). Secondly, they display magical qualities (ibid.), possessing talents that the mere mortal could not achieve. By closely analysing Prince's lyrical, musical and visual outputs, we will now examine how Prince enunciates his faith, constructs his identity and proposes an ideology through a star status that indeed transcends any limitations ascribed to a specific religion.

Lyrical and Musical Representation

Shifting our focus to the religious subject matter inherent in Prince's output, we will look at the ways he treats his music through the parameters of production, harmony, melody, timbral dynamics, textural material and rhythm. As we argue, it is the process-driven dimension of his composition and, in particular, his playful vocality that shapes lyrical meaning, the result of which is a matchless performance style.

On the B-side of the 'Purple Rain' single, released in 1984, is one of Prince's most religious songs, 'God'. Referencing the book of Genesis, the song is executed with a high dose of emotions in a reverent, hymn-like style, with no bass lines or rhythmic backing in the form of drums or percussion. Painfully slow and rubato, Prince preaches, 'love your enemies, there isn't much time, there isn't much time'. Towards the end of the track, Prince refers to another one of his songs in the phrase: 'Wake up children, Dance the Dance Electric, There isn't much time'.[3] Euphorically, the song culminates with the question: 'who screamed? Was it U?' This moment of transcendence is achieved through a series of the most primeval screams and wails imaginable during the last minute (3:02–3:22); the whole effect is in no uncertain terms spiritually orgasmic. Directly following this is a dramatic harmonic shift to E7 (from Em) that refuses cadential resolution as it morphs into a series of suspended altered chords, following the root notes of C and then turning into D♭ (F-E♭-D-B♭/C ---- D♭-E♭-F). The lushness of this progression and its sense of rising and climbing intervallically can be read as a metaphor for struggle and endurance, adding tremendous weight to the song's overall message of salvation. Throughout, harmonic and melodic material is made poignant by the textural and timbral features of the instrumentation (mid 1980s synth pads with an Oberheim touch),[4] while the layering of the vocal parts is subjected to high doses of delay and reverb.

---

[3] André Cymone, bass guitarist in one of Prince's first touring band's (prior to The Revolution), was given as a gift the funk song, 'The Dance Electric'.

[4] Undoubtedly, the keyboard sounds and style of playing were inspired by the keyboardist, Dr. Fink (Matthew Robert Fink) of The Revolution, who won a Grammy Award for the *Purple Rain* album in 1985. Dr. Fink continued playing with Prince until 1991, and was one of the early members of the New Power Generation.

Details of scoring, production and arranging situate Prince as the One within God's created universe, his deployment of a wide range of vocal techniques engendering a great sense of presence. Without fail, his musical material is controlled by an adventurous approach to melodic material, which shifts from the tuneful, easily memorable phrases with a natural voice to abstract squeals and shrieks of ecstatic affirmation in a screeching falsetto. The soundscape depicts Prince's religious reflections, as his voice merges with the backing instruments in temporal suspension. Climaxing through a vivid display of dynamics and effects in the mix, the song transports a heavenly voice. While extolling God, Prince also reminds us that there is not much time left here on earth; life is a mere trick of time.

Delving further into the question of music and spirituality, let us turn to 'The Ladder' from *Around the World in a Day*. Through the song's biblical narrative, Prince tells us about an uncaring king who was not worthy of his throne. Sentiments are built up eloquently through the slow gospel-type ballad, supported by lush chord sequences around the tonal centre of Db. Harmonically, things feel ambiguous through the slipperiness between major and minor modes. 'Everybody's looking 4 the ladder, everybody wants salvation of the soul', Prince cries out in the chorus, and while the path might not be an easy one along the way, salvation will be attained '4 those who want 2 go'. He tells us that to achieve this, 'U gotta climb, U have to climb all of the steps in between'. Musically, the metaphor of climbing and preaching the love of God's creation is achieved through a number of compositional devices: melodic and harmonic repetition on a lengthy chorus (the song's duration is over five minutes), a soaring backing chorus of mainly female voices, and great freedom in scatting. These compositional ploys work to intensify his phrases, and are set against a general dynamic curve upwards that leads to the density of the textures in the mix. A sense of spiritual fervour is reached by the unleashing of yells, screams and yowls on the final cadence points.

Returning to the issue of harmonic ambiguity, it is worth emphasizing that this is one of Prince's prime musical trademarks. Take the song, 'Anna Stesia'. Based around what at first seems the simplest of harmonic structures, an aeolian C chord, this track, from the *Lovesexy* album, released in 1988, develops twists and turns of the most elaborate nature as Prince goes on a crusade. Brimming with religious connotations, the pensive lyrics in the beginning grow out of a frail piano riff that is hesitant in its shift between a Csus2 and F minor chordal riff. Gradually the harmony develops into extended and altered chords, culminating in a full-blown hallelujah chorus. At this point the dynamics soar, as do the effects in the mix, as Prince summons all his passion to proclaim, 'Love is God, God is Love, Girls and Boys, love God above'; and his channel to God is through his adoration for a girl called Anna Stesia. The ambiguous Csus2 chord that starts the journey also ends it, and, symbolically, befits the narrative of searching until one finds.[5] Skilfully, Prince treats harmonic and melodic material in a way that musically

---

[5] This chord is ambiguous in that it is neither major nor minor; it perches in tonal uncertainty, creating a tension in the harmonic fabric throughout the song.

gravitates to the lavish 32-bar gospel chorus, driven by the progression, Cm add9 – Fm7 – Cm add9 – B♭ – Gm7 (see Hawkins 1992a). This elaborate sequence, coloured by a wealth of other features (rhythmic, instrumental, melodic, textural), demonstrates how Prince stretches himself in every way to deliver the sentiments of his spiritual desire. Characteristically, even in the most profound moments of musical intensity, there is a sense of playfulness, often in the form of ironic retort, as in the word play on the title (anesthesia – the sensation of having feelings of pain taken away). We are left wondering, could it be that the song's object of desire, Anna Stesia, succeeds in turning him into the crazed and obsessed religious fanatic we encounter at the end of the song? The One might well ask.

Themes of carnal and religious desire are prevalent in so many of Prince's songs. 'Thunder', from *Diamonds and Pearls*, has a narrative of the redemption of the soul as it endures thunder 'all thru the night'. A steady, pounding rock groove propels the song forward, its rhythmic tightness charging the song with a forcefulness and sense of conviction. The dramatization of the song's narrative is decidedly down to its stylistic idiom, with the word 'thunder' being surrounded by an overdose of 'oooooos' and frenzied guitar licks. Unlike 'Anna Stesia', 'God' and 'The Holy River', this song starts in full throttle, with Prince sermonizing through a simple minor melody, almost chant-like, 'Thunder-all thru the night, promise to see Jesus in the morning light'. When it comes to the last phrase of each chorus, 'c'mon save your soul tonight', there is a sharp break in the backing instruments as the vocals are left hanging raw and exposed. Compositionally, the technique of sudden instrumental dropout, leading to dramatic textural thickening, serves to focus the listener's attention on specific lyrics. Prince ensures that the religious message is communicated as dramatically as possible. And, to this end, the vocal parts in 'Thunder' are given the highest priority.

With reference to this point, mention should be of Prince's use of the word 'thunder', which involves unison two-beat crashes by all performers on the two syllables, 'thun-der'. Alliteration is a powerful technique in driving the weight of the sonorous quality of words, and Prince has mastered this technique throughout his career. For instance, his exceptional way of emphasizing 'thunder' forcefully on two identical pitches in the low register, granted with more of an accent on 'thun', gives the word an immediacy of unprecedented magnitude. Repeated incessantly with his characteristic yelps of 'ohs, yeahs and heys', the word 'thunder' opens and closes the song, made demonstrative through the booming timbral quality of its articulation. Once again, the music shapes the theme of salvation in the lyrics themselves.

Spiritual redemption also forms a thematic strand in the mid-tempo song, 'The Holy River', from the 1996 album, *Emancipation*, written during a period in Prince's life when he had decided to marry Mayte Garcia. The single, released in the UK in 1997, appeared as two separate CDs that were placed in an ornate jewel case. A fervent guitar solo (5:02–6:56) forms the goal of the song as Prince repeats the chorus hook time and time again: 'Let's go down 2 the holy river, let's go down 2 the holy river'. As well as functioning in an improvisatory role, the guitar provides an important descant part to the tune of the hook. Once again, Prince makes substantial use of his vocal technique through the details of the recording. Already in the first minute of the song the timbral variations of his voice shift swiftly as he tells us why we are going down to the holy river. For example, the opening of the song (on the hook) is sung in a gentle falsetto with a high level of overdubbing drawing out the choral effect. This then gives way to the start of the verse, 'U can still see the picture upon the wall', where his voice moves into a mid-range croon. When Prince croons he takes a relaxed approach to vocal performance, opening his timbre to a multitude of dynamic nuances, with phrases that routinely result in touches of tremolo on final sustained notes. The touch of tremolo in this first verse is extraordinarily discrete with an ever so slight build up to the final word 'fear', which elegantly swells to heighten the significance of the phrase, 'U got 2 find the answers 2 the questions that U most *fear*'. An array of vocal timbres are sensitively handled by Prince's attention accentuation and breathiness. When he sings, 'puttin' your faith in things that only make U cry' (1:11–17), the 'cry' is split into two notes, falling down a major 2nd, the accentuation on the final note. In the treatment of this word the two notes are detached (cry-eye), the effect of which is made more fragile and precious by the breathy quality of his vocalization. The recording of 'The Holy River' signifies much about the role of the vocal palette in the delivery of songs with spiritual meanings, and Prince's performance is made striking by the detail he affords to his lyrics in a manner that comes across as effortless. Through the technology of mixing he is able to juxtapose his voices in a fluid way, where minute attention to every vocal positioning contributes to the overall effect of a tightly controlled large-scale choral backing. His propensity for play is a crucial ingredient in the aesthetics of a song, such as 'The Holy River', as he draws out the sentiments of the lyrics with a mastery that is implicitly consistent in its originality. Above all, Prince's vocal interpretation of spiritual-oriented lyrics is rooted in the gospel traditions and practices of African American culture, which he has managed to reconstruct within the parameters of his own musical identity.

Lyrical Content: A Very Dirty Mind?

The lyrical content of Prince's songs has borne the brunt of outspoken critics who have highlighted the perceived political and religious threats posed by his work. Complaints and crusades against popular music by conservative, religious factions would prevail over several decades with Elvis, the Beatles and the Rolling Stones being particular targets. Emerging youth-oriented cultural forms were viewed as a threat to the morals of young audiences. As Sullivan, who has produced a history of such protests, concludes:

> … media which cater to the young are a prime target for all moral crusaders. Campaigns against comic books, television programming and rock music, even crusades against pornography and 'adult' movies, are housed in the language of

saving the young from corruption. In turn, youth culture draws few supporters – the young consumers are not thought to have sufficient maturity to know what is really good for them. This opinion is held most strongly among the conservative faction. (Sullivan 1987, p. 316)

Beginning in 1980, the year of Prince's *Dirty Mind* album, Sullivan identifies a dramatic increase in anti-rock publications. The incoming Reagan administration signalled an atmosphere conducive to numerous conservative causes, including Christian fundamentalism (Sullivan 1987, p. 319). One such group took particular exception to Prince. As we mentioned earlier, the Parents Music Resource Center (PMRC) believed that music could be cleansed by surgically removing certain anti-social lyrical trends. In a media interview, PMRC member Susan Baker said:

What we are trying to do is let parents know that the rock 'n' roll that they danced to and that I danced to growing up, has changed from the swinging of Elvis' hips and saying, 'I want you, I need you, I love you', to people like Blackie Lawless going around in his codpiece with a chainsaw between his legs singing, 'I F-U-C-K like a beast'. (featured in the report 'Inside Greater Washington', WJLA News, 6 September 1985, cited in Sullivan 1987, p. 321)

Prince's work came in for particular derision in 1985 when PMRC founder Tipper Gore, wife of the former US vice president Al Gore, bought the album *Purple Rain* for her 11-year-old daughter. She was horrified by the overt references to masturbation in 'Darling Nikki' and urged Congress to draft legislation requiring parental warning stickers to be placed on album covers. She said: 'It's a quantum leap from the Beatles' 'I Want to hold your hand' to Prince singing 'If you get tired of masturbating ... /If you like, I'll jack you off (Gore cited in Sullivan 1987, p. 321).

Amidst this context, it seems inconsistent that a recurring theme in Prince's work from the mid 1980s onwards is human cultural decay. Yet through *Sign o' the Times* and the *Black Album*, which was withdrawn at the eleventh hour, and then *Lovesexy*, Prince found a way to condemn moral turpitude both ethically and politically, whilst still promoting sexual expression as a means to greater self-determination. Prince stopped the release of the *Black Album* just a week before its release date at the very end of 1987. Rumours abound on the internet as to his reason for this, although the formal explanation was that Prince felt the lyrical content to be too dark and disturbing. Originally titled the *Funk Bible*, the *Black Album* had been intended to reference Prince's black musical roots, but tracks such as 'Dead On It' actually criticized rather than embraced emerging African American music genres such as hip-hop. His subsequent release of *Lovesexy* in 1988 was, by contrast, high-tempo pop synth positivity, extolling his rebirth with his naked, androgynous figure on the sleeve. Tracks such as 'Eye No' and the title track promote upbeat godliness, though he cannot resist overt double entendres, such as when proclaiming his attachment to his deity: 'I want it so much in every single way/I want it morning, noon and night of every day'.

How were non-religious Prince fans meant to respond to this quasi-sermonizing, which might have distanced many artists from their secular fans? Thinking about Cliff Richard, his later career has firmly segmented him within a specifically Christian market. But while Richard's incorruptible asexuality signifies a Jesus-like figure, Prince's brand of faith heads in quite a different direction. Two recurring characteristics of Prince's work are his rooting in humanity and his conscious referencing of his own construction as a black male artist. His output continually makes reference to cultural decay, such as on the single 'Sign o' the Times', where he draws on abstract discourses, such as faith, as mainstream discourses of politics which fail to find a solution. Prince does not want other official discourses to speak of his formation and experiences – he seeks an authoritative voice, a notion that sits at the heart of his faith, ethnicity and sexuality. Anthropologist James Clifford, whose work focuses on who has the authority to speak for any group's identity and authenticity, writes:

> Twentieth-century identities no longer presuppose continuous cultures or traditions. Everywhere individuals and groups improvise local performances from (re)collected pasts, drawing on foreign media, symbols, and languages. This existence among fragments has often been portrayed as a process of ruin and cultural decay. (Clifford 1988, p. 14)

Prince can be thought of as one of these twentieth-century identities, yet it is clear that he does not view himself or his music as a harbinger of cultural decay, but rather he sees his mission as the enlightenment and betterment of all humanity.

The Pictorial Representation

Like so many other individual stars, such as Michael Jackson, Madonna and Robbie Williams, Prince has created images of himself that reflect a clearly religious semantic field. He has utilized technical means – through posture, use of lighting and props, and positioning of the camera – alongside creative design to distinguish himself as a charismatic spiritual missionary. However, the accompanying strong erotic overtones serve to subvert this image. Indeed, Prince uses conflicting signifiers in order to jumble consensual binary symbols of spiritual identity.

Crucifixion Pose

A good example is the artwork that accompanied his 1980 album *Dirty Mind*, which was to elicit the most controversy over his image. Allen Beaulieu photographed Prince in a staged shower scene in colour, naked but for black bikini pants, with a crucifix hanging on the wall behind him. Prince's pose, with his arms raised, and hands behind his head appears sacrificial, mimicking the figure of Jesus on the cross that hangs next to his head. As Beaulieu said himself, 'he wanted it to be this underdog thing that people would tell other people about, not something that advertising would kill' (in Hill 1989, p. 147). The depiction of Prince is highly eroticized, drawing on soft-porn depictions of women rather than men, with unflexed muscles and a wholly exposed, soft torso. It is also reminiscent of another major popular cultural and sexually-ambiguous figure – that of Tony Manero, John Travolta's narcissistic character getting ready for a night at the disco in *Saturday Night Fever*. He is shown contemplating his image in a mirror, torn between the family adherence to faith (symbolized by rosary beads) and that of popular cultural icons (signified by Al Pacino).

Prince is not alone in terms of contemporary male pop stars utilizing crucifixion-like imagery in promotional material, but the effect is quite different in comparison. Anja Lobert (2008, p. 82) has identified how Michael Jackson recurrently used the crucifixion pose. In his video for 'Earth Song' (1995) he was filmed from below, arms outstretched grasping tree trunks as the world undergoes a final judgement one imagines has been unleashed by Jackson's own power as redeemer. Prince's pose has more in common with the homoerotic display of Take That in 'Pray' (1993), in which they throw their bodies open to heaven, though like Prince with similar sexual connotations. '… these recurring associations are expressed in the same socio-cultural sphere, namely the genre of Western popular music', says Lobert (2008, p. 82). Whereas Jackson's representation has anchorage in the image of a redeemer figure akin to Jesus himself, Prince's does not. There is positive religious framing but also something ironic – the use of sexuality in the shot.

Halo Effect

The use of light in a religious vein has also being recurrent in Prince's imagery since the halo-like backlighting on the cover of his first album *For You*. Likewise in live performance, for instance, Prince's figure is surrounded by light radiating from his body throughout the video of the *Sign o' the Times* live tour. Christian art frequently depicts divine figures that are marked as such by an aura of light, called 'aureole', or halo. The latter originates as a zone of light from behind the head of a divine or sacred person (Didron and Millingston 1851, p. 268), whereas the aureole frames the body of Jesus Christ (Dick 2002, p. 57). In some cases, according to George Ferguson (1977), 'it is removed from the body and is composed of many luminous rays issuing from a central point' (Ferguson 1977, p. 267). If we more closely examine the *Sign o' the Times* video, specifically the close of the track 'U Got the Look', we see the image of Prince elevated onto a platform at the rear of the stage, in silhouette with a halo of light and a blast of dry ice creating an apocalyptic image of ascendance. According to the narrative, Prince has managed to resist the temptations of an attractive woman (Sheena Easton) and ascends onto the stage pulled by his female dancer Cat. As they strike a triumphant pose, the biblical connotations are undercut by the emphasis on Prince's phallic guitar neck. Unlike images of Christ or stars such as Michael Jackson, Cliff Richard or Robbie Williams, Prince has ascended with a woman. Cat's muscular arm is flexed to emphasize her toned bicep, which is viewed in parallel with Prince's guitar neck, indicating a further ambiguous undercutting of Prince's symbolism. Whereas the image of light surrounding Cliff Richard might allude to his embodiment as a redeemer and his Christ-like propensities, with Prince it is something different. It is as if he is representing agency as a means to redemption, with femininity at its heart.

Superhuman Elevation

As evidenced in *Sign o' the Times*, the use of camera angle to raise the star aids the visual construction of a 'heavenly figure' (Lobert 2008, p. 88). In her close analysis of Cliff Richard, Lobert notes the use of low camera positions to create the effect of body enlargement. She also identifies the recurrent 'blue screen' superimposition of Cliff so that he is located in the sky. Prince has used these techniques frequently but, once again, they connote faith in quite a different manner, such as on the cover art for his 1993 album *Come*. The star commissioned Terry Gydesen, a documentary and political photographer rather than a pop culture image-maker. Gydesen was Jesse Jackson's staff photographer during his 1988 presidential campaign and, besides politics, she has documented the plight of refugees in El Salvador, women and children living in homeless shelters, and women in recovery from drug and alcohol abuse.

The gothic imagery for the album centres on its location, La Sagrada Familia, one of the architect Gaudi's most famous works in Barcelona. It is a giant temple that has been under construction since 1882 and is as yet unfinished. Most of the photographs are taken at night, creating an intimidating backdrop of iron gates, flying buttresses and stained glass windows. They are overlaid with Roman numerals and back-to-front lyrics, which add to the imposing, uncanny mood of the visuals. On the front cover Prince is shot from below, giving him unnaturally long legs, while he holds a cane across his body to connote control. It has all the trappings of power, with Prince portrayed as if he is otherworldly, almost floating, and the overall effect is malevolent and oppressive.

But from another perspective, the image undercuts its own otherworldly power through quite an overt vaginal reference. The shape of the top of the gate is akin to the shape of the female body, while Prince's slightly parted legs standing atop of the word 'Come' allude to the vaginal entrance. He literally, and figuratively, is a spiritual figure standing before an imposing entrance. Hence, for Prince, the elevated symbol of power is femininity, through its representation in the curvaceous architecture of the religious monument.

Other images from the same shoot are similarly complex; one in particular, which became the cover image for the single 'Letitgo', shows him high in the cathedral as if hovering over Barcelona. His cane sits across his shoulders, with his arms hooked over in a crucifix position. Prince, at this time, was in conflict with his record label, Warner Bros., and changed his name to The Artist Formerly Known as Prince. The cover bears his birth name Prince but carried his date of birth and the year of 'Prince's' death as 1993. The crucifixion pose might be a double message. Prince's highly exaggerated make-up, hair and clothing is in synch with the cathedral's excessive Gothic-inspired architecture. His cuffs look like stone carvings, and his overall appearance is reminiscent of a Batman-like avenger, or hero figure. In contrast, the chosen perspective on Barcelona is banal – Prince is above it all, and excessive with a glimpse of bare midriff to remind us of his physicality.

A more stark and literal depiction of Prince's ascent into heaven occurs at the end of his second feature film, *Under the Cherry Moon*. It enjoyed none of the success of *Purple Rain*. It won eight Raspberry Awards, the alternative Oscars, losing only one to Madonna in *Shanghai Surprise* (1986, dir. Jim Goddard). It opened to negative reviews in the UK in August 1986, with press reports that audiences were demanding their money back. Shot on location in the south of France, *Under the Cherry Moon* cost between $10m and $12m to make, twice as much as *Purple Rain*, and made only a third of its budget back in box office receipts (Jones 1997). Though seemingly set in the present day, the film stylistically resembles the classic narrative romantic comedies made in the 1930s and 1940s. Shot in colour, Prince is reported to have wanted it to be black-and-white and persuaded the producers to re-process the final film into monochrome. As such, the finished movie came as a shock to audiences who associated Prince with the colourful, formal excesses of his promotional videos on MTV.

The narrative is a love story with Prince playing Christopher Tracy, a pianist and gigolo, who unintentionally falls for an heiress from whom he had hoped to simply glean cash. The opening commentary of the film tells us that Christopher and his friend-cum-valet Tricky had travelled to Nice from Miami in the hope that the doe-eyed Christopher could win the heart of a rich woman and marry her. Heiress Mary Sharon, played by the then-unknown Kristin Scott Thomas, disobeys her overbearing father (Steven Berkoff) by falling in love with Christopher and hanging around with him and his sidekick, Tricky, played by Jerome Benton. Mary's father has set aside a huge trust fund that will be released to her upon condition that she marries a business associate, played by Victor Spinetti, whose links would greatly enhance Sharon's own prestige. Initially, the haughty Mary sees Christopher as a 'peasant', causing him to mock her airs and graces. Eventually she rebuffs her family and elopes with him. On realizing Mary is determined to defy him, Berkoff's character has Christopher shot dead.

Prince played a major directorial role, demoting the nominal director, Mary Lambert, early during production. In contrast with *Purple Rain*, there are no conventional on-stage rock performances – Prince is only seen playing the piano and, once, dancing on it to a ghetto blaster – and it features no autobiographical elements. The *mise-en-scène* is highly stylized. The audience can ascertain that it is set on the French Riviera, but it is hard to locate the narrative within any specific epoch. As Roland Barthes writes, 'it often happens that representation takes desire itself as an object of imitation; but then such desire never leaves the frame, the picture; it circulates among the characters; if it has a recipient, that recipient remains interior to the fiction' (Barthes 1975, pp. 56–7). Prince's representation of the *mise-*

en-scène uses an intense style of visual signification that strips away the familiar, not to make it strange but to allow the spectator to witness the strangeness there.

One of Isaac's henchmen shoots Christopher in the back as he stands on the quayside from where he hopes to launch his and Mary's bid for freedom. The death scene itself, on a cinematic level, is hugely camp and melodramatically played, 'one of the most self-indulgent and protracted since Brando popped his clogs in *Mutiny on the Bounty*' (Jones 1997, p. 86). The religious connotations of CHRISTopher lying dying in Mary's arms, dressed in long white robes, while Tricky prays over them like an angel, are overt and tongue-in-cheek. Christopher is a martyr, reduced to flesh, bought, sold and exchanged, and now destroyed for the sake of Isaac's business empire. But there is a resurrection for Christopher, where men and women are united in a utopic realm. Prince and The Revolution perform the song 'Mountains' on a cloud: 'There's only mountains and the sea, there's nothing grey there, just you and me'. From the huge gender, economic and class divisions that existed in the opening of the film, Christopher's transcendence represents a salvation, an affirmation that has required self-exertion rather than self-assertion. *Under the Cherry Moon* expresses the desire for a new openness and honesty and an examination of the subjugation of particular classes and groups.

However overt the Christian symbolism might be in the film, it bears little relation to the self-aggrandizing religiosity of other stars, notably Michael Jackson's infamous stage performance of 'Earth Song' at the Brit Awards in 1996, at which Pulp lead singer Jarvis Cocker leapt to the front of the stage and wiggled his bottom at Jackson. Speaking on BBC1's Question Time soon after Jackson's death, Cocker told host David Dimbleby that he disrupted the Brits because of the pomposity of Jackson's performance. 'He was pretending to be Jesus – I'm not religious but I think, as a performer myself, the idea of someone pretending to have the power of healing is just not right', Cocker said. 'Rock stars have big enough egos without pretending to be Jesus – that was what got my goat, that one particular thing.' Lobert said Jackson's performance 'leaves no doubt about its biblical references and the singer's self-portrayal as Jesus Christ' (Lobert 2008, p. 89). She describes how he descends and eventually touches the hands of the cringing masses. Prince's signification, though sharing some religious connotations, does not convey him as the embodiment of redeemer but as subject, as a channel and as a recipient of God's 'blessings'.

The Incorruptible Body

The track 'Mountains' connoted transcendence and also suggested Prince's immortality and ever-youthful body. Lobert has identified how images of Cliff Richard, like those depicting Jesus himself, show a perpetually youthful figure who by some potentially divine power has managed to overcome the natural process of ageing. Cliff's official website contains a gallery of images that suggest the star has barely aged in the past 20 years.[6] Michael Jackson used plastic surgery and other medical techniques to similarly construct himself as an eternal youth. Prince has certainly been a constant in many of his fan's lives since their teens, and has physically changed very little, lending a timeless quality to his appearance and to his music. From more candid press photography, as opposed to his own visual outputs, there is no evidence that he has undergone any facial cosmetic surgery and is maturing gracefully and with dignity. Like Madonna, Prince eschews any artistic compromise based on his physical age, though, unlike his female counterpart, his promotion of his own sexuality is much more subtle. But he remains agelessly beautiful, extremely slim and effectively uncorrupted physically. His vocal disapproval of alcohol, drugs and animal products reinforces the idea of purity through self-denial and control rather than a deliberate act to reverse nature. For example, on his two-part interview with US chat show host Tavis Smiley on 27 April 2009, Prince revealed that he had been born epileptic:

'I used to have seizures when I was young and my mother and father didn't know what to do or how to handle it but they did the best they could with what little they had. My mother told me one I day I walked into her and I said "Mom I'm not going to be sick anymore." And she said "Why?" and I said "Because an angel told me so." Now, I don't remember saying it, that's just what she told me.'

He continued by saying that he compensated for constant childhood teasing by being as 'noisy' and 'flashy' as he could. 'I looked forward to this time in my life when I could reflect ....'

Connections between creativity and denial of death have been analysed by Ernest Becker (1997) who, drawing on Otto Rank, asserts that every act of artistic imagination has a spiritual underpinning. Rank (1884–1939) became distanced from his close working affiliation with Freud when he suggested that separation anxiety is an influential and resonant phase in an infant's emotional development. Whereas Freud maintained there was no such phase, and that the phallic Oedipus Complex is the main determinant of future drives, Rank believed that separation from the body of the mother was a more powerful moment (1929). Rank sought to explain how this separation resonates through an enduring desire for oneness and unity, which is expressed through cultural production in forms such as art and music. Thinking of Prince and the incorruptible body, Becker extends these ideas to consider the human as essentially struggling against the inevitability of its decline and demise. The ever-youthful image beckons the audience who might also be able to transcend their condition, with Prince's help.

---

[6] At the time of writing, Cliff Richard, 70, has released his 2011 calendar in which he is depicted shirtless with a muscular abdomen, no grey hair on his head or body, and looks no older than 40. He has given media interviews saying his youthfulness is simply down to good nutrition.

Asexuality

Prince's public declaration of celibacy in 2008 did not convince his fans that he was asexual. Writing in *USA Today*, journalist Edna Gundersen noted: 'On a love song, his voice takes on yearning as he pines for the feel of a lover's lips and the move of her hips.' Prince told her: 'That's what happens with years of celibacy, it all goes into the music.' Prince's sexuality continues to drive his musical output, such as in the throbbing bass line to '3121', whereas Cliff Richard and even Michael Jackson, despite the crotch grabbing, were not typically associated with sexiness.

Michel Foucault's account of the modern control of sexuality parallels modern control of criminality by making sex (like crime) an object of allegedly scientific disciplines. In his first volume of the *History of Sexuality*, Foucault posits that what is thought of as repression of sexuality actually constitutes sex as a core feature of human identities. In other words, it is repression that paradoxically creates the sexual obsession, encouraging talk in the interests of liberation and self-understanding. Foucault explains:

> Why has sexuality been so widely discussed and what has been said about it? What were the effects of power generated by what was said? What are the links between these discourses, these effects of power, and the pleasures that were invested by them? What knowledge (*savoir*) was formed as a result of this linkage? (Foucault 1998, p. 11)

This may help shed light on the significance of Prince's knowing transgression of his own celibacy or, moreover, his refusal to be asexual despite his proclaimed lack of sexual activity. For example, during Prince's half-time performance at the Superbowl in 2007, three year's after Janet Jackson's 'wardrobe malfunction', he was shown in profile silhouette playing his symbol-shaped guitar through a white sheet. The guitar neck is quite clearly held at crotch level and it would be hard for anyone to believe, knowing Prince's mastery of stagecraft, that this was anything but deliberate. The spectacle coincided with Prince's declaration of celibacy, itself against a backdrop of the high-profile rise of virginal pop acts in the US such as the Evangelical Christian teen group Jonas Brothers, who wear 'promise' rings as symbols of their purity. A Foucauldian reading of their abstinence could clearly elicit claims that an avowed absence of sexual activity in fact predicates their whole public identity on sex, as if the fact they are not doing it ensures the act is never far from their minds. Prince therefore breaks the typical connection between sex and guilt and dirtiness in pop. Whereas Mick Jagger, Tom Jones and Elvis promote physical raunchiness and transgression, Prince sanctifies sex, especially in his later years.

Conclusion

Prince's work has continually negotiated the boundaries of freedom by seeking to blur the sexual and the spiritual, the political and the personal. His performances are a celebration of the earthly pleasures and gifts that his God has bestowed upon him, which we can also access individually to help us be like Prince. In this way, Prince's offering of points of identification with himself also offers us a route to his God through him. While identifying with Prince is pleasurable in itself, he is saying that we can also access earthly pleasures if we can see the world through his eyes. Therefore, his religious songs are often gently sermonic but not proselytizing, offering a much more genuine and less self-seeking image of faith than numerous other artists. In later years, Prince has shifted away from the profane and more fully into the realm of his faith; a superficial move, possibly? One thing is certain: with a Foucauldian twist, his apparent silencing of his libido has made this middle-aged superstar's name synonymous with sex.

Chapter 4
Voicing the Erotic and the Sublime

Introduction

As highly ritualized events, replicating ordinary behaviour in the most spectacular ways, pop performances are disseminated in recorded or live form. Having fun is what pop music is all about. And in Prince's performances the entertainment factor is high, resting on the sublime and the erotic. Fun is mediated through all his performances with great passion to a dramatic effect. Proceeding from this observation to an examination of his vocal sound, we want to consider in this chapter what makes his music so well-oiled, unrestrained and explicitly sensual.

The focus in this part of our study falls on the role of the voice as a sonic signifier – a veritable 'sign of the times'. Prince's vocal expressivity has carved out his niche in the pop world, and we will turn to various songs to exemplify his elaborate techniques. Of the numerous issues we address, vocality-at-play surfaces as the most central. Prince's music, after all, is meant to entertain; it becomes ritualized in a vibrant cultural and social context where his virtuosity never ceases to woo his fans over.

What then are the musical functions, idiosyncrasies and properties of singing one encounters in his music? And, how does his specific brand of vocality ritualize his performances? Of particular relevance here is the question of musical *affect*. One might say that the recorded voice negotiates a path that reveals its ideological positioning within a cultural sphere that is constantly transforming. During the past 50 years, the revolution in recording has profoundly shaped the pop aesthetic. Indeed, the transition between analogue and digital technology, the advent of the compact disc in 1982, and the spread of mp3 files on the internet from 1994 onwards, mirror the rapid changes in the music industry. Consequently, technological changes have greatly impacted the creative space of the recording, where the sculpting of the voice becomes an art in itself; for it is in the process of recording the voice and instruments that musical ideas are conceived, negotiated and imagined.

Enticing us into the mix, Prince's recorded voice brims with affect, offering up all sorts of attendant pleasures. Certainly, his recorded vocal imagery and singing practice produces the structures of every musical event through which feelings of desire are transmitted from performer to receiver. Yet, as Sean Cubitt reminds us, within the performance space even 'the most flagrantly erotic of spectacles is still a discourse' (2000, p. 148) – to be sure, the material content of a recording is elusive.

Prince exerts utmost control over his recorded and produced sounds. Take his vocal 'drop ins' during any recording process. Always these are about enhancing, altering and individualizing the voice. In particular, his form of sonic processing prompts one to ask: how is the recorded voice 'staged' as an object of desire, and what renders it sublime? Tracking this idea throughout this chapter, we argue that recording techniques not only contribute to enhancing musical accuracy, intensifying expression, but they also determine empathy. In a studio context, expressive devices, such as 'riding the fader', employing compression and editing in countless ways, offer the artist a potent site for re-affirming the ego. Notably, Prince's voice commands a central position in all his songs, attesting to an idealized depiction of something tangible and real. Luringly, his voice escorts us into a virtual domain where his *presence* is felt through technological realization. Precisely it is this conjunction of technology and musical expression that induces the feeling of another's presence through the voice. Moreover, it is the fetishization of the recorded voice that is made so explicit in Prince's songs, which works to foreground the gendered structure of his subjectivity.

Assessing vocal presence as a constructed entity, we argue, cannot bypass the non-verbal, non-sung aspects of a style that are so grounded in African American history; for vocal utterances, both sung and non-sung, are powerful elements of musical narrativity. In the various analyses we provide in this chapter, vocal embellishments are situated as carriers of primary musical meaning. In fact, vocal sounds of any kind adhere to a musical practice that forms part of the call and response vocal tradition that has substituted for words. For sure, Prince is one in a long line of black artists – James Brown, Michael Jackson, George Clinton, Aretha Franklin, Little Richard – who have turned to this expressive device. One might say that it is ultimately his vocalizations that contribute to a palette of timbres, textures and techniques that become part of his rich vocabulary, with one goal in mind, to entertain us from start to finish. With this in mind let us move into the 'purple zone'.

Sounding Out the Purple Zone

The process of songwriting generally consists of four stages:

1. creating a musical event out of a story that makes it worth sharing;
2. playing around with a range of musical codes and structures together with other performers;
3. exhibiting one's dexterity as a singer and instrumentalist; and
4. subsuming all of these approaches into the fantasy of one's private world through utopian projections.

Indisputably, the challenge of working out Prince's approach to songwriting is a daunting task by any measure, and this has much to do with the multidimensionality of his compositional approach. Allan Moore has insisted that the 'streams of sounds a listener hears is composed of rhythm *and* harmony *and* instrumental timbre *and* lyrics and, quite possibly, other elements as well' (Moore 2001, p. 33 – author's emphases). In Prince's case, we would suggest that the 'other elements' include the recording techniques he employs as compositional tools. Subsequently, the mediation of his stylistic signature has everything to do with the meticulous techniques he turns to when arranging and mixing sound through spatialization, an issue we will concentrate on in more detail in Chapter 6. Invariably, Prince's musical textures are porous, with an abundance of gaps, pauses and moments of silence; by this we are referring to the stratification of processed sound in a constantly mobile virtual space. Essentially, it is the vertical and horizontal layering of musical elements and their processing through technological procedures that spice up the song. And, in terms of responses to Prince's music, one might say that fans construct their own subjectivities through listening processes: this implies that the reception of the artist takes place through a highly imaginative involvement. Sustaining this idea throughout the chapter, we want to consider the kinds of performance that go into the surrealistic creations of an artist's songwriting, and how these furnish the interior and exterior dimensions of their fantasy world.

'I only want 2 see u, only want to see u in the purple rain', Prince crooned in 1984 at the close of his very special title-track hit from *Purple Rain*, his sixth album. This, the first album that credited Prince's backing band The Revolution, showed the emergence of a distinct rock style that instantly broke through into the white mainstream. For the first time since The Beatles an artist would reach the top of the charts with an album, film and single at the same time – a tumultuous achievement that rocketed Prince to the heights of international stardom. No wonder, then, that in almost every tour Prince has showcased 'Purple Rain' in a multitude of arrangements. The song has become a major component of his musical persona, symbolizing, one might say, a very special shade of purple. In the album version of 'Purple Rain' the music is erotically charged throughout with extraordinary vocal panache. Lengthy in duration (8:45), the song structurally comprises a drawn out introduction section with three verses followed by a chorus with a dramatic, slow build up. Effortlessly, everything develops into a memorable extended guitar solo in the final chorus, a transcendent moment of immense outpouring that is unashamedly self-indulgent. And then, almost as an afterthought, the song culminates by resolving to a gentle piano solo cushioned by gentle strings.

'Purple Rain' is one of those mighty rock ballads with all the classic ingredients that make a song a success. Numerous details account for its alluring quality and an unforgettable recorded performance. In performance terms, the challenge of 'Purple Rain' is to maintain the musical momentum through a variety of devices. For example, phrasing in the verses and choruses comes across consistent while the final chorus opens up for a good deal of exposure and musical elaboration. In terms of the musical arrangement, the vocals in their juxtaposition, with the guitar backing and solo passage, provide the song with its edge. Narratively, the symbolism of purple is vast and derivative. References to 'purple rain' in pop songs can be traced back to the 1970s US group America, and their song 'Ventura Highway', where, in the second verse, the protagonist, while waiting for a train, sings, 'sorry boy, but I've been hit by purple rain' – a sense of restlessness and indifference, brought upon by boredom, leads the male singer to leave his whereabouts. It is also quite likely that purple rain refers to a hallucinogenic drug, a form of LSD, which causes cloud shapes to appear like 'alligator lizards in the air'. A further reference to this is found in the song 'Someone to Call My Lover' from 2001, where Janet Jackson samples 'Ventura Highway'.

Plainly, much mileage can be derived from the idea of 'purple', the most regal of all colours, luxuriant in its hue. In literary criticism, however, this colour has been portrayed as disparaging, referring to prose that is so embossed that it disrupts the flow, extending things well beyond their context. In this sense, the term 'purple prose' describes the rhetorical effect of sentimentality, pathos and extravaganza, conjuring up intended responses on the part of the reader. For instance, stylized and highly formulaic pulp genres (inexpensive fiction magazines and mass market paperbacks that have been around since the 1950s), doomed excessive by critics because of their prose, are deemed purple for prioritizing sentiments over factual documentation. Most certainly, the sentimental weight of Prince's 'Purple Rain' can be interpreted along these lines when it comes to the song's musical prose, which, incidentally, bear an uncanny resemblance to Bob Seger's song, 'Night Moves', from the 1976 album, *Night Moves*. This reached number 4 in the Billboard Hot 100 singles charts. Another more obvious reference is of course Jimi Hendrix's 'Purple Haze', from 1967, inspired by LSD, based upon a very weird dream Hendrix had of walking under the sea. Not coincidentally, the legendary Hendrix chord from 'Purple Haze' – a dominant seventh with sharpened ninth – is transplanted in Prince's 'Kiss', a symbolic gesture of affection to his hero?

Well worthy of consideration is the relationship of musical features to the 'sublime'. To start with, the term sublime refers to a divine quality that connotes a spiritual value of magnitude, something overwhelmingly beautiful, created by the wailing melodies and poignant vocal delivery. Our turning to the sublime in this context is in antithetical contrast to that of Kant, Schopenhauer, Hegel and the later *Kunstwissenschaft* movement that charted primary aesthetic forms. The way in which the Prince-experience involves an intricate conception of the sublime is more Lyotardian, where the artist's creative sensibility exposes the multiplicity and excess of the fun-loving postmodern subject. Because sublime codes fall on the edge of human reason, where the beautiful is replaced with an excess of startling signifiers, they threaten to destabilize conventions through the power of musicalized sentiment.[1] Therein lies the aesthetic appeal.

---

[1] See Lyotard (1994). An important point to stress is that postmodernism does not correlate aesthetic value with beauty. In a Lyotardian vein of thought, this is because of the aesthetic of the sublime. Lyotard claims that the sublime's aim is to present the unpresentable in ways that transcend moral categories that relate to feelings of good, bad, nice and unpleasant. The de-differentiation that distinguishes postmodernism, exemplified

Musically, then, how does Prince render his sound sublime? What colour purple is illuminated through instrumentation, harmonic, rhythmic and melodic structuring, and technological production? Once again, his vocal mannerisms warrant close attention, and to understand their workings we will now to turn to a range of compositional properties. Throughout 'Purple Rain' the harmony is distinctly diatonic, centred around B flat major, with the main chord progressions comprising, B♭-Gm-F-E♭-B♭-Gm-F-B♭ in the verse, and E♭-B♭-Gm-F-B♭ in the chorus. While the bridge and solo sections consist of similar chords, the general movement of the entire song is from tonic to subdominant (B♭-E♭) with no dominant resolution to F major. This gradual progression secures the melody with nuances of blues notes and inflections that spell out its rock aesthetic. In the verses, Prince's singing style is more spoken than in the choruses (Example 4.1) – a more spoken dialogue in vocal delivery heightens the dramatic feel, with Prince's rhythmic 'speeching' function in stark contrast to melodious singing.

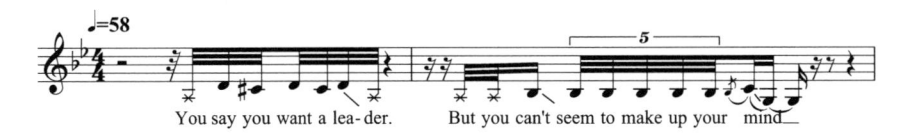

Example 4.1   Speech forms in musical dialogue in 'Purple Rain'

Things quieten down considerably in the chorus sections, with the melodic rhythm levelling out into longer, sustained notes, painting in wide strokes the majestic grandeur of the 'purple rain' hook. Extracting every drop of purple from his main melody, Prince stretches out his message with heartfelt sincerity. This occurs through extensive repetition and prolongation making the sing-along chorus hook so memorable.

Consisting of only three pitches, this hook circles the tonic during the first two phrases, ending on the dominant of the third phrase (Example 4.2). It only takes two bars respite to hinge the second half of the chorus. This occurs prior to a leap of a major seventh (F-E♭) that transports the voice to the repeated pitch of E♭ before resolving stepwise to the tonic (B♭). For a brief, precious moment the voice is suspended in time, teasing and pleading. Directly following this Prince releases an avalanche of emotions. In melodic terms, something as simple as an intervallic leap offers him the chance to unleash all his sentiments as he croons, 'I only want to see u bathing in the purple rain'. In this poignant moment, it is the timbral and dynamic shift in his voice to a more rounded, pure sound that makes the words

---

in the pop texts of Prince, succeeds in bridging the gaps and alerting us to borders we need to cross. This also entails a dismantling of the barriers between music and other human activities, such as politics, fashion, design and gender representations.

overwhelming. And, with full backing (guitars, bass, drums, backing vocals), the vocal fabric intensifies and thickens, easing out the passion in the lyrics.

Example 4.2   The melodic hook of 'Purple Rain'

Technical details of vocal production and treatment within this mix are highly intricate, making explicit the erotics of Prince's vocal articulation. Certainly excessive, it is this kind of vocal delivery that transports with it the rhetoric found in African American song traditions. David Brackett, in his study of James Brown, addresses the performative aspects of the vernacular that are based upon toasting and preaching traditions associated with black power and nationalism (Brackett 2000, pp. 124–7). Drawing attention to the critical difference between European American and African American music, Brackett points out Brown's affirmations of these complex distinctions. In contrast, Prince's performativity in 'Purple Rain' veers more towards a crossover into white mainstream rock, although he still manages to sustain an African American idiom in his vocal heritage. This is discernible in the wistful, beautiful self-consciousness of lines such as, 'I never wanted 2 be your weekend lover', in the second verse, which gain their full effect from the characteristics of vocal embellishment found in soul, blues, gospel and funk. Throughout the song melodic flow and idiomatic inflection become objects of expansive magnitude, inspiring and spiritual.

Not only is the length of the bar unexpectedly halved for tuneful phrases, such as in Example 4.2, but also the deployment of a sudden moment of silence greatly enhances its effect, directing our attention to the accent on 'rain'. Maximizing the feel of the purple rain phrase through a slow tempo, Prince languidly fluctuates between rapid and slow rhythmic units to extract the sentiments of the lyrics. Out of this emerges the contour of the melody that moulds into the guitar performance, comprising the now famous majestic solo.

Recorded live at the Minneapolis Club First Avenue in 1983, the song's vibrancy is a direct result of its production. On close inspection, the abundance of echo on Prince's voice and the guitar parts contrasts starkly with the dryness of the strings, while the slow, pounding rhythmic drive, with reverbed kit beats on the second and fourth beats, provides an underlay for Prince's voice. Gradually the guitar solo (3:47–5:17) turns the song into an extravaganza that pays tribute to a legacy of guitarists. Measured and expressive, the solo never quite goes into the same overkill as Hendrix's 'Purple Haze'; rather, its improvisatory character emulates a dignity that is melancholic. Mostly, the effect of this solo is attributable to Prince's capacity to achieve an exalted state of elation in the guitar's fullness of tone and technical articulation.

There is no doubt that during the twentieth century the amplified electric guitar idealized a wealth of popular music styles, and, unmistakably, the solo in 'Purple Rain' aspires to a powerful rock idiom. Extending the sung phrases, the solo's angular, virtuoso gestures weigh down the words, functioning as a powerful instrumental interlude that finally gives in to Prince's voice.

Aesthetically, the guitar solo complements the voice. Starting mid-way in the song (3:47) and continuing to 5:17 much happens musically as Prince wails in his upper register, turning on his best falsetto. The climax occurs in the form of the descending four-note pattern, GFE♭D, FE♭DC, and E♭DCB♭, performed in unison with guitar. Of the various tension-building devices appearing in the solo, it is a sustained string tone on a high F pitch (3:47–6:32) that stands out. Significantly, this is the dominant degree of the home key, providing an anchor point, a backdrop, to the entire solo. A main function of this pitch lies in its continuity as it overarches the orchestral swirls, keyboard motifs and non-verbal vocal sounds, all of which cushion the solo. Pensively, Prince draws out the main melody with a melancholy that befits his unique colour of purple. Basking in the glow of his glorious virtuosic eruptions, great solace is achieved; in moments like these his pause for reflection extracts the erotic quality of his performance style.

As has already been suggested, one way of understanding the 'Purple Rain' solo is through Jimi Hendrix, whose experimental approach to guitar playing undoubtedly rubbed off on Prince. Recorded in 1967 and wild for its time, 'Purple Haze' created a stir in the rock and pop world. Played through an Octavia (an effects pedal which raises notes by one octave), Hendrix's solo literally electrified the lines, 'purple haze, you go on and on till the end of time'. The imagery of this narrative owes much to the treatment of sound as much as the guitar playing. Echo, fuzz, distortion, wah wah, filters and octave doubling are just some of the effects that ignite the guitar solo. Fuelled by a wide range of unconventional performance techniques, gestures and textures, Hendrix's guitar playing displayed an eccentricity that was passionately hot. By comparison, Prince's 'Purple Rain' solo is less pyrotechnical, and not on quite the same psychedelic route of travel. Moreover, the technical proficiency that encodes the Hendrix guitar solo is from another era than Prince's. That said, both guitar solos are conditional on similar narratives, where virtuosity in guitar performance becomes a striking metaphor for the pent-up feelings of the frustrated male musician. By this we are reminded that rock solos are all about the sensations of aural movement in spectacularized ways, their prime goal being to propel constructs of identity into the purple zone.

Before leaving 'Purple Rain' let us linger a little longer on Prince's vocal and instrumental soloing and what this signifies compositionally. Because instrumental solos are musically exploratory, they exhibit a performer's skills through virtuosic freestyling – with this we are referring to a form of recitative that gives the impression of a non-rehearsed performance. Engineered to produce a commentary on what has already been stated vocally, guitar solos of the kind found in 'Purple Rain' are *impromptu*, giving the impression of things being spontaneous. In his studies of African American music performance practices, Derek Scott observes that as 'important as the ability to improvise is the manner in which the improvisation is played' (Scott 2003, p. 198). Prince's improvisatory manner is all about the transformation of musical material figuratively and rhetorically, where devices of call and response serve as commentaries that are full of parody and fun. Moreover, his flair as improviser is self-validating and linked to an African American tradition of music-making, where the appropriation of styles and practices map out his heterogeneity as an artist. Alone, extemporizing provides a useful key to understanding musical performativity, and through his extempore in 'Purple Rain', Prince speaks an ideology that accesses emotions that are erotic and sublime.

From Purple to Raspberry: Donning the Beret

At eighteen, Prince had almost moved permanently into the recording studio, often catching a few hours sleep on a couch there. A local eight-track production studio, owned by the British entrepreneur, Christopher Moon, gave Prince full access to a studio console that enabled him to spend countless hours developing his music production skills. Consequently, this led to a spate of demos. In these early days, Moon's assistance would have a profound impact on Prince's songwriting. Moon urged him to angle his lyrics in a way that were risqué, but not explicit enough to be stopped by the radio censors. Eager to experiment with a lyrical framework suggested by Moon, Prince learnt quickly about building up songs in a specific style through studio production. As well as producing the music, he would perform, sing the vocals, mix and arrange everything. Remarkably, he was only nineteen when Warner Bros. signed him to a deal that made him the youngest performer-producer in the label's history.

His first hit single, 'Soft and Wet', from his first album, *For You*, with lyrics co-written with Moon – would be a sign of things to come. Instantly, his vocal sound established something fresh and new. Matthew Carcieri has insisted that it 'introduced Prince's falsetto – a disco-era holdover and a more comfortable range for the post-adolescent teen – and it gave birth to his ethereally sexual identity' (Carcieri 2004, p. 4). Evidence of Prince's desire to control everything was blatantly apparent in the presentation of the credits on the album's sleeve: produced, arranged, composed and performed by Prince and a listing of the 27 instruments he played. Things moved rapidly from the first album onwards.

Winding forward to his seventh album, *Around the World in a Day*, released in 1985, there is plenty evidence that music technology and recording practices had evolved radically in a period of several years. Prince's adapted his performance techniques accordingly. Rooted in the 'Minneapolis Sound', his inimitable sonic identity would now spawn a thriving music industry in his home city, and, in the wake of the success of *Purple Rain*, he was soon big enough to be granted his own label by Warner, Paisley Park Records. This label became manifested physically in the building of his own recording studio with the same name. *Around the World in a Day*, the first album on this label, depicted a different world from the concept behind the film and album *Purple Rain*. Not only did the cover work of this album have obvious references to the Beatles' *Sgt. Pepper's Lonely Hearts Club Band*, but also the music bore a wealth of similarities. Enhanced with more exotic sounds (in the choice of instruments) and a new sonic world, the songs on this album signalled a departure from all he had done during the previous four years.

Charting in the Top 10, the single, 'Raspberry Beret', propelled *Around the World in a Day* into the album charts – to date it remains the label's fastest selling record. Originally recorded in 1982, Prince would thoroughly rework this song with his band, The Revolution. Featuring a funk-driven intro, the 12″ single is experimental in its instrumental and vocal performance. In addition to a string section with Novi Norog on violin and David Coleman and Suzi Katayana on cello, Prince would include Middle Eastern finger cymbals and harmonica. The duo Wendy Melvoin and Lisa Coleman provided backing vocals. 'Raspberry Beret's' huge popularity, and its subsequent inclusion in the majority of Prince's tours, owes much to specific features: its haunting melody, the tricky chords, the nostalgic flavour in musical gestures reminiscent of the Beatles, and, most of all, the sheer magic of his vocal delivery.

In terms of harmonic flavour, 'Raspberry Beret' joins a group of famous songs written in the mixolydian mode: 'Norwegian Wood' (the Beatles), 'Satisfaction' (the Rolling Stones), 'Dark Star' (the Grateful Dead) and 'The Visitors' (Abba). Based primarily around the diatonic scale, the mixolydian has the fifth as its relative major tonic. In 'Raspberry Beret' it is the A mixolydian, that consists of the tones ABC♯DEF♯G (relative key being D major), that provides the song with modal colouring. Generating a dominant seventh chord, with its fourth degree (D) positioned dissonantly alongside the dominant seventh chord (by comparison to the fourth degree in the major key), the mixolydian possesses a 'luring quality' that owes much to the sub-dominant alignment to the leading tone. Notably, Prince stresses this through his main harmonic riff throughout the song (A-G-D/F♯).

A typical harmonic device used by Prince involves breaking with the regularity of a mode or key during the course of a song – the effect of this is teasing through its ambiguity. Take the C section of 'Raspberry Beret' (2:15–2:47), on the 'speeching' vocals, 'the rain feels so cool when it hits the barn roof and the horses wonder who u are': here a chord shift to D-A/C♯ occurs in each bar, while the bass oscillates between D and C♯ via B. This effect of this is to establish tension by preparing us for a two-bar melodic riff (see Example 4.3) when the entry of a G♯ occurs, which belongs to the tonic major scale of A mixolydian (A major). Such subtle harmonic shifts register a degree of uncertainty, serving as a cunning ploy for alerting the listener's attention to what is being said. Ambiguity is further increased by the commencement and completion of melodic riffs on the pitch D, suggestive of a transition into D lydian rather than the related A major scale. These devices heighten one's sense of anticipation, and it takes little time before we return to a G major chord (the seventh degree of A mixolydian). Modal slipperiness is a trademark of Prince's expertise in pulling things off in ways that are harmonically unique. Musically speaking, risk-taking in such harmonic devices requires an extraordinary amount of technical proficiency and confidence. Ultimately, Prince's handling of modality is a central compositional strategy that highlights his originality – we will return to this aspect in Chapter 6.

Of the many features that distinguish Prince's compositional signature is his elegant handling of simple forms and structures that involve complex twists and turns. 'Raspberry Beret' is based on a compound structure, AABA, which props up a host of musical ideas. The micro-details of his compositional working are located in the organizational function of formal division. In the B section of the song, for example, Prince does not only restrict himself to harmonic subtleties when instigating change. Melodic intervention, rhythmic precision and vocal variation are also decisive techniques. His meticulous attention to melodic riffs deserves some comment. Take the main riff in Section B (Example 4.3), flanked by another two-bar syncopated cell designed to create contrast. Here, the tight precision in its performance and production offers a compelling template for conveying the song's message. Delivered in the mid-register, in an improvisatory manner, the lyrics convey a sense of urgency, which is further supplemented by the dissolution of the backing vocals. All in all, the material in this section owes much to the bass and kit parts, which regulate the even accents on the weak beats, with the occasional handclap on the fourth. These instrumental lines contribute to the measuredness of the musical tempo, over which Prince's voice is animated and intensified.

Example 4.3   Main riff in section B of 'Raspberry Beret'

As the climactic point of the song is approached, Prince departs from his lyrical lines to non-verbal sounds (howls, screams, yells), with one final lap before fading out. This is the point where Wendy and Lisa take over the main melody from

Prince as he flirts with them through his infectious style of scatting. Delivered with great fervour, this call and response passage involves a host of humorous embellishments around the hook. In these final bars of the song the singularity of Prince's vocal style communicates something richly diverse, displaying the extent to which he pushes himself. Mostly, his melodic ornamentation shows us how ideas can be reconfigured and enhanced during short spurts. Consistently, his vocal techniques converge with his compositional ones as he kneads the tessitura of his voice into the musical fabric. Artfully, the details of every one of his musical mannerisms relay a style that is about recycling and implementing with subtle nuance. In the end, what contributes to the richness of his performance is a vocal style that is full of melodic angularity and pitch colouration.

From this music analysis, one might say 'Raspberry Beret's' huge popularity is a direct result of Prince's vocal delivery. Stylistically, his voice frees up enough space to grant us access to a wide range of emotions that connote fun-loving parody. The narrative, about a girl who wore a raspberry beret, more than subtly hints at his fantasy about her first sexual experience. In his way of telling us this story, Prince's vocal expression is naughty, edgy and wickedly pleasurable. The recording of 'Raspberry Beret' stands as a progressive rendering of untold pleasures and intent.

Cries of Redemption, Yells of Remorse

With this let us return to the album *Purple Rain*, now turning to its sixth track. Amongst the very last songs written for the *Purple Rain* project was 'When Doves Cry', released in May 1984. Epitomizing pain and redemption, it became Warner's fastest selling single to date. Elegantly arranged, produced and performed, this track wryly captures the anguish of a broken family with all its troubles. At the same time as despairing over numerous troublesome aspects of his relationship to his parents, Prince seeks peace with his father. The backdrop to all of this is the theme of peace symbolized by doves: 'why do we scream at each other, this what it sounds like when doves cry'.

Starting with a guitar solo superimposed with gyrating vocals and a classical music keyboard motif, 'When Doves Cry' connotes the individual's inner search through turmoil and pain. The vocals are offset by a punchy, mechanic 4/4 drum pattern. Most prevalent in the arrangement of this song is the absence of a bass instrument; that Prince alone decided to remove the bass part in the final mix was both daring and radical for its time. Interestingly enough, the track still maintains a bass register through the heavily compressed bass drum in the kit, which gives the song an eerie feel. Generally in pop, the symbiosis between bass and drums is critical, and disturbing this can entail risks. Allegedly, when it came to the final mix of 'When Doves Cry' Prince would make a last minute decision to avoid a clichéd-type Larry Graham-type slap lick. The decision to do this would hardly seem obvious. For in most of Prince's music the bass pre-empts snare beats on 2nd and 4th beats, with an added single slap or even fill for syncopation to underline the strong beats in the kit. In other words, the bass steers the groove, shapes the feel, and completes the audio image. Take as an example the track 'Automatic', from the album *1999*, where flourishes in the slap on the last quaver beat of the following bar fully determine the song's feel; texturally, rhythmically, melodically and harmonically, the bass flavours not only the drums but the entire mix. On most of the *1999* album the intricacies of bass and drum counterpoint are distinguished by kicks on the first three beats with snares on the fourth. And, as a rule, fills and breaks in the bass part rarely detract from the groove, the only exception being in 'When Doves Cry' from the *Purple Rain* album. In this track, while the drum programming is precise and rigid, the feel of the music is altered considerably without a bass part; the attention is thus diverted elsewhere. So, where? Most definitely to the voice and the storyline.

Told in the first person, the lyrics are deeply personal: 'Maybe I'm just like my father 2 bold', 'Maybe I'm just like my mother, she's never satisfied'. Conveyed by verbal and non-verbal utterances, this message is delivered with pained yowls, screeches, wailings and yelps, so sublime in their effect that they open up a vulnerable space for reflection. Throughout the song Prince's vocalizations are dramatically punctuated, executed and enhanced by pauses stops, and silences. One of the obvious results of such effects (and especially the non-verbal vocalizations) is an erotic sensibility that is in direct lineage with the visceral sexy utterances found in soul and disco. In a brash, showy manner, Prince's vocalizations are imbued with self-proclaimed sexual prowess, something that is inherited from a legacy of artists before him, James Brown, Little Richard and so on. Hence, one is drawn to the desirous appeal in his voice as it lets loose within the sphere of the arrangement and the mix. Indeed, the specifics of Prince's singing style are coloured by the technologization of his amplified voice that further fetishizes his role in the song. Moreover, the homoerotic appeal of his voice asserts his own brand of masculinity through the testing out of an agency that is predicated upon androgynous representation. The eroticized manner of singing in 'When Doves Cry' has much to do with vocal fetish in song form. As Ian Biddle puts it, song 'intensifies the voice, turns it into formidable material, into stuff *beyond speech*, draws attention to its limits, its texture, its ontology but it does not fundamentally change it – it just makes it *more audible*' (Biddle 2009, p. 276 – author's emphases). Accordingly, Prince's gendered representation through vocal fetishization fashions desire, intrigue and even perversion, as a result of its audibility through sonic production.

The consistent use of non-verbal sounds in 'When Doves Cry' transmits an erotic sensibility that becomes operational. These sounds militate against the production of sonorous melodic lines as vocal noise blends with melodious phrasing. Technically, the conditions of these utterances are determined by the amount of muscular force exerted in singing. Take the first non-verbal sound, occurring in the introduction material (0:13–0:25), located in the mid-register and unaccented by rhythmic motion. Starting on the right side of the audio image, superimposed over the distorted Hendrix-like guitar solo, the voice gradually pans over to the left side, acting as a bridge into the introductory material of the first verse. At this point, Prince's utterance is grinding, jeering and impudently frank. Loosely definable as a guttural vocalization, his articulation has strong associations with babbling and moaning. This is situated in strong contrast to the entry of the sung lyrics (0:34), where, raw and exposed (without any harmonic/melodic cushioning), Prince's voice is superimposed over the mechanical groove of the drum machine. As the song develops so the vocal texture thickens, a common trait in all his productions. That is to say, his voice(s) progressively becomes more processed through the effects in the mix, with intricate vocal over dubs thickening it out. Another prime non-verbal sound appears at the end of the first chorus, during the instrumental interlude into the next verse (1:41) in the form of a 'falsetto cry'. Delivered as an enunciation of vowels absent of any syllabic articulation, the resulting sound is evocative of a dove's cry. Articulated in short interjections that little by little form part of a longer phrase, the dove-cry weaves around the tight drum pattern. The angularity of this non-verbal utterance is blatantly metaphoric, conjuring up impressions of doves as they swoop around, fight and circle overhead. Highly stylized, this 'falsetto cry' is a superb example of the vocabulary that comprises Prince's rich repertoire of sounds.

Constituting a vital component of the pop performance, vocal sounds – sung and un-sung – enhance the rhythmic syntax of the groove. This is an apt moment to consider the rhythmic material of Prince's music. Vocal rhythm is a distinct feature of lyrical transmission. In 'When Doves Cry' the rhythmic figures in the melodic construction function as a counterpart to the heavily reverbed riff in the drum part. Mostly, it is the detailed interplay between the kit riff and the vocal and instrumental parts that establish the track's vibrancy. What then actually comprises melodic rhythm? Simply identifying the main rhythmic riff of a track is not enough, for rhythmic patterns are inherent in the verticality and the horizontality of all the musical events, working in counterpoint with one another. Indeed, the groove is also determined by the vocal parts. In her study of grooves, Anne Danielsen has found that the basic unit of a groove comprises 'different rhythmic figures and the basic pattern of rhythm might be described as a stable of separate figures played on top of each other, or perhaps in parallel' (Danielsen 2006, p. 43). Observations made by Danielsen suggest that the phenomena of beats rest on the fact that they are weighted very differently according to style and feel. In funk-style grooves, for instance, the rules are generally governed by a tension 'between the basic pulse and its alternative, between rhythm and counter-rhythm' (ibid., p. 70). Findings of this type provide evidence of polyrhythm occurring when a sense of counter-rhythm derived from cross rhythm is 'used to create small stretches in time that fall between a dominant basic pulse and hint at its virtual alternative' (ibid., p. 71). For instance, the strokes of such cross-rhythmic figures are often anticipated, delayed or almost played on the beat, thus becoming a prime source of rhythmic appeal. Groove configurations constitute everything from the 'small-scale musical gestures, to displacements and variations on a micro-level' (ibid., p. 71), and, as Danielsen argues, it is essentially the *manner* by which rhythmic phrasing is articulated that determines musical meaning. Inheriting so much from James Brown, Prince's grooves are highly sculpted musical events that exhibit his technical skills as a performer as much as a producer. Much stress falls on the nuances of rhythmic inflection, the micro-rhythmic features of a rich vocabulary, and their polished processing through rigorous studio production.

'When Doves Cry' is a first-rate example of a deceptively simple groove, where the kit and percussion survive, astonishingly enough, without a bass line. Yet the bass is nevertheless felt through its very absence, and close examination reveals that this is a direct result of the production work that designs the performance. In other words, the sheer abundance of details and processes produced on the famous LinnDrum provide the groove with its vibrant charge throughout. Bass-less, the groove is, however, all the more dependent on other musical elements, and, Prince's experimentation with the LinnDrum remains revolutionary for its time.

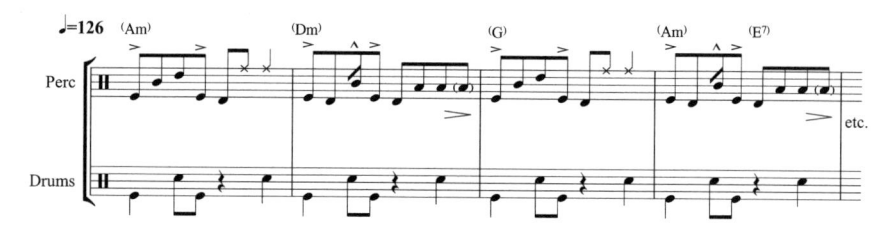

Example 4.4   Groove from 'When Doves Cry'

Incorporated into recordings by numerous mainstream artists of the 1980s – Sting, Sheila E, Jan Hammer, Peter Gabriel, Jean-Michel Jarre – the LinnDrum pioneered drum programming and new-sounding grooves. This was largely due to an increase of sampled sounds from a rate of 28 to 35kHz. In addition, its 15 sounds – bass, snare, rimshot, hi-hat, crash, ride, three toms, cabasa, tambourine, hi- and low congas, cowbell and handclap – contributed to its status as the most professional drum machine on the market in its day. Designed for the studio with 15 individual outputs for every sound as well as external sync and trigger, its sequencing features were exceptional. Never before had quantizing and memory storage of this kind been encountered – there were 56 user patterns for storing drum patterns and patterns could be arranged into songs with 49 memory locations.

The technological implications of new instruments, such as the LinnDrum, logically lead us to the matter of cultural heritage and instrumental proficiency. In the footsteps of James Brown and others, Prince has developed his rhythmic propensity through regulating vocal utterances, such as 'yeahhh', 'ooooooo', 'ah', with open vowels rather than fricatives (consonants produced by turbulent airflow). This also discloses a chief ingredient of humour in his style, not least in terms of scatting where the 'nonsensical' use of language is attained through quotation. Techniques of this kind can account for the pleasures inherent in the recorded performance of 'When Doves Cry', which is delivered through sung melodies, harmonic fills and the falsetto 'dove cries', and realized through the meticulously worked-out production process. Overall, the production of 'When Doves Cry' maps the past on to the present, its representation offering a snapshot of a very special moment in pop history. Most of all, this track reminds us that the recorded image of Prince's voice mediates the pleasures of listening, as he colours in things with a profound sense of imagination. Vocal signifiers found in 'When Doves Cry' thus ensure the intimate and erotic dimension of listening and participating in the performer's musicking. In the end, 'When Doves Cry' offers us a close-up audio image of Prince, ushering us into an extraordinarily vulnerable and intimate space.

Chronicling 1999 through 1982

Something in the performed, engineered and recorded voice enables us to escape the normality of our daily lives. Idealized through recording technology, the voice's affective charge induces pleasures that are often indescribable. During our listening to a recorded voice, a sense of desire is mediated through a consciousness that is about feeling in the here and now with the artist. This is how the recorded voice is made meaningful. It is a salient point that the voice never sounds the same no matter how many times one encounters the same recording. That is to say, every time we return to a sonic representation we are open to more of its details and differences. Being musically engaged is about discovering new elements every time we experience a recording.

Much can be said for comprehending the performing voice in pop music, for it preserves the ambivalence of fantasized desire; it is a huge force of redirection and emotional uplifting. Aware of this, Prince discharges a vocal energy that abounds with wit and self-indulgence, his voice bridging one's consciousness and repressed desires. Always there is a yielding of pleasure through his singing that is based upon pent-up psychical energy. Rife with farcical actions in the form of musical gestures, his songs are strong social and political signifiers. Through farce, he frequently ridicules and overturns rules of conduct, delighting in the celebration of the obscure and the 'different' as much as the banal. From this position of intention, his strategies of 'musicking' are eccentric while thoroughly entertaining. As Christopher Small has theorized, musicking 'establishes in the place where it is happening a set of relationships, and it is in those relationships that the meaning of the act lies'. For Small, musical meaning lies in the 'totality of a musical performance' (Small 1998, p. 13). Musicking, at any rate, is a sociopolitical matter, which raises critical questions relating to reception.

With this in mind, let us turn to one of Prince's all time greatest hits, '1999'. Released in 1982, this song, the title-track of his album, provided a comical yet cynical statement on the future. Fuelled by rhythmic entities of a pop-funk style, Prince would convert apocalyptic gloom into farce while singing about a world on the brink of Armageddon. Epic in its scope, the arrangement of '1999' brilliantly mirrored a narrative about the current Cold War, the threat of nuclear weapons, and the worrying rise of fundamentalism in the Middle East. Quite ingeniously, the emotions depicting doom and gloom would be translated into the most hedonistic song about partying away until its 1999. In 1982 there was still some time left. The huge success this song brought with it of course turned it into an anthem for the 1990s, preparing us for 'two thousand zero zero'. Few could disagree that '1999' provided a momentous vision, a prophetic arrival point for a new epoch, and a foreboding summing up of the twentieth century. Production-wise, this track's creativity lay in the major changes afoot in recording technology, which Prince had used to advance the compositional possibilities in pop music.

Before turning to aspects of vocal production in the album version of '1999', we will consider this track's arrangement and mix. Much of the sonic image is defined by the Oberheim 8-voice synthesizer, which Prince used for arranging horns in the style of groups such as Earth, Wind and Fire. The groove and drum programming was produced by the Linn LM-1 drum machine, the sounds of which characterize many pop songs from this period. Without question, Prince's programming was original for its time, with him deploying this machine in almost any kind of compositional way he wanted. Significantly, as we have already mentioned, this was the first drum machine of its kind with digital samples of acoustic drum sounds. As one of the first programmable drum machines, it encapsulated the pop scene of the day, its sound instantly discernible in the music of artists such as Michael Jackson, Madonna the Human League and others.

With a robotic, slowed down, electronically distorted phrase, '1999' opens with the lines 'Don't worry, I won't hurt you. I only want you to have some fun'. Assuming a put-on God-like authority, Prince comes across farcical, his sermon-voice framed by a cymbal crash and entry of the emblematic four-chord synth riff; the effect is dramatic, like a curtain rising slowing on the first act of a show. Throughout the song the vocals are cleverly varied, alternating between Prince and other members of The Revolution, Dez Dickerson, Lisa Coleman and Jill Jones, their voices recorded separately at the start of each verse. Within the mix, they are tightly interlocked in three-part harmony at specific points through dubbing and multi-tracking, and distinguishable by their palpable funky performance in a whoosh of fervour.

Lavishly assembled within a dazzling arrangement and punishing, tight groove, '1999' exemplifies Prince's approach to funk and epitomizes his creative wizardry. Much of this is due to his clipped guitar riff work, an aspect all too often overlooked at the expense of his lead and solo playing. For instance, the wah-wah licks that eroticize the groove also complement the teasing funk bass line as the song develops. Added to this are the guitar fills that become more ornate, albeit still low in the mix. In the final round (5:45), the four-chord riff (Example 4.5) breaks into a chicken-scratch riff, the rhythm guitar changing from a wet wah-wah effect to a bone-dry, clipped pattern that is raw and sensual. Culminating with the lines, 'Mummy, why does everybody have a bomb', '1999' finally snaps shut with the same dose of farce with which it opened.

Example 4.5   Four-chord synth riff in '1999'

The vocals on this track reveal a wealth of features that extend numerous ideas we have already aired in this chapter. The constantly changing vocal tones in the recording not only belong to Prince's voice, but also to the others who perform with him. While Prince's voice is mainly located in its mid-register, the others are registrally above and below his, flanking him. Alan Leeds, Prince's tour manager and vice-president at Paisley Park until 1992, has explained how all three singers would originally sing in their parts at the same time. It was only later that Prince decided to mix out the other two voices on each line so as to avoid the impression of a well-rehearsed chorus. Aesthetically, this provided the verses with a more natural yet adventurous feel. Also discernible in the mix is the clear distinction of each vocal track, a notable detail when working out the textural fabric of the arrangement. Subtle use of effects, such as contrasting reverb settings, panning and eq-ing, further add colour to the vocal parts making them stand out in the mix. Perhaps what characterizes the production most is the diverse range of processing techniques that regulate the voices. In particular, their multi-track overdubbing renders the lines unusually 'live' in their feel, drawing all the more attention to the sentiments expressed in the lyrics. Another prominent detail found in the vocal treatment in '1999' is that of reverberation, which serves to assist levels of dynamic contrast as much as a sense of space.

Almost double the length of the single hit, the album version of '1999' would offer Prince the possibility to jam away to his heart's content in the track's final three minutes. Jamming has always been a prime element when showcasing his vocal flair, and this is intrinsic to Prince's musical style. Occurring at the end of a song, the jam passage draws all the performers on the track together. Based on the main thematic of the song, Prince turns to jamming for creative commentary. Certainly, its effect is carnivalesque, its technical virtuosity and extemporizing quality directly linked to the cadenzas in the common practice period (1600 to 1900), where the musician was expected to demonstrate his improvisatory skills.

When jamming, Prince turns all his vocal assets to full throttle, exercising the control of his register brilliantly by inserting non-verbal exclamations, picking out key phrases from the lyrics, and articulating the urgency of his message in one voice. There is something burning about the jam in '1999', which is highly activating in dance contexts. Slickly, the groove consists of Prince's vocals set against the others in a full-blown stint of the chorusing on the word 'party' (4:35 onwards, see Example 4.6), the word mutating into a two-bar riff. Commencing with single voices, in their respective registers, on 'party', the arrangement builds into a magnificent chant of the two syllables 'part-y'. Signalling the final arrival point, this passage is reached with full harmonic regalia; it is the song's plateau, where Prince jams impulsively. Stretched over three beats at the onset of the riff, the word 'party' is blissfully delivered, repeated *ad lib, ad infinitum*.

Example 4.6 'Party' in '1999'

The features of vocal style inherent in '1999' broadly typify many of Prince's songs and consist of:

1. rhythmic coordination of his voice with his other voices (vocal dubbing), as well as vocalists and instruments;
2. projection of an image of unity through the vocal blend of the band – the effect is one of call and response, where Prince's voice stands out as independent;
3. the use of *parlando rubato*, whereby the speech rhythm of Prince's quasi-spoken lines departs from the steady rhythm of the sung lines in order to accent specific words differently;
4. non-verbal interjections that are designated to flavour the flow, consisting of yowls, melismatic phrases (where syllables and vowels are stretched out) and high-pitched screams;
5. glottal shakes, appogiatura[2] inflections and slurred articulations in the pronunciation of words, creating a quavering effect in an over-enunciated manner.

Generally speaking, Prince's arrangements consist of pent-up energy in the vocal tracks, often in a talkative (or for that matter babbling) manner, all of which heighten the rhythmic propensity. After all, vocal articulation through multi-tracking involves manipulating the way the voices fill spaces, change positions, extemporize and extend melodic and lyrical elements. Intrinsic to this is the art of phrasing the melody and lyrics, a main ingredient in getting the narrative across.

Such vocal idiosyncrasies define Prince's oral narration. And, as we have seen, much of this takes place through jamming, scatting and speeching, where

---

[2] An appoggiatura, from the Italian verb *appoggiare* is an ornate, decorative embellishment to a note or theme that usually falls on the strong beat and is reached by an intervallic leap.

the mannerisms of vocal expression become the rhetoric of his style. Indeed, the minute characteristics of the vocals in '1999' offer a way into understanding how vocal gesturing establishes his aesthetic on a broader level. In the end, it is his virtuosity that stages the live-ness of the recording. '1999' is delivered by the unveiling of the subject's desire through a bewildering mix of intersecting vocal and instrumental voices; no wonder it has succeeded in becoming a main signature of our time. Prince's recorded voice in '1999' represents a fabulous construction of desire and passion, at the same time it stands as a disquieting commentary on the gloomy political events of the early 1980s and the years to come.

Conclusion

In this chapter we have attempted to argue that the sublime is a prime feature of Prince's musical vocabulary, an element always inherent in his songs: the *jouissance* of his music is a result of this. Richly excessive, Prince's recorded style helps us access a world of fantasy constituted by multiple narratives, histories and approaches. His emphases on the sonorous quality of words can be read as invocations of a set of practices that underscore musical processes through pitch, rhythm and repetition. The function of repetition of musical ideas owes much to the compositional technique of ostinati – the repeating of an idea in the form of a rhythmic motif, tune or complete melody. Styles such as funk, rap and hip-hop are predicated upon ostinati, and, as Brackett points out, rap elevates the practice of ostinato through the use of sampling. This is evident where 'fragments of previous recordings overlap or are superimposed onto the basic rhythm track, or even used as the basis for the rhythm track' (Brackett 2000, p. 137). Sampling in Prince's music can be understood as a prominent compositional technique in the troping of vocal and instrumental gesturing. The impish and provocatively familiar sound of Prince's voice (set against his samples) signals all kinds of connotations: invitation, seduction, appeal and ecstasy.

The pleasure derived from pop is largely about the listener identifying with the sensuality of the human voice and, in the case of Prince, there is scarcely cause to emphasize the importance of the erotic aspect of his sonic representation. His voice establishes a phallic order, an order of obsessive control that is organized around the tactics of subversion that displace the norms of heterosexual display. Remarkably, the performative dimension of his recorded voice reveals the ambiguities of the African American male, vulnerable and emasculated. Prince's politics is to weave in and out of the discourses that fetishize the black male in popular culture; this he does by eroticizing his own androgyny. One is almost without words to explain how the erotics of an anti-macho black male are disseminated through the sung voice (and here we can even beg the question of what signifies the 'sung voice' in terms of symbolic signification?). As we pointed out at the start of the chapter, the sung voice communicates via the temporality of conscious experience, creating the conditions for which the listener becomes a conscious participant.

Most of all, the act of singing is a byproduct of the symbolic, reproducing our conceptions of who we are and what notions we have of our cultural settings. Prince's erotic sensibility thus gives way to a powerful musical agency that is grounded in race, corporeality and gender-related struggles. The same is true for his sexuality and sensuality, whose display is ambiguous and therefore threatening to many social orders. Prince's musical performance is sensual at every point, and located in the intricate dynamics, the mimicry, the groove, the jam and the studio production. Vocally he is present even when he is silent – his voice represents his responsive understanding, his inner speech. Indeed, Prince's music shows us how the recorded voice acquires a lifelike reality, making available exciting and disturbing avenues for new forms of identification. When all's said and done, Prince's voice fashions an aesthetic that falls outside the domain of verbal communication – this is because his vocal sensibility functions as a barometer for sublime play within a highly charged context of erotic desire.

Chapter 5
'Take Me with U, Prince': Female Identifications with a Male Pop Icon

Vivian Ward: Don't you just love Prince?
Edward Lewis: More than life itself.

(*Pretty Woman* (1990), dir. Garry Marshall)

Introduction

At the time of writing, Prince has just made another of his headline-hitting appearances in the front row at a fashion show, this time at British designer John Galliano's catwalk parade at Paris Fashion Week. Dressed from head-to-toe in tomato-red satin, black sunglasses and vertiginous heels, his appearance upstages that of the professional supermodels sashaying in the latest couture designs. As other celebrity guests, including retro-inspired pop star Katy Perry, gaze at him in admiration, Prince coolly pouts and checks his cufflinks; it is just like any other day in the life, and wardrobe, of the man who sang 'life is a parade'. Prince's style of 'parade' is rather more than surface appearance, though. It is part and parcel of his career-long alignment with the characteristics and practices of femininity. Prince is renowned for his association with women; be they his legions of female followers, collaborators or even through his own controversial displays of gender ambiguity using his voice and appearance.

Prince's feminine, non-threatening visual appearance provides, for his female spectators, a point of access to a meaningful engagement with his identity. Looking at Prince suggests the possibility of an active female gaze on the part of his fans, which casts doubt on some of the most abiding accounts of the female spectator and cultural studies' approaches to women consumers of pop. Far from seeing Prince in the context of 'lack' – so that he fills some kind of Freudian gap in their psyches – Prince's young female fans use his on-screen image as a site of negotiation, as a point of access for reflecting upon their own identity. If young females have the capacity to actively read images of Prince, it is necessary to utilize theories of female subjectivity that are not founded on lack to better understand the nature of fans' identification with the star.

Therefore, this chapter will delve deeper into the theories of the psychoanalyst Melanie Klein (1882–1960), whose emphasis on the power of the mother object may help unlock how Prince's female fans might 'use' his on-screen image towards the formation of their subjectivity. Furthermore, by identifying with

Prince's on-screen persona, what meanings and messages might his young female fans have derived about femininity in the context of the mid 1980s, when Prince's first motion picture, *Purple Rain* (1984), was screened?

As with his still images, a distinctive feature of Prince's first full-length musical film was the emphasis on the star as spectacle. The female spectator is beckoned to contemplate Prince's image above all others within the diegetic space, through his employment of feminine practices such as certain types of clothing, hair, make-up and gesture. His use of these female signifiers serves as more than a reversal of gender codes, subverting conventional theories of gendered spectator power relations asserted by Mulvey (1975) and others.[1] According to Jon Lewis, in his review of *Purple Rain* for *Jump Cut* magazine in 1985: 'women are (so clearly it's silly to argue this) rendered as willing objects of the male performer's gaze and song and sexual interest' (Lewis 1985). Indeed, this power relationship was enacted in many music videos at the time, such as David Lee Roth's 'California Girls' from 1985. In contrast, it is possible *Purple Rain* offered his young female fans a space for identification with a male star, through, in a Lacanian sense, his subversion of visual gender codes and transgression of female viewing positions.

Moreover, the idea of studying this weird, 'black gay fag'[2] pop creature went against the grain of the well-grounded rock aesthetic, whose visual iconography constrained the pleasures for the female spectator. Following on from our study of the music in the song 'Purple Rain' in Chapter 4, selected scenes from *Purple Rain* in this chapter will demonstrate how this film offered young female fans a space for identification with a male star.

In a similar vein to some of his publicity photographs, Prince's play on sexual and gender identity in *Purple Rain* provoked strong, negative – and positive – reactions, particularly in his portrayal of women in the mass media. Critics

---

[1] It must be remembered that the majority of studies of rock music and its visual iconography denied the possible pleasures for the female spectator. Much of the early research into rock music and gender relations focused on the positioning of female fans, taking as a starting point the 'natural' links between rock music and the masculine and analysing the space created by/for female performers and spectators. It was only in the 1990s that scholarship in popular music and gender theory took off with publications such as *Sexing the Groove*, *Queering the Pitch*, *Queering the Popular Pitch* and *Running With the Devil*.

[2] Over the years it has been apparent that a distinct majority of non-fans think of Prince as gay and that this is down to his feminine image. While Prince's androgyny has been a compelling subject and an extraordinary source of fascination within the context of a postmodern pop subjectivity, his imagery and behaviour has provoked much debate. Homophobic comments regarding his possible gayness (coupled with his black-ness) still abound as any internet search engine will verify. On his 35th birthday, when changing his name to the symbol (consisting of a glyph that constituted both male and female signs), the question of his possible bisexuality was raised. Many of his songs' lyrics play on sexual ambivalence and deviation. For example, take 'Anna Stesia': 'have you ever wanted to play with someone so much you'd take anyone boy or girl', or 'Controversy': 'am I black or white? Am I straight or gay?'

castigated its depiction of women as misogynistic. For example, Lewis wrote that the film was:

> ... a violent misogynist, adolescent male fantasy ... as a result nothing undercuts the adolescent male fable of success. Rather the unswerving development of that myth falls into place within the film's allegiance to music video and the dream of becoming elite. (Lewis 1985)

Furthermore, O'Brien (1995) suggested women in Prince's acts, such as Apollonia 6, who features in the film, have been little more than fantasy glamour figures. Nonetheless, women who have worked with the star, such as Sheena Easton and Mavis Staples, have proclaimed him to be respectful and indeed a promoter of women (Jones 1997, p. 106).

The film tells the story of The Kid (Prince), a young, gifted musician who is trying to overcome personal difficulties and professional rivalries to achieve stardom and fulfilment. Set in Prince's home city of Minneapolis, this semi-autobiographical text is centred on tensions between band members in a real-life club, First Avenue, and the domestic violence at The Kid's parental home. On the surface, critics' allegations of misogyny would appear to have weight, for the spectator witnesses both The Kid and his father inflict violence on their partners as if aggression towards women is to be justified in the context of desire. Furthermore, black characters such as Morris Day are presented as two-dimensional objects of jocular derision. Moreover, The Kid appears to use the legacy of his father's eventual suicide bid to obtain commercial success and acceptance in the patriarchal music industry, regardless of his appalling behaviour theretofore. Lewis suggests that even The Kid's androgynous appearance is cultivated in an attempt to ridicule his own femininity, to send it up and thus defuse its power (Lewis 1985). However, from another perspective – a feminist reading using psychoanalytic theories that are not predicated on lack – *Purple Rain* serves as a metaphor for the instability of patriarchal masculinity, and illustrates the limitations on femininity that it seeks to impose. The film seeks to cast light on the institutional foundations for the perceived fixity in gender-based identity, and undercut them. This quote about Prince by the journalist and biographer Dave Hill (1989) crystallizes the power of the star's identity at the moment in question, and his direct assault on conventional notions of gendered subjectivity in this film:

> Purple Rain would turn Prince into a superstar, but more than that, into a symbolic personification of a bunch of ideas about the world, which were certain to polarise opinion. His eventual trivialising portrayal by particular bastions of reactionary thinking as nothing more than a deviant head-case is a clear indictment of the blind fear that the success of the 'wrong' kind of outsider can induce. Young, black, strong, prosperous, self-directed, unnervingly mute and sexually programmed to subvert – this is some people's recipe for hell on earth. (Hill 1989, p. 145)

Prince's visual persona in the film may be read as being on a ceaseless quest for his own subjectivity. This is significant because his search mirrors the ceaselessness of the search for the elusive female subject in psychoanalytical theory, primarily through the discourses of Lacanian-derived film theory. Furthermore, this quest was mirrored in other popular cultural messages aimed at young women, such as magazines. That the search for an authentic feminine identity might bear fruit through identification with a male star is a major challenge to established principles of psychoanalytical, cultural and feminist theories, but must nonetheless be accounted for. There has, to date, not been any in-depth positive analysis of the film, other than some favourable media reviews, suggesting this hugely commercially successful film demands a closer re-reading.

Narrativity and Visual Scenario in *Purple Rain*

A $6m production, *Purple Rain* was written by Albert Magnoli and William Blinn, the latter of whom was an executive producer of the *Fame* television series. As a brief plot synopsis, Prince plays The Kid, leader of a struggling band, The Revolution, who suffers crises in his family life, the effects of which filter into his relationships with friends, lovers and colleagues. Professionally, he is struggling to retain The Revolution's top-ranking status as resident band at the First Avenue club against rivals The Time, led by charismatic spiv, Morris Day. In a bid to revitalize The Revolution's success, two female band-members, Wendy and Lisa, offer The Kid tapes of their own composition, but their arrogantly authorial leader mocks them and refuses to contemplate their intervention. However, in private, he is impressed. The Kid's ambitious girlfriend, Apollonia, who is new to town, is lured away by Morris Day to front his risqué, suspender-clad female trio, Apollonia 6. The Kid resorts to hitting Apollonia in anger, as he has witnessed his father do to his mother and to himself on numerous occasions. The epiphany arrives dramatically when The Kid's depressed father shoots himself and is placed on a life-support machine in hospital. Devastated and guilt-ridden, The Kid is also on the brink of committing suicide but is distracted by the discovery of his pianist father's sheet music. He is jolted out of his pessimistic impertinence and composes a new track that incorporates his critically ill father's legacy with the input of Wendy and Lisa. The climax is The Revolution's last-chance stage performance, when The Kid is transformed from derided has-been into rock messiah using the new track.

Thematically, the film addresses innumerable tensions between The Kid's inner and outer worlds. His relationship with Apollonia, and his employer's threat to place commercial interests over loyalty to the young star, bring to the fore traumatic responses to his masculinity, his femininity and his relationship with his parents and collaborators. The relational identities and tensions arising might find parallels with the context in which young females were negotiating their subjectivity in the mid 1980s. Significantly, the struggles of the main protagonists are enacted in the context of a shift in fortunes within the context of

First Avenue. The club, which has clearly served to nurture the talents of its young stars, is threatening to withdraw its loyalty to their creativity and instead demand commercial acts to bring in larger audiences. The characters are struggling for some order against the shifting social and institutional contexts of their lives. The Kid and his contemporaries are undergoing rites of passage into independent adult identities, and their familiar home of the club is also re-evaluating its commercial priorities, which may no longer have them at the centre. Thus, the film might be interpreted as an allegory of the transition from teenage years into adulthood, from dependence to independence. The attempts to link Prince with The Kid and thus coax the spectator into assuming inherent authenticity in the film's messages are apparent throughout. The film's advertising slogan was 'Before he wrote the songs, he lived them'.

One way this is achieved is visually, in the way the film combines elements of a range of cinematic genres, making it difficult to categorize via the conventional demarcations of classical Hollywood cinema (see Bordwell and Thompson 1997, pp. 108–10). The classical narrative sequences are interspersed with spectacular musical stage performances by the bands in the film, though the film could not be neatly categorized as a musical, as singing is confined to spaces in the film where it would be appropriate. However, the use of musical sequences, it is argued, opens the film up to more 'against-the-grain' readings than classic narrative cinema. Might this offer a space for an active female gaze in *Purple Rain*?

Films examining the lives and roles of young rock stars proliferated in the late 1960s and early 1970s. *Privilege* (1967, dir. Peter Watkins) starred Paul Jones as a singer forced by the British government to become the leader of an evangelical crusade. *Stardust* (1974, dir. Michael Apted), starring David Essex, sees an icon of messianic status fall victim to temptations foisted upon him by those supposedly with his interests at heart. The film coincided with the release of religious-themed rock films including *Godspell* (1973, dir. David Greene) and *Jesus Christ Superstar* (1973, dir. Norman Jewison). Subsequent musical films such as *Grease* (1978, dir. Randal Kleiser) referred back to earlier musical movements, intermingling contemporary forms such as disco with 1950s doo-wop. While Peter Steven argues that music films such as these reside wholly within a realistic depiction of time and space, 'by this I mean that the singing and dancing are all at times motivated by natural locations and plausible characters' (Steven 1980, pp. 13–16).

Furthermore, generically, parts of the scene would already have been seen by the spectator in other extra-textual contexts. For example, the scene with The Kid arriving at First Avenue's 7th Street Entry on his motorcycle was used in the promotional video for the single, 'Let's Go Crazy', and in advertising for the film. There is, therefore, slippage between the character of The Kid and Prince because not only will Prince's fans have seen the promotional materials, they may also have followed the highly-publicized progress of the film's production in the music press and other media. The 'Let's Go Crazy' performance, and other songs from the film, were live recordings from actual concerts, including a fund-raising gig for a charity (see Nilson 1999, p. 129). The scenes of The Kid and Morris arriving at the club were in effect documentary shots of the real-life applause the artists were receiving from real fans rather than mocked-up crowd shots. Thus, for the young female spectator, the context of viewing the opening sequence would likely have been important in providing her with something of an active and privileged view of the construction of the scenes. This inevitably problematizes any foreclosed concepts of female spectatorship, such as in Mulvey (1975), or foreclosed narrative texts, as described in Bordwell and Thompson (1997), and instead proposes an active female viewing position, which recognizes contextual factors.

The interplay between The Kid's traumatized psyche and his struggle to maintain professional credibility, renders the film thematically in common with the Gothic genre, which could be found expressed in many areas of popular culture in the 1980s (see Jancovich 1992). This style is illustrated through the *mise-en-scène*; most of the film is shot at night and indoors in dimly-lit, confined spaces, such as dressing rooms and The Kid's basement bedroom. These familiar places, such as the home, become uncannily defamiliarized. Indeed, The Kid's parental home is depicted throughout as a site of horror and violence; his subterranean, nocturnal world represents his tension with his socio-cultural backdrop, which may have corresponded with his young female fan's feelings of distance and confusion in relation to their familiar environments.[3]

Ultimately, it is Prince's visual persona which will be scrutinized in this chapter as we consider the way he amalgamates, embodies and problematizes these generic and gendered juxtapositions and conflicts within the film. The star employs his body as a site of contemplation, for the female spectator to negotiate the myriad messages in popular culture that sought to categorize gender within foreclosed pre-given identities. The Kid's visual identity, as Gothic, androgynous, simultaneously vulnerable and aggressive, presents the young female spectator with a range of viewing positions from which to envision the star's identity. This chapter will focus attention on how those images and identifications might relate to the development of female subjectivity using popular culture, and in order to do this it will draw on the positive potential of femininity in the theories of Klein.

Applying Klein: Theories of the Female Subject's Use of the Media

Klein's theorizations of the formation of the subject have rarely if ever been applied to cultural texts. This may be partly explained by the powerful influence and popularity of Lacan's theory of the gaze, and film studies' application of it to develop concepts of spectatorship. Yet Klein's theories of object relations and of the pre-Oedipal attachment to the mother offer significant potential for furthering knowledge into how the female subject might use popular cultural

---

[3] As such, it may be helpful to look at the work of writers who argue the Gothic can serve as a powerful textual strategy for conveying the themes of alienation felt by the female subject. See Jancovich (1992) and Botting (1996).

texts in developing her identity, and this is for two main reasons. Firstly, as the previous chapter demonstrated, while Lacan's theory of the gaze and its use by feminists has helpfully illuminated patriarchal structures and representations in dominant cinema, it has never been able to conceive of an active female gaze which causes stumbling blocks in relation to the on-screen image of Prince. Klein's (1940) emphasis on the object of the mother, and how that figure is forever internalized, offers a female subjectivity that is fundamental, powerful and active and not defined by lack in relation to masculinity (Klein in Mitchell 1986, p. 148). Secondly, Klein's theory is distinguished through her notion of fantasy, describing the arena in which psychic processes are played out. For the child, the outside world is nothing more than a series of images and passing forms that are used to characterize an inner world of fantasies (ibid., p. 149), which suggests popular cultural texts, including film, photography and music, contribute to the gendered messages and meanings that impact in some way on the inner landscape.

In her paper 'Mourning and Its Relation to Manic Depressive States' from 1940, Klein describes the earliest stages of infantile psychic life in terms of a successful completion of development through certain positions (ibid., pp. 146–74). A position, in Kleinian terms, describes a set of psychic functions that correspond to a given phase of development, always appearing during the first year of the infant's life, but which are present at all times thereafter. The transition through these phases can also be reactivated at any time in later life. Klein described two major positions, the paranoid-schizoid position and the depressive position. The paranoid-schizoid position occurs at the earliest stage of development and is characterized by the relation of part-objects, notably the mother's breast, the prevalence of splitting in the ego and in the object, and paranoid anxiety. The depressive position is ushered in when the infant recognizes the mother as a whole object. It comprises a multiplicity of object relations and anxieties which correspond with the infant's experience of attacking a loved mother for withdrawing the breast and losing her as in internal and external object. This experience gives rise to guilt, pain and feelings of loss.

For either paranoid-schizoid or depressive identification to occur, two processes are needed. On one hand, an object is introjected into the ego, which then identifies with some or all of the object's characteristics. Alternatively, the projection of parts of the self into an object results in the object being perceived as having the characteristics of the projected part of the self, which also results in an identification. This process is described by Klein in detail in her later paper 'Notes on Some Schizoid "Mechanisms"' (1946, in ibid., pp. 175–200). For instance, in the paranoid-schizoid position, the ego will split the object into an ideal satisfying part, and a persecuting part, in order to achieve a partial identification with a good object. The result of this defence mechanism, which is essentially a denial of persecution, may be that the ego itself is split into two. In this way identifications can be made with a persecuting part object that can then be projected outwards. But the projection is now in danger of infecting the good object, threatening to destroy it, or provoking the possibility of retribution. For Klein, the form of the mother is central to this process.

She describes the depressive position as a process of early 'reality testing' and argues that this is a prototypical form of what will later become the process of mourning:

> The object which is being mourned is the mother's breast and all that the breast and milk have come to stand for in the infant's mind: namely, love, goodness and security. All these are felt by the baby to be lost, and lost as a result of his uncontrollably greedy and destructive phantasies and impulses against his mother's breasts. (Ibid., p. 148)

So, for Klein the earliest active relation to reality begins with the infant's awareness of its own uncontrollable greed and an inconsolable sorrow for a plenitude it feels it has destroyed. The form of the mother, in the infant's fantasies, is 'doubled' and 'undergoes alterations' as it is internalized (ibid.). In this way, external reality can be 'read' as long as the forms of the outside world can be:

> ... fitted into the patterns provided by the psychic reality which prevails at the time; whilst the psychic reality of the child is gradually influenced by every step in his progressive knowledge of external reality. (Ibid., p. 150)

It is important to recognize that for Klein the child's use of external reality is never anything more than an attempt to better understand inner psychic drives. Reality is itself understood in terms of the doubling bifurcation of images. So there is, in effect, nothing but unconscious fantasy, on the one hand, and the forms and images that flit across the perceptual screen on the other. This seems to be close to the experience of the mass media. In Klein's version of reality, objective truth is suspended, so that the active subject applies meaning based on its perceptions, feelings and experiences.

One of the reasons why Freudian and Lacanian psychoanalytical theories have been widely applied to analysing the experience of cinema viewing is their emphasis on loss, borne out of the castration complex. Bordwell and Thompson (1997) have deconstructed the form of classical Hollywood cinema to reveal how typically films commence with a sense that something has been disrupted in the order of things, something is missing or lost, usually motivated by desire (Bordwell and Thompson 1997, p. 109). The trajectory of the film ensures that the loss is made good, or the disruptions to the world are repaired:

> Leaving no loose ends unresolved, these films seek to complete their causal chains with a final effect. We usually learn the fate of each character, the answer to each mystery, and the outcome of each conflict. (Ibid., p. 110)

Kleinian desire, in comparison to Lacan or Freud's theorizations, forces the spectator to work harder. In Klein, the loss of the part object of the mother and ensuing paranoid-schizoid position is not as terminal as Lacan's notion of lack. The infant's desire to make good, to repair the damage, suggests that the child has the strength and capacity to return to and confront anxiety head on. To move forward into the depressive position, the infant must learn to move backwards into terrifying territory, into the neo-natal environment that produced the violent, destructive fantasy. In cinema, it is possible to read films as a version of this state, a scary landscape in which reality is suspended and fantasies are confronted and re-enacted. In the following section, *Purple Rain* will be critically analysed according to Klein's theorization in an attempt to re-read the film as an account of the ravaged world of infantile fantasy. In this way, it may be possible to open a space for conceiving of the female spectator in active negotiation with the text as a point of access to her own identifications.

Underlying *Purple Rain* in Kleinian Terms

Purple Rain can be read as a fantasy played out almost entirely in the paranoid-schizoid position, culminating in The Kid's move to the depressive position. There are four main themes underlying the film, which will be taken into account during this analysis. Firstly, the role of the mother is central to the film's thematic development. She is the archetypal Kleinian object, who is symbolically troubling and fragmented from the outset in *Purple Rain*. The Kid finds it almost impossible to identify with his mother because she allows herself to be brutalized by his overbearing and depressed father. She is rarely seen in the film, except in glimpses through windows as she fights or makes up with The Kid's father. There is little or no interaction between mother and son within the narrative, yet it will become evident how profoundly important her symbolic presence is in furthering the plot and in The Kid's journey to self-realization.

The second theme, which relates to the first, is what might be identified as the excessive gendering of the main protagonists throughout the film, both in plot and in visuals. Conventional representations of masculinity and femininity are disrupted and subverted throughout the film with the male actors displaying camp, narcissistic characteristics, while females like Wendy and Lisa can be read as demonstrating roles and practices normally associated with males in the context of the music industry. The Kid in particular is excessively feminized in his clothing, hair and make-up, an external signifier of his internal struggle to reconcile his femininity with his masculinity. Ultimately it is the power of the mother object which enables him to embrace his inner femininity to help him to forge positive and non-patriarchal relationships with the women in his social sphere. The gender struggles within the film also provide an opportunity to unpack thoroughly the themes of misogyny underlying several of the scenes, which reveal something of the psychic organizations at work in the text. The feminist critique of the film can be re-evaluated when exploring the film using Klein's perspectives.

Thirdly, there is the delineation of The Kid's home as the scariest place imaginable, symbolizing the scene of the infant's neo-natal crisis on entry into the paranoid-schizoid position. The home is the scene of his parents' violent battles, where The Kid witnesses their mental breakdown and his father's suicide attempt. It is also the place where The Kid hits Apollonia and has a hallucination of his own death by hanging. The Kid's home becomes uncannily defamiliarized into a site of almost unimaginable horror, though it is also the place where he is forced to confront his reckless and immature behaviour, acknowledge that he is vulnerable when he begins to rebuild his life, coinciding with his move into the depressive position. Last but not least, there is the fourth theme of doubling which serves as a structural key to the entire film. As The Kid relives the neo-natal paranoid-schizoid position, the image of his mother is doubled and aspects of it projected onto other female characters within the diegetic space, notably Apollonia, Wendy and Lisa. It is with these three women that The Kid has the most conflicts and, significantly, it is their actions, rather than his, that serve to propel the plot and move The Kid further towards his epiphany and transformation. In this way, the female characters represent agency and it is The Kid's projection of fantasies onto them, rather than any inbuilt characteristic of theirs, that causes conflicts.

These underlying themes propose a viewing position for the female spectator that can be active in its negotiation of the meanings emanating from the text. They will be demonstrated and critically unpacked through an analysis of the 27 scenes from the film, as they appear chronologically, drawing on Klein. Specific scenes will be focused upon in depth, because they foreground femininity within the narrative and visual signification, and consequently may problematize a reading predicated on a fixed spectatorial position, as would be determined from a Lacanian-informed perspective. Instead, these scenes encapsulate the way the film – and specifically the on-screen image of The Kid/Prince – may offer a space for the female spectator to envision and negotiate femininity as a fundamental presence and agent of subjectivity. Klein herself illuminates the complexity and sophistication of identification with the mother even in tiny children, and the importance of images and fantasy in that process:

> ... in the quite small child there exists, side by side with its relations to real objects – but on a different plane, as it were – relations to its unreal imagos, both as excessively good and excessively bad figures, and that these two kinds of object relations intermingle and colour each other to an ever-increasing degree in the course of development. The first important steps in this direction occur, in my view, when the child comes to know its mother as a whole person and becomes identified with her as a whole, real and loved person. (Klein in Mitchell 1986, p. 142)

Thus the experience of viewing media images, like the infant witnessing and recognizing its emergence as a whole and separate being, can be reflexive and productive on the part of the female subject.

Opening Scenes 1–6: Gender Disruption, Part Objects and The Kid's Femininity Complex

The first six scenes establish The Kid's position as an up-and-coming musician, and introduce the ambitious new arrival in town, Apollonia, as a love interest. His interest in Apollonia corresponds with a violent breakdown in his parents' marriage, which he witnesses. The scenes depict The Kid's increasing difficult relations with his band-mates, especially the women, as he descends towards inner crisis. It is not so much the narrative but the visual cinema rhetoric of *Purple Rain* that makes it so interesting for analysis in relation to female subjectivity. The seven-and-a-half-minute opening sequence of the film is important in introducing the key protagonists while immediately problematizing the stability of their gender identities and practices. These scenes are also important in introducing a series of objects that surround the protagonists, notably The Kid, which serve as metaphors for their inner worlds. The sequence opens with the sound of Prince's voice reciting a sermon, which introduces his hit song, 'Let's Go Crazy'.

From a silhouette of Prince on stage, holding his guitar, the scene switches to a rapid-edit montage of images of androgynous faces of club-goers, a mixer desk, a pin-ball machine and close ups of Prince applying eye make-up. As the tempo rises, the scene switches back to the stage where Prince launches into a performance of the track with his band, The Revolution, to a rapturous audience response. There is a cut to a night-time street scene and a taxi pulling up. A young women (Apollonia) leaps out and sprints away to dodge paying the fare. Then the view cuts to a young black man (Morris Day), wearing a headscarf, camply vacuuming his room, before another quick edit to Prince checking his appearance in his bedroom mirror. The camera looks over his shoulder, sharing his gaze at his reflection. He is dressed in a full-length, purple, silk, Edwardian-style overcoat, white shirt and cravat and wears full make-up and bouffant hair. Framing his reflection are objects and images attached to his mirror – pierrot dolls, silk flowers, candles, pre-Raphaelite images cut from magazines and taped onto the glass. Reflected in the background are the walls of his room, which are covered in art sketches of women's faces. It is evident his personal space is ornate and feminized, though all the props denote copies – fake flowers, torn-out art pictures. Indeed the image of Prince we see is of his reflection.

Back to Morris's bedroom and we see him holding a plastic-wrapped jacket against himself and looking at his reflection. He narcissistically pulls comical but appreciative faces at himself. In contrast to Prince/The Kid's feminine and cared-for space, Morris's is messy, with underwear – male and female – hanging out of drawers, carrier bags stuffed behind the mirror, and banknotes and a hipflask strewn on his dresser. Instead of 'tasteful' art, we see Polaroids pasted up. Next, we witness The Kid self-assuredly riding past the fans waiting outside First Avenue Club on his fetishistic Batman-style purple motorbike, with his guitar strapped to his back.

In stark contrast to both the men's spaces, the audience sees Apollonia surveying her new hotel room, reluctantly handing over rent money to a landlord. The room is dark, dusty and ugly. She stands with her back to two mirrors – we never see her look at her reflection – but they are too dirty to reflect much apart from dark corners. Her prerogative is to throw open the shutters and gaze at First Avenue over the road. Morris has just arrived, stepping out of a yellow cab, and preens himself in a mirror held by his valet, Jerome. We see The Kid in dark silhouette playing his guitar solo in an onanistic fashion, while brightly-dressed Morris makes his way to the bar surrounded by numerous women. The next few shots secure Apollonia as a powerful and active female character. Having successfully fair-dodged, she now squeezes her way past club security, using her physical strength to wrench open an automatic door in a bid to meet the manager. Once inside, she is distracted by the final bars of The Kid's on-stage performance as he completes a guitar solo. She gazes at him as he plays, the camera cutting between presenting the audience with her view of him, and her appreciative expression.

This sequence establishes three important themes in the film's narrative and its visual rhetoric that underlie the ensuing text. Firstly, the film cannot be neatly read as a classic realist text, because of overt temporal and generic slippages. This contextual fact must impact on the subsequent reading of the gender representations within the film, as they cannot be taken necessarily literally, as Mulvey (1975) proposes. Secondly, the sequence presents a series of visual objects that signify the gender affiliations of its key protagonists that are of interest to a Kleinian analysis. The memory of the form of the mother, for instance, is evoked from the outset and is key to the construction and development of The Kid's identity. Thirdly, the on-screen female protagonist, Apollonia, cannot be read simply as passive or decorative as Mulvey would assert, but rather she beckons the female spectator to identify with her as she identifies with The Kid. These points will now be discussed in more depth.

In this sequence from *Purple Rain*, with the events being out of order, we see The Kid preparing for his performance while already on stage. The spectator is not so much witnessing a logically ordered sequence of events but rather a series of juxtaposed images that serve as present themes and relationships. This, in turn, offers opportunities for a reading of the sequence using Klein. The production values of the scene, the distorted and often disembodied, decontextualized images of people and things, such as dancers and mixing desks, correspond with how Klein describes the imagos created by a then-infant in the paranoid-schizoid position:

> ... which are a phantastically distorted picture of the real objects upon which they are based, are installed by it not only in the outside world but, by the process of incorporation, also within the ego. (Klein in Mitchell 1986, p. 116)

Objects in this sequence serve as signifiers of the gender identities of the main protagonists. The evidence for this is in the distortion of the use of recurrent objects in relation to each character. In Kleinian terminology, part objects in the unconscious – such as the bad breast or vagina – take the forms of other objects in the conscious (ibid., pp. 117–45). This formulation may correspond with a visual landscape of cinema's rhetoric, such as props and other iconographical devices. Prince's character, The Kid seems to acknowledge and embrace femininity, which is evident from his stylized appearance, but in particular in the nature of objects that he surrounds himself with and uses in the opening sequence. As if in reparation, The Kid's chosen objects are like part objects of the form of the mother – the overt femininity depicted in the pre-Raphaelite paintings and in the poster portraits, the scent and warmth of the red candles on his dressing table, the touch of the fabric flowers, the richness and folds of material draped over his body and thrown over tables and chairs. These all suggest that the idea of the mother is central to The Kid's sense of security, and that he has projected imagos of good mother objects onto his external world, or at least into his room. It immediately sets up a series of gender contrasts within the identity of The Kid, which make any gender-specific identification on the part of the spectator difficult. In contrast, Morris's object relations suggest a more patriarchal, narcissistic and competitive identity. While The Kid's objects are based on nature, femininity and childhood, his objects are unnatural – Polaroids, plastic bags and hard cash. These 'bad' objects might indicate an anxious relationship to the mother, to the feminine, from a Kleinian perspective.

Apollonia's relationship to the feminine is more ambiguous than that of The Kid or Morris. She seems to be more autonomous, active and self-defined than the male protagonists, which is not easily explained in dominant Lacanian-informed accounts of the female subject in cinema. For instance, according to Mulvey, Apollonia's appearance would render her as object of the gaze, not bearer of it, with no possibility of identification with her on the part of the spectator (Mulvey 1975). This is because she cannot exist in the Lacanian conceptualization of femininity, she is *pas-toute*, not-one (Lacan (1972–73) in Benvenuto and Kennedy 1986, p. 190). This does not satisfactorily account for Apollonia's agency and active gaze, which the spectator is invited to experience simultaneously through subjective shots. She eschews gazing at her own reflection, directing her gaze outwards – at First Avenue where she wants to work and towards the on-stage image of The Kid. Her gaze at the star as he plays his solo is ambiguous – does she desire him, or does she desire what he has, his power, creativity and success? She may be projectively identifying her dream of success as a performer onto The Kid, so that he becomes a good object. Though the spectator, male and female, may simultaneously be encouraged to share in her erotic desire for the figure of The Kid, this would seem to reverse the model of female to-be-looked-at-ness in Mulvey, and offer the possibility that film may serve as a site for projective identification for the female spectator. Indeed there are a number of moments within the film where women actively gaze at The Kid.

Femininity and The Kid's relationship with the mother figure are swiftly established in the film in order to contextualize the ensuing narrative. After the spectator witnesses scene two, the on-stage performance by The Revolution's rivals and arch-enemies The Time, led by Morris, the third scene shifts rapidly to The Kid's home and to his parents. This is important in establishing, firstly, that The Kid's parents have a destructive and violent relationship, and are in turn unable to show him any attention or nurturing, and secondly, through visual rhetoric, that the house and its basement in particular are the site of unimaginable horror for The Kid. The Kid arrives at his parental home, which is depicted like a crime scene, with its unlit windows and creaky porch, like the seat of horror in many US films.[4] All is clearly awry in his world, and it would be interesting for further research to explore the film in relation to its Gothic visual and narrative themes. For this interpretation, it is important to focus on the home as the site of family breakdown. The Kid storms in to see his father cornering and hurting his mother. He tries to break up their fight but is punched to the ground by his father. His mother, instead of going to the aid of her injured and distressed son, appeals to him to recognize his father's brutality and to nurture her: 'He wants to kill me, he's crazy, look what he's doing to me!'

This scene is key in establishing The Kid's status within the father-mother-child triad. His name, The Kid, is significant, for he is very much locked in the pre-Oedipal attachment to the mother, and is finding his father's presence overbearing and threatening. In 'The Early Stages of the Oedipus Complex' (1928), Klein wrote that the child experiences frustration towards the mother on withdrawal of the breast at weaning, causing the child to turn away from the mother and feel sadistic impulses to her. Klein adds that this characterizes the boy's femininity phase:

> ... the femininity phase is characterised by anxiety relating to the womb and the father's penis, and this anxiety subjects the boy to the tyranny of a super-ego which devours, dismembers and castrates and is formed from the image of the father and mother alike. (Klein in Mitchell 1986, pp. 74–5)

The Kid, starved of affection from either parent – who he views as monstrous and describes to Apollonia as 'a freakshow' – feels pain (ibid., p. 75). Instead of directing these sadistic impulses towards the mother, whom he feels sympathy and compassion for on the conscious level, he projects them onto other women. The commercial context for the ensuing disavowal of females, and The Kid's struggles, is set in scene four when Billy, First Avenue's manager, is talking to Morris in the street about the need to boost the venue's trade. Billy talks about The Kid and his troubled father messing up his own career. He fears history will repeat itself with The Kid. Morris proposes creating a new female band which will be 'sexy-but-not-dirty' to boost the club's fortunes, with the promise that the The Revolution

---

[4] See *Last House on the Left* (1972, dir. Wes Craven), *A Nightmare on Elm Street* (1984, dir. Wes Craven), and *Hallowe'en* (1978, dir. John Carpenter).

will be evicted if his plan succeeds. The scene cuts to the club where waitress Jill hands The Kid a tape recording of a composition by his band-mates, Wendy and Lisa. It is evident from their exchange that they are friends and respect one another as equals, unlike in scenes where Morris talks to women condescendingly and predatorily.

Scenes five and six feature, firstly, a musical interlude during which The Kid accosts Apollonia in the street and takes her for a ride into the country on his motorbike. The track 'Take Me with You' plays in the background. His first humiliation of Apollonia takes place when The Kid says that in order to help her with her career she must first bathe naked in Lake Minnetaka. Apollonia swiftly removes her clothes and leaps into the freezing water beside them, despite The Kid's faint protests. As she re-appears, he says: 'That's not Lake Minnetaka', and rides off on his bike as she struggles to put her clothes on. But he returns and praises her 'guts' for going in the water, and they drive off on good terms. It would seem that as a defence mechanism, The Kid is using aggression which, Klein states 'has its source in the femininity complex. It goes with an attitude of contempt and "knowing better," and is highly asocial and sadistic; it is partly conditioned as an attempt to mask the anxiety and ignorance which lie behind it' (ibid., p. 75).

Middle Scenes 7–23: The Kid Enters the Paranoid-Schizoid Position

In scenes 7 to 22, the film depicts The Kid's deepening emotional crisis as he is locked in the paranoid-schizoid position. As his home life grows ever worse, his defence strategy is to project bad mother objects onto Apollonia. He finds it impossible to bear witness to her as a whole being, and instead attacks – verbally and physically – facets of her behaviour that suggest her independence of him. These scenes are important for developing two key themes that underlie the text's subversion of conventional ideas of patriarchal spectator positions. Firstly, The Kid is no longer a powerful and potent character, in control of his band. Instead, he is unsympathetic, especially in terms of his inability to communicate with women. Secondly, and following on from the first themes, The Kid begins to use props to 'speak' for him, either directly to others through puppets, or symbolically via his powerful motorbike and phallic guitar. The narrative drives these themes as The Kid, under growing pressure to succeed in his career, does not divulge the impact his destructive home life is having on him. His new relationship with Apollonia is already under threat as, in scene seven, Morris agrees on a password with his valet/sidekick, Jerome, to be uttered when Apollonia enters the club. He wishes to put her in his new band, as a means to seducing her. Meanwhile, The Kid's growing hostility and emotional distance from his friends is demonstrated in the way he behaves badly towards Wendy and Lisa when, in scene eight, they prompt The Kid over the song they have composed.

Wendy and Lisa's recording of guitar work on tape for The Kid might be read, from a Lacanian perspective, as a statement towards a contradictory wish for acceptance in the phallic structure and their simultaneous willingness to masquerade in their phallic fantasy. However, it is significant in the scene where Wendy and Lisa ask The Kid if he has listened to their tape, that he uses a puppet to speak through.

The Kid's silence, and use of an object as a symbolic mouthpiece, suggests that, under the threat of competition from Morris and the anxious feelings he experiences in relation to Apollonia, he has moved from a relatively stable depressive position, where he is comfortable with others' and his own femininity, to one of splitting and defensiveness. Hannah Segal (1955) drew on Klein to develop an understanding of the meaning of symbols in analysis, and their relation to good and bad objects. Klein (1923)[5] had tried to show that children's play is a symbolic expression of anxieties and wishes, and Segal investigated the link between Klein's theory of projective identification and communication. Segal surmised that where an object came to be lost or absent, the subject might substitute a symbol for it: 'The symbol proper, available for sublimation and furthering the development of the ego, is felt to represent the object' (Segal 1955, p. 168). She says that the symbol becomes a way for the subject to deal with loss, in the same way that Klein stated projective identification serves as a defence against depressive anxieties (ibid., p. 169). The symbols are an important way of the subject communicating with the outside world but also a way of connecting with their unconscious:

> Symbol formation governs the capacity to communicate, since all communication is made by means of symbols ... One of the ever-recurring difficulties in the analysis of psychotic patients is this difficulty of communication. Words, for instance, whether the analyst's or the patient's, are felt to be objects or actions, and cannot be easily used for purposes of communications. (ibid.)

He has split off his feminine aspects and projected them as bad objects onto Wendy, Lisa and other women. He is both speechless and powerless in the midst of their feminine revolution. Critic Jon Lewis interpreted this moment in the film as The Kid's self-protective misogynistic gesture:

> He seems to fear not only them but also their female song – one that may arouse the feminine side of him, an aspect of his young male identity that he finds troubling. Such a fear of the female extends to Lisa and Wendy, Apollonia, his mother and we can assume women in general. (Lewis 1985)

However, as will be seen in the film's conclusion, The Kid addresses his issues and realigns his relationship with the mother object so that he re-embraces his inner femininity and moves to the depressive position. The misogyny is not implicit in the text – it accordingly serves as a function within the text to illuminate its existence as a problem. For instance, The Kid's silence is significant throughout

---

[5] In Klein's paper, 'The Role of the School in Libidinal Development' (1923).

the film and up until its conclusion, and it represents how profoundly the film overturns conventional representations of femininity and masculinity.

It is interesting that The Kid talks to his band members, Wendy and Lisa especially, via his mirrors rather than looking at them directly. According to Jon Lewis, their use by The Kid suggests narcissism and masculine power: 'Prince seems to feel contained enough to depend on his charisma to succeed on a far larger scale than Morris Day and The Time' (Lewis 1985). Indeed, from a Lacanian perspective, it might be shown that they signify The Kid's narcissistic identification with his more perfect reflection, in comparison with the lack of the females, doubly castrated by his refusal to countenance their offer of creative input. However, a Kleinian reading of this scene might uncover how, by gazing at his image in a mirror, he avoids bearing witness to his real identity and confronting aspects of his masculinity that are far from ideal. He splits his identity and works only with the positive projection. For he cannot bear to see his real self reflected in the eyes of the females before him, who are autonomous and signify mastery of their instruments and their own identities. In his paranoid-schizoid state, he is a figure without a gaze and without a voice in the company of women, defending himself through splitting and projecting onto his props. As a consequence, the spectator is confronted with a split and fragmented projection of The Kid's identity, preventing any seamless identification with his on-screen image. A Kleinian reading of this text may indicate active identification on the part of the spectator, which moves from character to character, or which might identify with parts of characters rather than the whole. At this point in the film at least, The Kid is no longer a sympathetic character, while the female characters offer a more consistent and potent site of identification and agency.

In contrast to The Kid's retreat into his inner world, Apollonia is emerging as an autonomous subject. In scenes nine and 10, Morris accosts her in the club and tries, comically, to seduce her. Morris then describes his luxury home in elaborate detail, intending to impress. However, Apollonia laughs at him throughout. In 'The Beautiful Ones', a ballad, The Kid plays at a keyboard, with Wendy playing lead guitar. Through this flamboyant song and performance, The Kid declares his devotion to Apollonia, and proclaims his emotional vulnerability. The song is about emotions, not sexual activity, denoted through the lyrics and further connoted through the high-pitch wail of a synthesizer throughout. During this three-minute sequence, we watch The Kid through the eyes of Apollonia. Approximately 40 seconds of the sequence focus on the face of Apollonia as she watches him intently. As at the start of the film, Apollonia subverts the gaze that has, in dominant accounts of cinema spectatorship, been ascribed to the male viewer. This does not correspond with Mulvey's denial of a pleasurable female spectator, that film must impose a masculine point of view on the viewer. Perhaps the pleasure of the gaze might be accounted for in Lacan's suggestion of something extra, *encore*, that permits female expression to be manifested beyond the symbolic order?

Drawing on Lacan, Jacqueline Rose writes of a place outside the 'dialectic (of imaginary and symbolic) to which (woman) is constantly rejected' (Rose 1996, p. 51). According to Rose, this moment is not quite a phallic pleasure and not entirely social exclusion, and may be best described as a *jouissance*, a 'something more' that 'goes beyond' the structure of phallic being (ibid.). Lacan notes: 'There is this jouissance ... a jouissance of the body which is, if the expression be allowed, beyond the phallus' (in Mitchell and Rose 1985, p. 145). The difficulty and caution of Lacan's attempts to define *jouissance* indicates that in many ways it is beyond definition for it speaks to the very essence of beyond. Alan Sheridan's translator's note to *Ecrits* says: 'Enjoyment conveys the sense, conveyed in jouissance.' It directs us to the close relationship to the French *jouir*, colloquial for 'to come' (as in an orgasm). The term can at best be defined as a life force, an essence from beyond that surfaces in fleeting moments of ecstasy. But Apollonia's gaze, and potentially that of the spectator identifying with her look, is active and desiring, so that The Kid is intended to be the signified Other to Apollonia's correct signifying self. The Kid is the blank figure onto which the phallus-bearing female signifier Apollonia projects her image of ideal maleness. Thus, The Kid is perhaps intended to masquerade as an artistic creation of female completion in order to define Apollonia's, and inherently the female spectator's, projections of power and authority.

The Kid takes Apollonia to his house and seduces her. There then ensues a significant love-making scene within the confines of the pre-Oedipal world of The Kid's basement bedroom. Attention is drawn in the scene to the *mise-en-scène*, as his shelves are filled with toys, masks and 'feminine' objects such as flowers, which catch Apollonia's eye as she looks around. She puts on a tape to hear sounds which further destabilize reality – she thinks they are the sounds of a woman moaning ecstatically, but The Kid tells her it is crying played backwards. The following day, his treatment of Wendy and Lisa worsens, ordering them to stop composing their own tracks, before he is warned by Billy the owner that his band's contract is on the line. Threatened with expulsion by the venue, The Kid is usurped of the phallic power that the structure of the music business and the club has endowed him with. Now he is subjected to the treatment that he once used in authority over his band. Furthermore, Wendy and Lisa, but Wendy in particular, now seem to replace The Kid as the phallic signifier in the eyes of the rest of The Revolution. From another perspective to Lewis, it might be suggested that this moment is one of the most gratifying strengths of the film from the position of the female spectator and female subjectivity. The women are asserting, powerfully, the need for The Kid to align himself more with the feminine.

Scenes 14 to 22 take The Kid to breaking point, during which he hits Apollonia several times, undergoes a nervous breakdown and envisions his own death. Forty-five minutes into the film, his parents burst into his bedroom. The contrast between the visual rhetoric of the *mise-en-scène* of The Kid's child-like room, which has toys on its shelves, and the physical and verbal abuse culminates in The Kid lashing out at his father before retreating to his bed like a frightened child, crying. Neither of his parents go to comfort him. It is significant that shortly after, Apollonia presents The Kid with a gift of a guitar that he has coveted in a music store window. The embellished and curvaceous stylized white guitar could very much be interpreted as symbolic of Apollonia's/female spectator's/The Kid's feminized vision of masculinity. It is a creative vision, a manipulation that is handed to The Kid to symbolically enable him to 'see' in a new and particular way. The gift of the guitar is thus not phallic in itself but a phallic gesture by a powerful female protagonist who is able to manipulate The Kid into seeing correctly or mirroring her femininity correctly. The Kid symbolically exchanges objects with her, giving her one of his earrings. Apollonia suddenly announces she is joining Morris's new female band, Apollonia 6, to which The Kid reacts with fury and hits her.

From a Kleinian perspective, The Kid seems to be projecting the bad mother object he has witnessed onto Apollonia, which is shown by the way he repeats his father's words to her: 'Don't I make you happy?' This scene was one which attracted criticism by feminists in its depiction of violence against women. But viewed from this perspective, the film appears to be criticizing violence, representing the gradual breakdown of identity under patriarchal conditions. As he approaches her lying on the floor, the following dialogue takes place:

> The Kid: Apollonia, don't I make you happy? Don't you like the way we are?
> Apollonia: You should trust me.
> The Kid: Do you know Morris? Do you know what he's about? He doesn't care about you!
> Apollonia (shouting): You jealous?

The Kid's relationship with Apollonia is tempestuous, as her presence in his life appears to be a metaphor for his mediation between his inner and outer worlds. She is a multi-dimensional female figure in that she is ambitiously and autonomously pursuing a career and succeeding in a male-dominated arena, and she simultaneously reminds The Kid of the passivity of his mother. She is powerfully attractive in that she looks like a mature woman rather than a girl, and her sexuality and confidence is reflected in her clothing. She constantly wears black, often leather suits and boots reminiscent of Catwoman. Her powerful physical and symbolic presence causes The Kid to projectively identify with her as a mother-object.

Klein's theorization of projective identification (1946) relates to an omnipotent fantasy that some part of the self is placed into another object. This can be an actual external object, such as an external mother, or an internal object in the mind, separate from a sense of self, such as an internal mother. It extends the simpler process of projection, in that part of the self as well as an emotion is located elsewhere, although the difference may not always be clear. Klein (1955) was aware that aspects of the process, such as the way one can put oneself temporarily into someone else's mind when empathizing with them, had been taken for granted before being incorporated into psychoanalytical theory. It may be a way of avoiding the mental pain of being oneself and having one's own feelings.

This projective identification falls apart when Apollonia asserts her autonomy, by stating her wish to pursue her career independently of him and through Morris

Day's sexually-explicit manufactured female trio. The Kid's stereotypical view of her as an unsullied mother figure is tarnished by her sexually-provocative stage act. It is significant that their relationship is restored at the end of the film, but on a different level with The Kid accepting her as an equal once he has achieved a positive inner mother-object in his own right. The fact that Morris makes her a quicker offer as lead singer in a strip-tease style girl trio, completely controlled and choreographed by Morris, much to The Kid's disdain, serves as an illustration of the sexist manipulation of females by the music industry. For instance, during rehearsals, the camera's focus is less on the women practising their dance steps and more on the men who are watching them, becoming aroused by them and simultaneously repressing them for the power they assert over the male spectator.

But could Apollonia's ostensible power be explained by Lacan's theorization of the castration complex, rendering her activity a representation of her ceaseless search for the lost object? In 'The Meaning of the Phallus', Lacan sets forth to explain the difficult type of phallus/non-phallus relationship that a female child experiences as she searches for her own identity when he states:

> Paradoxical as this formulation might seem, I would say that it is in order to be the phallus, that is to say, the signifier of the desire of the Other, that woman will reject an essential part of her femininity, notably all its attributes through masquerade. (Lacan in Mitchell and Rose 1985, p. 84)

As Jacqueline Rose also notes, '(t)he absolute "otherness" of the woman, ... serves to secure for the man his own self-knowledge and truth' (Rose 1996, p. 50). Lost between desire for acceptance and completion, and incorrect identity, Apollonia subjects herself to the demands of the music industry embodied in Morris Day, donning suspenders – an identity mask which Lacan believes 'femininity takes refuge in' (Lacan in Mitchell and Rose 1985, p. 85). But this formulation does not allow for any pleasure for the female spectator. How can a woman realistically achieve her position in the symbolic order by blending her masquerade as the object of male desire with her need to retain the freedom of the imaginary? Women find themselves caught in the duality of wanting to be accepted in patriarchal society while breaking the phallus in search of their own female identity. In the workplace or public sphere, Apollonia does not wish to become subjugated to the rules and regulations set by the phallic signifying Kid or Morris; rather, she wishes to gain their acceptance, willing to masquerade in a Rivierian sense as an object, but at the same time desiring subjective freedom. Subsequently, The Kid learns to do the same from her.

Apollonia is constantly reminded of the harsh male superiority surrounding her, cut off from her imaginary fantasy by the unromantic voice of Morris. As in his earlier attempts to chat her up, Morris wields his subjugating phallic power as a means to stifle, not to set free, her confined identity. The humiliation of Apollonia illuminates the disruption of her own phallic drive or completed identity through the vehicle of the Other, The Kid. Apollonia desires equality with The Kid and thus, by extension, control over her own identity, but she is victimized by The Kid, who is seeking to identify himself not according to anyone else's wishes but through his own desire. This is his downfall. The Kid's inner voice, as opposed to the set of practices he has adopted in common with those around him, will later be the answer to his – and the female spectator's – liberation. The Kid reaches self-definition through his widening range of experiences, but also by constant transcendence of each experience, a constant rejection of and separation from what he is not.

Initially, The Kid's interest in Apollonia is one of self-assured subject who is attracted to Apollonia as a means of verifying his own identity and correctness. But after he hits her, he is cut from his means of phallic verification and he is expelled into self-doubt. The Kid dislikes her independence of him, which she displays through sexualized performance. This is interesting, as her sexual display functions in a more complex way than Mulvey would assert. She functions as an independent real being, as opposed to The Kid's puppet representation of himself. For fleeting moments, therefore, such as when she puts her foot in the door of First Avenue during the opening sequences, Apollonia is real by transcending the symbolic. Apollonia becomes The Kid's phallic mother and he fears she will devour him. In order to regain control, he can try to destroy her in the manner of the infuriated child he acts like when near his parents. But the mother/child battle The Kid goes on to have with Apollonia involves him expelling her so that she is out of his sight. This corresponds with Klein's description of the infant's sadistic impulse towards the mother, whom he fears:

> It does not seem clear why a child of, say, four years old should set up in his mind an unreal, phantastic image of parents who devour, cut and bite. But it is clear why in a child of about one year old the anxiety caused by the beginning of the Oedipus conflict takes the form of a dread of being devoured and destroyed. The child himself desired to destroy the libidinal object by biting, devouring and cutting it, which leads to anxiety, since awakening of the Oedipus tendencies is followed by introjection of the object, which then becomes one from which punishment is to be expected. (Klein in Mitchell 1986, p. 71)

The Kid's downfall – that he will self-destruct in the manner of his father's fall from grace – is cemented by Billy who warns of rivalries ahead, and of the continuing problems his hostility towards Wendy and Lisa will cause. In reflective mode, The Kid jumps onto his motorcycle and heads to the countryside to reflect. This scene, which served as the promotional video for the single 'When Doves Cry', depicts The Kid seeing visions of his parents fighting and of his happier times with Apollonia. The song's lyrics demonstrate his problematic identifications with both parents, and the issues he faces in reconciling the mother and father objects with his femininity and masculinity: 'Maybe I'm just too demanding, Maybe I'm just like my father ... too bold. Maybe I'm just like my mother ... she's never satisfied. Why do we scream at each other. This is what it sounds like, When doves cry.' (Also see analysis of this song in Chapter 4.)

On returning home, he discovers his mother, beaten, sitting in the street, and he rushes in to angrily confront his father. This scene takes The Kid to the site of intense dread, the place where he is forced to confront his own relationship to masculinity and his father. Hearing the piano, The Kid becomes disarmed and enters the dimly-lit basement where his father is playing some of his own compositions. His father talks of his deep love for his mother, then asks The Kid if he has a girlfriend. When he replies that he has, his father says: 'Never get married.' His father's disavowal of marriage propels The Kid into mental breakdown, manifesting itself in lascivious on-stage performances in the following scene. These scenes display very different power relations between himself and Wendy and Lisa, which would seem to match academic perceptions of the inherent patriarchy of rock music. However, The Kid's performances, being so strikingly different to the tone in which The Kid had been seen to work with women in the early scenes, make them unpleasurable, and potentially subversive of the power relations they display.

The Kid has entered into a state of inner crisis, shown by his projection of imagos of the bad mother onto the females around him, notably Apollonia but also his band-mates Wendy and Lisa. His ensuing on-stage performance is of two lurid tracks, 'Computer Blue' and 'Darling Nikki', during which rhythm guitarist Wendy falls to her knees before The Kid and feigns fellatio. Until that point, Wendy had always stood alongside The Kid on stage as an equal in a role conventionally reserved for males in rock music performance. In the audience, Apollonia and The Kid's friend Jill, who works at the club, look on in disgust and sadness at his stereotypical representation of phallic guitar playing and sexual humiliation of his talented female guitarist. The scene culminates in The Kid pacing his dressing room in crisis, interrupted by an angry Billy. Billy attacks The Kid for the vulgarity of his act and says The Revolution will be fired if they do not clean it up. His parting shot is the most painful for The Kid: 'Like father, like son.'

It is interesting that in the ensuing 'Sex Shooter' sequence, where suspender-clad Apollonia 6 make their debut performance at First Avenue, we see The Kid negotiate the male gaze. Morris Day and Jerome Benton, the girl-group's Svengalis, don sunglasses in a camp gesture suggesting they are bedazzled by the bright spectacle of the three scantily-dressed women. At the back of the club, The Kid enters and also puts on his sunglasses. However, the expression on his face suggests he is repulsed by the women's objectification and the glasses help conceal his emotions and protect him from the horror he finds in their show. This is important – we have witnessed The Kid's emotional breakdown as he witnesses his family's breakdown and self-destruction, both physical and mental. The Kid now feels no empathy with his blood family and has abjected the unstable mother and father objects within him. The metonymic vision of Apollonia 6, not least their respective representations as three facets of stereotypical femininity – vamp, lesbian and angel – is abhorrent. Apollonia, The Kid's mother-projection, is fragmented and subjected to the demands of the socio-cultural context. The Kid gazes not on the women, but at the men who are lasciviously enjoying the show.

He is neither masculine nor feminine, he is outside the symbolic, an abjected other. But he wants to identify with Apollonia, and to do so, he must actively rebuild his inner mother and father objects outside the symbolic order. In this way, he will be able to find an accommodation with political and cultural forces through a sense of inner integrity.

After the show, a drunken Apollonia is being lured into Morris's car. The Kid emerges from the darkness on his motorbike, she perceives, to rescue her, knocking Morris over in the process. Morris is clearly not intended to be viewed as a rounded character in his own right, but rather as a symbol of predatory, ill-equipped masculinity which uses financial power to hide inherent weaknesses. Falling to the ground, Morris calls: 'Ain't that a bitch. I just got my coat from the cleaners .... You long-haired faggot!' Apollonia is later horrified to see that The Kid has only rescued her to oppress her even further, as he kisses her roughly, hits her, then throws her to the ground and barely manages to hold back from beating her. She manages to flee, and The Kid rides home to find the house smashed up. The following scene, number 23, represents breaking point, the life or death moment, where The Kid is forced to confront his worst inner fears.

Entering the basement, which has been established as the scariest place in the house, The Kid sees the silhouette of his father in the darkness smoking a cigarette and holding a gun in his hand. The Kid's hand flicks the light switch and the gun fires. The next shot is of the father being taken away alive on a stretcher. The Kid sits in his house surrounded by police who ask him questions. The dialogue is obscured by a sound effect of screeching, and the spectator focuses on The Kid's childlike, vulnerable expression as he looks up at the faces of authority, who then leave him entirely alone. In a series of fast edits, the spectator is forced to engage with the paranoid-schizoid crisis The Kid experiences as he sees visions flash before him and hears sounds: the chalk outline of the body, the sound of his father's shouting voice, then the image of his own dead body hanging by a rope from the rafters. In this life or death moment, The Kid picks up a stick and destroys the contents of the basement, as if re-enacting the Oedipus complex on the withdrawal of the breast. As Klein (1928) stated, the infant's disappointment with the mother leads to sadistic impulses to destroy the contents of her body, and is accompanied by feelings of guilt and dread at the damaging thoughts (in Mitchell 1986, p. 70). The problem for The Kid is that he is simultaneously unable to 'turn to the father'. Klein wrote:

> The boy ... derives from the feminine phase a maternal superego which causes him, like the girl, to make both cruelly primitive and kindly identifications. But he passes through this phase to resume ... identification with the father. However much the maternal side makes itself felt in the formation of the super-ego, it is yet the paternal super-ego which from the beginning is the decisive influence for the man. (Ibid., p. 81)

In other words, the boy's original identification is with the mother, but because he is 'made in the image of his ideal' (ibid.) he must find an accommodation with the paternal super-ego. The Kid's crisis forces him into bearing witness to himself as a separate being from his mother and from his father, which enables him to enter the depressive position. The Kid stops wrecking the basement when he finds his father's sheet music. His father had earlier sanctimoniously denied that he ever wrote down his compositions, instead committing them to memory. The discovery of these objects is pivotal in The Kid's ability to identify with his father and move to the depressive position in the closing scenes.

Scene 24 to End: The Kid Enters the Depressive Position

The Kid awakes next morning lying on the strewn sheets of music. The daylight shining in from an unknown source is golden, and he hears birdsong. The *mise-en-scène* of the basement is transformed from the site of horror it was the night before. The Kid goes to the piano and starts to play the song Wendy and Lisa had composed, incorporating his father's tune. The scene represents The Kid's projection onto a good father object, the manifestation of the sheet music serving as the embodiment of his father's positive creativity. Klein wrote of the father's relationship to the infant and mother, and the need for the male infant to always acknowledge the power of femininity in his identity, which is The Kid's next step after recognition of his father. Identifying with the father is not enough, as Klein wrote: 'the attainment of complete potency ... will in part depend upon the favourable issue of the femininity phase' (1bid.).

Accordingly, the closing scenes of the film demonstrate The Kid's dual accommodation of femininity and masculinity, which endow him with an otherworldly potency. In the final scenes, depicting his crescendo performance of 'Purple Rain' that incorporates the tunes submitted by Wendy and Lisa, we see The Kid's loosening of textual and linguistic structures, so that in a moment of *jouissance*, the audience witnesses the birth of his new, autonomous subjectivity. He becomes a complete signifying agent and has control over meanings attached to the vision of him. His performance of 'Purple Rain', an anthemic declaration of future hopes, centres on his face and his expression of the sentiments of the lyrics. He introduces the song by dedicating it to his father, tears in his eyes as he vulnerably stands subject to the hostile glare of the crowd. As the song reaches the guitar solo, the guitar takes on emotional resonance. The crowd applauses and The Kid plants a kiss on Wendy's cheek. He runs off stage in crisis and tears, in death, believing himself to have been fully expelled by his fans and his band. But on realizing the audience is cheering rather than booing, he returns to the stage joyous, and performs 'I Would Die for You'. The song's lyrics play ludically upon Prince's real world ambiguity as portrayed in the popular media.

His dancing and the way it is filmed make this scene hilarious in comparison with the earnest tone of previous performances. He pirouettes, preens and teeters around on tip-toes and his face is pulled into camp expressions. This rebirth, punctuated by shots of his achievement of a different relational accommodation with his parents, represents not only the cyclical rhythm of familial continuance, but also the spiral towards independence and self-actualization. Indeed, The Kid breaks beyond social and familial confines as well as linguistic codes – in his rebirth there is no dialogue, just music and gesture entirely about him. In 'Baby, I'm a Star' he transcends into an almost mystical identity. Even Morris Day and the sceptical club owner leap around excitedly in the audience, commercial forces now under the control of The (ambiguous) Kid's new authority over his personal and creative identity. The final shots show The Kid on a piano sending up Michael Jackson's 'Thriller' video, and impersonating Sly Stone, before taking up his guitar and ejaculating white liquid over the audience from the machine heads.

This conclusion to *Purple Rain* showed the way a male star could overturn meanings about the nature of female subjectivity. Prince achieved this intervention on a textual and narrative level, but also in relation to the cultural context of production and reception. The film and the visual iconography of Prince provided a mediating category between self, other and the outer social world, and a space for his young British female fans to negotiate their femininity in the mid 1980s. This reflexive analysis of that reception illuminates the potential for female agency in responding to pop texts, and in negotiating that subjectivity. As such, the film illuminates the limitations of Freudian and Lacanian models of identification, even where utilized in feminist accounts of film spectatorship, by foregrounding female identification and the search for the mother object. Furthermore, this confounds cultural theories around women's reception of music performance, and the female characters provide a site for directly contesting both the objectification and oppression of women performers in the diegetic space and in the music industry.

Key psychoanalytical notions of subjective development, specifically vision and linguistic acquisition, are central themes of the film, as The Kid is both silenced and mesmerized by the authoritative display of Wendy and Lisa's phallic words and stance. In the midst of his family breakdown and inner crisis, The Kid is caught between two worlds. In negating the women's creative contribution to the band's musical oeuvre, The Kid refutes the imaginative element of aspiration in his own career. Furthermore, he simultaneously becomes susceptible to the tenets and methods of authoritarianism meted out by his own father and by the commercial forces of the outer world. The Kid's psychological defence to the imagined threat of the mother is to utilize the power and authority of the male phallus. The Kid accepts patriarchal, commercial forces as true and correct, further severing his link with the pre-Oedipal order of his parental home. By being unable to identify with his father or mother, he is in crisis and there is no-one to turn to for help, nowhere to go to escape.

This realization that something has broken inside him forces The Kid into an identity war in which he becomes isolated from his childhood and from the identifications with both his mother and his father. By adopting the phallic power of the father, and negating femininity, he finds himself dependent on, and subject to, a world to which he does not wholly belong, and in which he is identified by those around him, notably Wendy and Apollonia, as false. While masquerading as a possessor of phallic power, through his identifications with women in the diegetic space The Kid defies the very system to which he masquerades, which submerses him into an endless chase of subjective desire. Thus his grasp for phallic being forfeits his feminine identity. His existence depends on his continued power over the musical landscape so as to retain supremacy in his rivalry (erotic, cultural and financial) with Morris Day and The Time.

But witnessing the near-death of his father, and simultaneously envisioning his own death, or the death of the father object within him, The Kid is jolted. Rather than forfeiting his feminine identity and becoming like his father, he embraces and celebrates the type of assertive femininity within him that he sees reflected in Wendy and Lisa. His symbolic castration by Wendy and Lisa propels him into an order concerned with fundamental and emotionally powerful forces of life and death and sexuality. As a result, he looks at things differently and stops seeing Wendy, Lisa and Apollonia as a threat, but rather as facets of his inner self that he has been repressing.

Conclusion

This critical analysis of *Purple Rain* demonstrates how this hugely successful mid 1980s visual phenomenon can be read in parallel with Klein's theories of the development of identity. Utilizing a Kleinian approach, as opposed to the dominant Lacanian informed film studies approaches to spectatorship, it is possible to see how the film charts the lead character's journey from the paranoid-schizoid to depressive positions. This is helpful in positing the film as a site of positive identification for young females. This view challenges simplistic notions that females are inescapably locked in passive spectator/consumer roles. The Kid's series of projective identifications, which he uses as defensive mechanisms to counter problems caused by undeveloped attachments to the mother and father objects, correspond with Klein's statement that the crises of the Oedipal stage can be relived several times throughout an individual's life. Furthermore, and most significantly for this thesis, a Kleinian reading of the text subverts approaches that position the female spectator as constituted by lack, as Lacanian approaches do.

Femininity as an essential and original drive and site of identification is the underlying theme of the film, which propels the narrative, the relationships, the chaos and the ultimate conclusion. This aspect demonstrates how Klein, who has rarely if ever been applied to cultural texts, can be helpful in accounting for pleasurable, active identifications for the female spectator in visual media. In turn, it might be possible to extend Kleinian approaches to identifying positive female identities in wider popular cultural forms. Thematically, the film addresses the end of familiar history for Prince's character The Kid, as formative institutions, including his own family, crumble. The ostensible autobiographical narration serves as an attempt by Prince/The Kid to identify some underlying psychological motive for his father's/ his own/ males' actions. Far from being a simple reversal of misogynistic power relations, metaphorically the males depicted are also victims of patriarchy, as represented by the strictures of the music industry, violence and misogyny. The site of horror or monstrosity in *Purple Rain* is not within women and their sexuality, but rather with their repression in the mid 1980s, and how that power relationship was manifested in the cultural sphere. The monstrous in *Purple Rain* is about the context – it is the unstable signifiers that represent the context of The Kid's world, and that of his friends and colleagues, that implodes. The monstrosity is manifest in this ambiguous figure's refusal to accept the misogyny, patriarchy of his father, male peers and the music industry (law of the father). The monstrosity is dissipated through his self-recognition of his femininity.

As such, a Kleinian reading of this film offers an alternative account of female spectatorship to those of Lacan or Mulvey, who position the female viewer forever subject to lack. The film focuses on the possibility of a femininity phase for boys, and on the importance of successful identification with the mother object, not only the father. This raises the possibility that femininity, as a set of identifications, might be something 'out there', fundamental to both males and females, rather than solely attached to the biologically female gender. This is a very exciting notion, as it enables psychoanalytical theories of female subjectivity to disassociate themselves from allegations of biological determinism, as outlined in Chapter 2.

Nevertheless, this attempt to apply a Kleinian analysis to *Purple Rain* highlights a series of three challenges, at least, to the efficacy of such a methodology for illuminating the nature of female subjectivity in the mid 1980s. Firstly, Klein's writings are not easy to apply practically to films. Unlike Lacanian approaches which draw on a lucid theory of the gaze, Klein's work was intended to provide clinicians with practical strategies for analysing children. Ostensibly, it was not Klein's intention to be a theorist to rival Freud or Lacan, and her formulations did not stretch to providing models for analysing texts. As a result, while her writings are lucid and accessible, her theorizations are dense and have not yet been remodelled into a theory of consumption. Secondly, and consequently, Klein does not provide an account of the female spectator or consumer, though there is little doubt that her theories can envision one. While in Lacan and Mulvey, the female spectator is rendered an impossibility, Klein's concepts offer the potential for an active, reading, self-recognizing subject. Perhaps one of the reasons a Kleinian-derived female spectator has not been delineated in subsequent scholarship is due to Klein's fixation on the inner world. This is the third challenge to employing her concepts to female consumption of popular cultural texts. For Klein, the inner world is paramount, with the outer world existing as a series of imagos that serve as catalysts for the organization of the psyche. In this sense, it is difficult to comprehend the film text as meaning anything in itself. *Purple Rain* is not a cultural text, in a Kleinian view, but rather imagos.

On a formal level, at least, research suggests that music film is linked with gender struggles in the socio-cultural and socio-political context of its production, which begs the question: to what extent do *Purple Rain*'s musical performances relate to young women's experiences in the Conservative mid 1980s? In addition, there is a growing body of self-reflexive writing by women music fans that speaks of a knowing and active contemplation of the on-screen male musical star that is not easily explained through foreclosed psychoanalytical models. Can a film text be read using psychoanalytical theories alone when it constitutes a cultural text? It is important not to forget the film's promotion as a music film, and the simultaneous high-profile release of the *Purple Rain* album. The film and album's emergence occurred as Prince rose to huge prominence in the mid 1980s in Britain. To what extent can Klein's theories account for the social forces, such as education or socio-economic circumstances, which might contextualize the viewing experience? The film occupies an ambiguous space generically, and it must be acknowledged that it is difficult to undertake a self-contained, discreet reading of The Kid when his on-screen identity slips so easily onto Prince's own.

Thus, a central problematic in Kleinian analysis is that it cannot conceive of cultural forces, of which entertainment is an important facet, in the development of female subjectivity. As such, it is difficult to use Klein to account for the practices of femininity that appear within the film beyond the gestural. What about the rich cinematic visual dialogue of clothing, make-up and dance? Object relations can be useful in theorizing the place of props, but it does not sufficiently interrogate the potential for alternative structures of meaning in musical films borne out of the feminine actions and appearances of male and female characters. It has been shown that the female fan, who has enjoyed the cultural products and iconography of an artist in a variety of contexts, is not necessarily locked into powerful patriarchal viewing positions when seeing that artist in a feature film. But it is necessary to find a way to account for the wider feminine practices, of which consumption is a part, in order to develop a deeper understanding of female subjectivity within a given socio-cultural context. By raising questions about prominent theories of female spectatorship, and a male star's search for his inner femininity, Prince established a direct link between the political cultural context of the mid 1980s and its impact on the female subject. In his next film, *Under the Cherry Moon* (1986), the star is much more at ease with his femininity than in *Purple Rain*, and much more demonstrative and celebratory of his female side. With femininity as a given and essential quality and drive, we now see how Prince negotiates his female subjectivity with socio-economic forces, and how he explores what Riviere (1929) called 'the masquerade' of feminine practice,[6] during the gender crisis that characterized the context of the film's UK release.

---

[6] This article, 'Womanliness as a Masquerade', was first published in *The International Journal of Psychoanalysis* (*IJPA*), vol. 10 (1929).

Chapter 6
The Princian Sonic Universe: Matters of Compositional and Performative Proficiency

If we accept that the Princian aesthetic is defined by a unique pop sensibility, then the artist's approach to music-making inevitably reveals his inner workings. This chapter returns to the issue of creativity, from a musicological entry point, in a bid to argue aspects of Prince's performativity. Adumbrating the ingredients of a musician's performativity is always the question of proficiency, and we approach this from two specific directions:

1. technical mastery and virtuosic display; and
2. production, engineering and recording.

As well as demonstrating all-round aptitude as a multi-instrumentalist, Prince also utilizes the recording space in unprecedented ways. We argued in Chapter 4 that this constitutes a major site for understanding his musical ingenuity. Based upon this assumption, we now argue for the phenomenon of his 'sonic universe' by considering the various techniques he employs to establish his musical signature. Our focus falls primarily on the performance and compositional strategies that stage his style, and through an examination of a number of tracks we attempt to unravel some of the ways his sound is incorporated in the mix. To this end, we seek to identify a range of musical features that characterize his style.

To start with, we return briefly to the question of his guitar playing, which, in performance terms, entails a remarkable amount of deftness. Up to this point in time the rock guitar has not had a lengthy history and Prince's influences have already been pointed out. As we discussed in Chapter 4, Prince's guitar playing needs to be framed alongside the developments that have ensued in rock, pop and metal. We want to argue that Prince stands alongside guitar heroes such as Eddie van Halen, Eric Clapton, Carlos Santana, Jimmy Page, Stevie Ray Vaughan and others. Guitar playing has long been a male-dominated instrumental domain, both in terms of reception and performance, and Prince's own style both inscribes and challenges the prevalent norms within guitar playing. For instance, showcasing and selecting female instrumentalists (on stereotypical 'male-based' instruments, such as guitar, bass and drums) in his countless productions (live and studio) can be read as transgressive. But, as we argued in Chapter 1, this is no simple matter. Whatever the case, Prince's guitar style is heavily gender coded, and while his style might exhibit masculine traits through a virtuosity and versatility that slots into a tradition of male instrumentalists showing off, the rest of the package is problematic: for his look, mannerisms and voice are without doubt anti-macho and arguably femininized, as we pointed out in Chapter 5. Significantly, this is what might well account for him being underrated as a top guitarist.[1] In the wake of this assertion, we are compelled to probe at the following question: what is it that has obstructed him from being hailed as one of the great guitarists of our time? As we set out to argue, his extraordinary expertise as a guitarist needs to be evaluated against the backdrop of not only how he performs, but also what he achieves in the studio environment when recording.

As has already been discussed in Chapter 4, the aesthetics of recording production are not only a matter of sound but also space; the recording exists as an imaginary platform for musical ideas. Lelio Camilleri theorizes *sonic space* by defining the recording as a three-dimensional space that is divided into the localized, spectral and morphological (Camilleri 2010, p. 202). Perceptions of sound in recorded form are directly related to experiences of depth, position and motion, while the spectral space might be perceived as metaphorical, 'since there is no such physical space, even though we can experience the sense of saturation or emptiness due to the spectral content of the sounds used' (ibid.). From this vantage point, it is apparent that sensations of sonic space are integral to the compositional procedures found in a musical production. Subsequently, the sensory perception of space, as Camilleri insists, impinges directly on the 'temporal unfolding' of a recorded track. Thus, the 'recorded space, the sonic space', allows the songwriter to 'organise the musical discourse at different levels' (ibid., p. 211). This notion helps open up the possibilities for exploring further any number of sonic directions.

Part of our aim in this chapter is both to analyse and to contextualize Prince's productions. Close attention is therefore paid to the range of techniques he employs, as we consider the sonic signifier and its articulation of a pop aesthetic. As we have repeatedly pointed out, African American music traditions have shaped Prince's stylistic expression and are moulded into his compositional procedures. Granted, most of his musical material is formatted by the standardized formula of the pop song, where the idiom of his style intersects with a range of performance and songwriting practices, yet it is how he exploits the relatively short duration of song form in so many diverse ways that becomes a major source for our inquiry. In this regard, we recognize that his improvisatory and jamming skills are integral to the compositional process, making apparent the virtuosity of his style. In this sense, virtuosity is about stylistic versatility (jazz, big band, rock, latin, funk, soul, disco, rap, R&B and even country), and this is intrinsic to the performance traditions of Prince's musical heritage.

Some words are also required on how his songs operate. Along a richly diverse scale, Prince's songwriting is extraordinarily assured. This is borne out by the vast palette of performance and compositional techniques that go into the production.

---

[1] We note with some surprise that Steve Waksman (2001) and Kevin Dawe (2010), in their respective studies of guitarists and guitar performances, omit any reference to Prince.

How this impacts the listener needs to be evaluated in relation to the circulation of his songs through marketing, fanzines, blog sites, documentaries, interviews and so forth. Moreover, it is the way his songs become linked together in numerous ways that also arouses curiosity, and the sheer web of references that circle his album and song concepts become salient in any study of the practices behind the production of songs. Thus, it is aspects of his creativity in songwriting and music production that we take up in this chapter in an endeavour to work out the practices that perpetually succeed in entertaining millions of fans.

Styling Pop through the Rock Guitar

Few would disagree that the amplified guitar has become an idealized form, a sonic image and a veritable extension of the performer. Large, godlike, it is commonly showcased as a daemon of sheer marvel in rock. What the guitar offers is a site for communicating the performer's inner self to the exterior world, often releasing a narcissistic desire. This grants access to pleasures otherwise bypassed. Themes of yearning, pain, humour and eroticism are emulated by the guitar in almost every Prince song, as it extends and supplements the emotional content of the human voice. The sonic world of the guitar is thus made meaningful within the context of all the parameters of a performance.

Turning his hand to a wide range of techniques in his guitar playing, Prince utilizes the recording studio as a palette for his sonic universe. Accordingly, his style of performing and recording chronicles the developments in the course of the electric guitar. Lest we forget, by the mid 1960s the electric guitar had emerged as the most popular instrument in Western societies, due to the commerciality of guitar-oriented music. The idea of the boy holding the guitar soon became something natural in the US, notably amongst white people. Of course there are subtleties in the development of guitar-based music, which relate to the cross-over between African American and white influences. Steve Waksman has pointed out that the electric guitar's arrival embodied countercultural desires that essentially spelt out new ideals. For instance, the 'putting on of blackness' through the guitar would often compensate for feelings of inadequacy in whiteness. This was best exemplified in the ideal types of African American bluesmen from which 'legions of young white musicians (like Michael Bloomfield) sought to pattern themselves' (Waksman 2001, p. 4). In identifying the phenomenon of the male bias towards the electric guitar, Waksman discusses the signification of gender, sexuality, class and race, out of which rock styles arose. Hendrix, whose influences are traceable back to minstrelsy, turned to the electric guitar to accentuate a lot more than just his sexual identity. Rather than aspiring to an 'ideal of authentic musical performance rooted in race and sexuality', Hendrix personified that 'ideal by many whites in his audience' (ibid., p. 5). Understandably, this was critiqued by black audiences who saw Hendrix pandering to white myths of how a black man should be. Waksman argues that the significance of Hendrix's performance skills lay in his ability to straddle a range of codes of racial stereotyping that were manifested in an innovative approach to playing the electric guitar. Prince inherited much of this.

Occupying a very special place in the history of popular music, the electric guitar and its sonic scope is distinguishable from the acoustic guitar in many noteworthy ways. To start with, its amplification and access to multiple effects corresponds to a relatively short period of development in terms of music technology and recording practice. More precisely, the very sound of the electric guitar is directly associated with the cultural politics of the twentieth century. As Waksman's trajectory suggests, the cultural significance of the electric guitar involves its normalization over several decades. To be sure, the electric guitar's historical moment corresponded to the innovative approach to electrifying sound, forming the basis for 'the expression and refashioning of rock music's economic base' (ibid., p. 289). In a broader context, though, there is little doubt that the electric guitar has profoundly affected the course of popular music, its performance practices, sonic entities and, not least, production trends. From the late 1970s onwards, Prince's musical output documents the close ties he has had with other guitarists, as well as the repertoire of mannerisms he as inherited and developed. On this matter of influence, Kevin Dawe's concept of 'guitarscape' is useful for pinpointing the range of phenomena that impinge on identifying the culture around the guitar. Dawe notes the centrality of the body in his theorization of 'guitarscape', and addresses the matter of sense of touch and playing positions when the guitar is performed. A range of movements contribute to the broad catalogue of gestures that are inherent in performing the guitar, as Dawe observes:

> I note the extraordinary attention that some guitarists give to their nails. But what happens if they chip or break? ... The care of finger nails is absolutely essential if one is not to continually break the means by which the guitar is played. ... Although strings are set vibrating (set in motion, activated) by the use of the left- or right-hand fingers, flesh or nail, guitarists may actually end up employing a wide variety of techniques to produce sounds (and notes): plucking, tapping, bending, sliding, scraping and slapping with fingernails, fingertips, the side of the fingers, the back of the nails, thumb, palm, full hand or various objects (such as a plectrum, bottleneck, violin bow, E-bow, pre-selected objects) upon the strings. (Dawe 2010, p. 119)

But guitar playing is not just restricted to the intricate details mentioned above. It also involves exertion by the rest of the body:

> (T)here is the 'twanging' or pulling, tapping and slapping, of the whammy bar, the body, leg and foot movements required to operate effects pedals and pedalboards, and (for some musicians) the movements to and from amplifiers or speakers to tweak controls or create feedback. ... All such movements contribute to series of gestures, different within certain parameters, for each and every guitarist, providing for what appears to be in some cases a choreographed performance. (ibid.)

The manner in which a guitarist performs thus has a crucial effect upon his repertoire of movements. One only needs to consider how Prince's lavish spectacle corresponds to the details of his guitar playing, which, indeed, form the characteristics of his moves when performing and dancing. The motions of his guitar playing are part of the profound process of construction that goes into him being a pop performer.

Self-taught as a guitarist, Prince would spend years as a youth experimenting with the technical side of the instrument, gradually importing his performance skills into the recording domain. Over the years, Prince would adapt his techniques of playing guitar to meet the requirements of the recording itself, and, by so doing, would standardize a range of idioms that now characterize his style. In this respect, his mastery of guitar playing has been transferrable into his other instrumental skills. This has relevance when evaluating his all-round instrumental versatility. Let us dwell for a moment on versatility, a central clue to Prince's musical expression, which entails a proficiency in performance at the highest level. Indeed, his aesthetic is shaped by a virtuosity that is flexible and always versatile. His multitalented standing as a recording artist and performer is borne out by decades of press reports, critiques and reviews of his music that have tracked his career. When it comes to fathoming out his adeptness in performance, what stands out is his originality (even when mapped against the inconsistency of musical quality from one album to the next). In our study we have noted that even though his tracks and albums may vary considerably according to personal preferences – a point we will address later in this chapter – his quality of instrumental delivery seldom drops in standard. This is due to him being a perfectionist who always delivers the goods, a central point we will bear in mind as we interpret a number of tracks that disclose his performance style.

'U Got the Look and the Sound'

'U Got the Look', from *Sign o' the Times*, opens the second disc of the album. For reasons not difficult to comprehend, this became the single that charted highest. The vocal and instrumental parts of this recording are quite remarkable. Turning to his 'Camille voice' – a funky, sped-up vocal strand that is affected in its falsetto register – Prince opts for a voice that is highly charged and decidedly 'girlie'. The concept of *Sign o' the Times* came from another intended album, *Camille*, which was meant to consist of eight tracks recorded by the singer anonymously in a voice not to be easily identifiable. While the album was never released, the majority of the tracks were. 'U Got the Look' was one of them. Featuring Sheena Easton, this song ended up as a fun-loving, completely over the top duet. In addition to Easton the other female who performed with Prince on this track was Sheila E, whose personality is stamped on the song through the vibrancy of her unique, solid, 'live' drumming. Set against a powerful drum groove, the guitar parts drive home the clichéd narrative of heterosexual love. Somewhat coyly (if not with parody), Prince whispers: 'the dream we all dream of, boy versus girl in the world series of love'. As it progresses, the song is appealing on many levels. A standard 12-bar blues format provides an ideal framework for facilitating Prince's and Easton's alternating parts in the verses and choruses, and, as one might expect, the track works up to an extended jam section. In terms of the instrumental performance on the recording, three features come to the fore: the guitar playing, the groove and the details of the mix in 'U Got the Look', which we will now turn to.

Prince's guitar playing highlights the idiomatic traits of his style all the way through this track. The guitar part reinforces the chords, as well as providing melodic embellishments in the form of tunes, fills and improvisation. Frequently, he doubles up with the bass and other guitar parts, grounding the material tonally and texturally. In terms of textural filling, the guitar sounds deployed are exploratory. For instance, his sound often borders on distortion when responding to the content of the lyrics. Facetiously, Prince uses his guitar licks to caricature the subjects he refers to in the narrative. He does this by combining funk and rock elements within the 12-bar blues format. Functioning as a continuous thread throughout the song, the guitar works up the lyrics to a frenzy, culminating with rich, full blown synthesizer parts that are eventually pulled to the front of the mix together with the kit. The hook, 'U got the look', is repeated in jam-style before fading the song out.

As a rule, guitar licks provide Prince the leeway to navigate his tightly controlled grooves, as they tug against the regularity of the rhythmic pull. In 'U Got the Look' there is a sense that the guitar parts open up for a dialogue that energizes the narrative content. Certainly, the skilful phrasing and steady building up towards the climactic point demarcates the compelling sonic hook. This is assisted by the processing of the guitar sounds, which, while converting into a great deal of distortion, are enhanced by a high dose of compression and use of a flanger – the delay and octave effects emanate from the Zoom 9030. The result of this is something musically intriguing.

For sure, everything is accurately aligned to the groove. Defined by a standard rock pulse, the groove in 'U Got the Look' is boldly strident, with strong snares hitting the second and fourth beats, and bass drum on the first and third beats. Added to this are rim shots, which help flavour the texture and rhythmic regularity of the groove. Most discernible is the groove's tightness, largely due to the programmed feel of the live drums performed by Sheila E. The feel of the song owes much to how the kit is recorded and positioned within the mix. Effectively, the drums complement the other instruments, all of which contribute to a persuasive sense of rhythmic propulsion. Placed to the fore of the audio image, the highly reverbed groove acts as a performative device for accentuating a range of sound sources. For example, the placement of the synth bass in the groove – a gentle, bouncy, staccato figure – regulates the overall feel while pacing the harmonic rhythm. By merging with the kit, the bass sets up an underlay for the groove. Intricately, the bass is threaded into the kit parts, enhanced by the lower sustained notes in the synth and guitar parts in a way that enables it to enter and exit the groove at random; its function is to provide diversity in terms of textural coloration and rhythmic nuancing.

Cohesiveness in the groove in 'U Got the Look' has a regulatory role, and the recurrent events found in the kit, bass and synthesizer parts mark out the pop-funk style. If the main compositional intention is to profile the lead guitar and vocals, then the groove has a unifying function; it operates to draw the instruments and voices together in new permutations along the way. Thus, during this process, the groove creates a rhythmic basis for extracting the gestures in the voice and guitar. Not only does it enable stylistic expression, but it also provides the sonic 'look'. What, then, can be said about the arrangement and mix of this track?

Given that recording processes are integral to Prince's compositional working, his techniques of arranging and mixing assume a major role in the creative process. To start with, the details of Prince's recordings can be perceived as arrangements in themselves; they are conceived, organized and rehearsed in the studio prior to any live performance. In this sense, the recording constitutes a live performance. This is a salient point when it comes to considering the arranging skills behind his productions. Recorded at the impressive studios at Paisley Park, 'U Got the Look' epitomizes the painstaking process of recording engineering that characterizes Prince's compositional thought. By now it is well known that Prince often records his vocals in the studio control room alongside the other tracks on the multi-track. Using a Sennheiser 441 dynamic microphone, Prince recorded his vocals on 'U Got the Look' alone with Susan Rogers, his engineer on *Sign o' the Times*. She then monitored his vocals with headphones so that his microphone would not pick up the desk speakers. Such details of making a recording remind us of the ad hoc phenomena that often characterize the arrangement and production. Ultimately, the arrangement is steered by what happens at the mixing desk, which is based upon the vertical and lateral placement of musical events through audio engineering. Prince's approach to performance through recording thus defines the content of the mix, and hence the arrangement.

Let us say, for argument's sake, that the aesthetics in 'U Got the Look' are predicated upon the engineering of sonic mobility within an audio space. Consider the backing vocals in this respect: centralized with the bass and kit, they are panned around within the audio image of the verses, while in the chorus, during the middle of the song, they shift from left to right. Notably, the lead vocals are more stable and centred, while the overdubbed voices appear more mobile. When it comes to the other instruments, the rim shots are panned around the centre of the mix, while the guitars vary considerably in their placement. Such features of staging sound demonstrate the painstaking care behind regulating the properties of the mix. More specifically, Prince's staging of musical elements in the final mix involves both lateral and horizontal spatialization, which define the ambience of space. This issue of spatial function, especially when it comes to staging the recorded performance, is critical in the compositional process. Simon Zagorski-Thomas has claimed that this is 'closely associated with the audience aesthetic and with perceived creative and performance authenticity' (Zagorski-Thomas 2010, pp. 257–8). Prince's ideology of recording integrates performance with production techniques, which becomes the basis for our perceptions of his creative style. Zagorski-Thomas ascribes the complex technological tendencies in recorded music to an audience's 'perceptions of the artist's communal or individual creative practice' (ibid., p. 261), also noting that perceptions of normative creative practice are influenced by the 'current cultural *domain* and the historical precedent which partially informs it' (ibid.). Which returns us to the broader picture of a Princian sonic universe and questions of proficiency.

'Thieves in the Temple': New Styles and Materiality

Instrumental and recording practices intersect with one another in the historical development of trends in popular music. Technology makes the recording a 'flexible artefact', which is malleable according to what is being performed (see Hawkins 2009a). Teams of engineers, producers, musicians and arrangers work behind the pop act to produce the final result. Pop music is therefore a result of complex patterns of collaboration. With Prince, his singular control over the recording and arrangement process from start to finish is unprecedented, and has a direct link to the signature of his production. In other words, his musical expression is bound up in the technologies of his personal preferences in recording. Performatively speaking, one might say, Prince's *musicking* takes place through a technological performance that involves manipulation and elaboration within the confines of the studio space. Musical creativity, then, emerges through the processes of production that shape the performance style. On this point, we should bear in mind that as well as recording software, music technology includes other forms of reproduction, such as effects processing that enhances and alters instrumental and vocal sounds during a recorded or live performance. Indeed, in its more contemporary usage, the term music technology refers to electronic and mechanical forms as much as the techniques of composition and production arising from digital software.

Prince is noted for his meticulous attention to recording quality and production, and any account of his subjectivity needs to address his engagement with technology. The manner by which instruments are employed in his productions might be considered as an outgrowth of a general tendency in pop to treat instrumental performance with technological proficiency. Undeniably, Prince demonstrates this through the moulding of his musical ideas as palpable entities. Of course, the tendency towards digitalized instruments, as Paul Théberge argues, has conferred new styles and materiality on the sound recording (1997, pp. 185–91). Obscuring all distinctions between the performance types and approaches, digital instruments have offered up new possibilities for realizing one's ideas, and, when it comes to pop music, Prince has led the way.

Prince's incorporation of the electric guitar within multi-track recording has reconfigured performance practice in pop. Underlying this assertion is evidence of his handling of music technology as a structuring device of instrumental creativity. Consider Prince's technique of regularly equalizing his guitar and keyboard parts to highlight the higher frequency. By doing this, he positions them in contrast with the harmonic backing (often taken by keyboards, synths, vocal choruses and guitars) that is generally low in frequency. Recording practices such as these shape a pop aesthetic, constituting the aesthetics of the produced sound. There can be little doubt that Prince has taken his sources of inspiration from the recording techniques of others, yet, at the end of the day, his creative impulse arises from the staging of the recorded event in a virtual space.

It was only in the eleventh-hour that the song, 'Thieves in the Temple', was added to *Graffiti Bridge*, saving this album from outright commercial disaster. Reaching the top of the US R&B charts, the single also became a hit in the UK. Released in July 1990, the song was a statement in itself of music technology for its day. Discernible in the arrangement of the song is a distinctive sound that owes as much to the mix as the performance. For instance, throughout, quantized kit parts and synth-bass lines dominate the mix with a wealth of catchy, syncopated figures. The main effect of this track is derived from the way the material booms in its lower range, with overlaid vocals spicing up heavily reverbed synthesizer chords and wailing guitar licks. Instead of predictably turning to a guitar solo, Prince rather samples a harmonica solo from The Chamber Brothers, which is mixed into the high-density areas of the track. Added to this is a quasi-Middle Eastern flavour throughout, provided by the melodic and timbral quality of the synthesizers used. Peculiarly, this complements the rock-opera feel of the track.

From what has been said so far it will be apparent that techniques such as mixing, engineering and programming play a decisive role in 'Thieves in the Temple's' arrangement. Blandly sparse, the opening material consists of dry, deep percussive sounds resembling a temple block, delayed and panned tambourines, and ascending synth chords in fourths on the triad of G minor in each bar. Following this eight-bar introduction, Prince enters with the words, 'Love come quick, love come in a hurry' (0:14), in unison with the top notes of the synthesizer part. His reverently sombre voice is treated with enough reverb to conjure up associations of a large temple. Apart from a touch of reverb on the snares, the instrumental accompaniment is kept dry and highly compressed throughout. This aspect of spatialization in the mix affords the vocal tracks a more live audio space. Close inspection reveals further subtleties in the use of reverb and echo between the lead vocal and dub tracks. On the entry of the first harmonica sample (1:45), for instance, the vocals ascend an octave, remaining in front of the sample, whereas towards the end of the song, during the climactic build up (3:00), the harmonica sample becomes distorted into an unpleasant screech at the same time as Prince emits a pained yell. The dramatic effect of these gestures is heightened by the regulation of echo and reverb amidst a dense mix that adds weight to the narrative, which is all about betrayal and deceit.

Of particular relevance is Prince's use of pause and silence, which Susan McClary has referred to as the 'erotic gaps'.[2] His vocal and instrumental technique of using break-off points to add poignancy to his performances forms a main ingredient of his musical vocabulary. Interestingly, Prince has attributed this directly to the influence of jazz on his music, not least through Miles Davis: 'I learnt a lot about space from Miles. Space is a sound too, and it can be used very inventively.'[3] In 'Thieves in the Temple' it is primarily *gating* that assists and regulates space. Gating in the recording process involves using hardware or software called a noise gate, which minimizes the bleed from other instruments in the mixing process. Effectively, noise gating adds a dimension to an instrumental or vocal sound that is more distracting than the original static. For instance, in the recording of 'Thieves in the Temple', there is evidence that Prince has used the threshold level of the noise gate to isolate the bass drum and snares with a release rate that is rapid enough to create the impression of abruptly chopping off the end of sounds. This functions as a surprise tactic, resulting in short gaps between each sound, thus contributing to the overall levels of musical tension. Indeed, the specific type of gated drums used reveals the song's era.[4] During the recording process, if the bass drum is slightly ahead of the snare it can be controlled via a gate's sidechain that is regulated by the snare's signal, pulling both parts together. Tension in Prince's recordings is cleverly nuanced by the meticulous control of 'musical breaths' and 'erotic gaps' that are accentuated by detail to gating. Commonly, he turns to noise gates to constrict the textural material in a way that emphasizes the rhythmic pull, and his way of tuning a gate to open at a specific band of frequencies over the threshold is a powerful marker of his kit parts and grooves.

From the outset, Prince has mastered the process of compression, and 'Thieves in the Temple' exemplifies this technique. It is worth stating that many different kinds of compressors are used in music production, which involve at least four basic controls that assist in shaping the sound: threshold, attack, release and ratio. Threshold controls exactly when compressions should be activated, and once the signal has exceeded the threshold value, the compressor starts to reduce the gain according to the attack, release and ratio. On the compressor, the attack control influences the leading transient of the sound, thereby determining the duration the compressor takes to reach the maximum amount of gain reduction. For example, a fast attack compresses the sound early and aids controlling sound that consists of loud spikes in volume. Employing such an attack results in the

---

[2] In her legendary keynote address at the IASPM conference, Stockton, CA, July 1993, McClary turned to Prince as one of her examples of gender ambivalence through male inscriptions, describing the pauses he invariably turns to as 'erotic gaps' in his material.

[3] Interview on *Larry King Live*, CNN, 10 December 1999.

[4] Per Elias Drabløs has pointed out that the gated reverb on the drums in this sound are the most era-specific features and similar to those used by Phil Collins on 'In the Air Tonight' some years earlier.

compressor instantly handling any signal that exceeds the threshold. However, as Prince well knows, using fast attacks can often lead to a reduction of frequencies that make the sound dull. Prince will therefore avoid this by increasing the attack time in a way that seeks a balance between reacting to fast dynamic changes and maintaining the transient of the signal. Contingent on release control, this organizes the length of time it takes for a sound to return to its pre-compressed state after it falls past the threshold. After compression the sound will instantly return to the audio image, creating an unintended gain in the form of a pumping sound. Whilst in some genres (electronic dance) this effect might be intended as desirable, if it is not carefully controlled the sound will come over as contrived and hard on the ear. Prince solves such problems by working meticulously on release times that complement his chosen attack settings. The effect of this is that dynamic contrasts can be maintained with just the correct amount of control. Finally, ratio in compression controls the amount of gain reduction that occurs when a signal goes over the threshold – the higher the ratio setting, the more the compressor squeezes the sound; the lower the ratio, the greater the risk is for losing dynamic control.

Compression makes a song such as 'Thieves in the Temple' particularly radio-friendly, with the dynamics built by layering and not by volume. This is especially discernible in the last minute of the song, where dynamic levels vary quite considerably. As the music reaches its highest plateau in terms of volume, compression is employed to aid the various instruments in 'sitting comfortably' alongside one another in the mix. Furthermore, the lead vocals are compressed to distinguish them from the other instrumental parts, adding greater clarity to his voice. Significantly, the technological devices used date the recording, mirroring the technology at the start of the 1990s, a period when Prince's use of compression was in no uncertain terms pioneering.

In addition to compression, sampling is prevalent in much of Prince's music, and as already mentioned, the sample used in 'Thieves in the Temple' comes from The Chambers Brothers' 1965 song, 'People Get Ready'. Easily recognizable, this sample is edited and ingeniously inserted into the song as a substitute for what normally would be a guitar solo. Sound collage has always been a part of composing and arranging and involves a well-recognized technique of quotation. In pop music this is regularly carried out through sampling. Serge Lacasse (2000) refers to two paired concepts of quotation, the 'autosonic' and 'allosonic'. Autosonic quotation 'is intimately linked with recording techniques' through sampling, while allosonic is about snatching, say, a snippet of a tune from another source and performing it in any number of ways (Lacasse 2000, p. 38). As Lacasse argues, 'autosonic' quotations, which frequently involve digital sampling (although analogue techniques can be deployed) help regulate alteration: 'one can speed them up or slow them down, loop them, modify their spectral content (through equalization), add reverb, echo or flanging to them, etc.' (ibid., p. 39). Such sampling processes involve a set of practices that entail modification, transformation, and citation, and in the context of pop music, it is important to grasp that the skills of imitation and copying assume an aesthetic value if carried out with flair and panache. As Lacasse argues, an autosonic copy per se 'would be of no aesthetic interest, being the equivalent of a new edition (from standing type) of a given written text' (ibid., p. 45). In Prince's case these issues of imitation and sampling spill over into the live performance, where one of his main challenges is to accurately reproduce features of his songs from their original recordings in the sense of copying the 'original performance'.[5]

In sum, so far, the connection between Prince's music and developments in technology during the decades following the 1970s document his constantly evolving sound. Alone, the practices and resources of the recording studio during half a century have altered enormously. During Prince's lifetime, stereo analogue tape recorders have given way to digital multi-track consoles, consisting of finely regulated editing and audio operational specifications. Highly flexible signal routing and digitalized automation has replaced the mixing desks of the 1960 and 1970s, with the modern recording studio tightly controlling the input of analogue signals (amplifiers, microphones, speakers). In sum, then, the gradual development of new technologies and software has provided Prince with ever-greater resources for experimenting with musical ideas through the varied tools of recording.

The Sound of '7': From Voice to Heavenly Voice

'7' would be the song that sold best from the *Love Symbol* album – officially titled with the unpronounceable sign and released in October 1992. While '7' did not go down that well in the UK, it was a Top 10 hit in the US, featuring Prince's backing group, the New Power Generation. It was in fact the song with the shortest title ever to make it into the US Top 10. For the purpose of this analysis we will turn to the version of '7' from the compilation album, *The Hits 1*, released in 1993, with a longer duration (5:09). Notably this three disc set also consisted of the various edited versions of '7' on Disc 3, the B sides. The thematic content of the song hints at references to the Book of Revelation; Prince more than likely refers to the seven deadly sins, which he sets out to ward off. 'I saw an angel come down unto me, in her hand she holds the very key', he cries out in the middle of the song. Yet, life still goes on with words of compassion and words of sorrow.

With great pathos, Prince delivers his message in a hand-clapping, gospel style. His choir-backing consists mainly of him in overdub, as he mixes his voice in ways that correspond to the structure as much as the thematic content. Throughout the song, the voice stands alone in the verses and is joined by large multi-voice

---

[5] See Middleton (1990), esp. chapter 3, pp. 64–99, for a thorough discussion of the technological practices in popular music and the ensuing implications of appropriation in a pop-mediated context.

build-ups in the choruses and a highly-charged bass quote from Otis Redding and Carla Thomas's 1967 hit, 'Tramp' (see Example 6.1).

Example 6.1   Bass line from 'Tramp'

Redding, Otis. 'Tramp' (Fulson, McCracklin, Yasinski). Donald Dunn electric bass. *The Dock of the Bay*. Rhino 80254.

A main musical characteristic of the chorusing involves the layering of material harmonically, and this is administered through a range of technological devices: pitch shifting, overdubbing, compression and so on. While the groove and guitar parts are kept quite simple in '7', the musical interest lies in Prince's style of singing. The opening chorus of the song (see Table 6.1) sets the scene for everything that follows, almost reversing the usual tendency to build up to the end. What this means is that '7' starts on its climactic point; the message is driven through the hook of the chorus that starts the song, with a high dose of reverb that creates a sense of spiritual bliss: 'All 7 and we will watch them fall, They stand in the way of love and we will smoke them all'. Languidly, the melodic rhythm of the phrasing is measured and brimming with confidence. (See Example 6.2.)

Example 6.2   '7' – 'and we will watch them fall'

Prince turns to *a cappella* to enhance the religious connotations of the lyrics. *A cappella*, literally meaning within the style of church music, refers to music intended to be performed without instrumental accompaniment, which down the ages has ended up meaning an all-vocal performance of any style. In Prince's recording of '7', the *a capella* style he adopts includes the overdubbing of his own voice into a rich, chordal textural carpet. The resulting effect of this owes everything to the production, emulating his characteristic Minneapolis sound through the horn-like arrangement of the vocal parts. Accents on specific words follow the downbeats of the moderately slow four-beat measure, with clean cut-off points and a precise diction brilliantly captured by his choice of microphones. In particular, the distinct sound of the words, and the message they communicate, become as important to the musical texture as the elements of pitch, register, vocal timbre and rhythmic articulations. Throughout the entire track, as with 'Thieves in the Temple', the use of pause is executed to great effect. The technique of pausing without warning is quite unprecedented in pop music, and it is the slickness with which Prince carries this off that entices us into the artist's world.

Vocal timbre is also a prime distinguishing feature in Prince's sonic universe. Affected vocal mannerisms transport a particular aesthetic that translates into sentiments that are captivating. A close look at Prince's vocal timbre reveals how he stages himself theatrically. Categoriizing timbre, however, is fraught with difficulties for, as Nina Eidsheim has argued, it 'depends on the perceptual paradigm through which it is experienced' (2008, p. 211). Because of the descriptive terms we use to describe timbral quality, it stands to reason that listening is predicated upon language. Eidsheim suggests that timbre 'is trapped in the performativity of language categories', which, in turn, are 'engraved onto the body' during the complex processes of singing (ibid., p. 212). If we concur with Eidsheim, vocal sounds are perceived in relation and by comparison to our memories of other voices: '(...) each voice, when heard in the present, is also carefully situated in a particular location within the texture of all voices we have heard in the past' (ibid.). Certainly, perceiving Prince's voice is about locating it in relation to what we have heard before. And in this sense, we would argue that his voice encodes a mode of vocal performance that is fashioned by a unique timbre that invokes a sensibility. We are referring here to a timbral sensibility that is linked to an expressive bodily display, which has gradually become a familiar marker of his identity.

Working in tandem with look and mannerism, vocal timbre plays a major role in triggering off responses. The processes of identifying with Prince, then, are based as much on the qualities of vocal sound as on visual display. Therefore, the signification of vocal timbre figures greatly in the articulation of musical performance, and serves to situate the performer socially, culturally and politically. Timbre contributes to the range of features controlled in the recording space, which is always an active and live performance arena for Prince; a space where the sound is realized and gains its significance. Upon listening to Prince's voice(s) in '7', it is blatantly clear that he knows how to stage it as a prime marker of his subjectivity, and when it comes to considering issues of ethnicity, his vocal sound broaches a gap between 'black' and 'white'. In '7' he assumes the role of the preacher in a style that is most close to gospel. This is discernible through his African American stamp of identity. There is an unmistakeable tendency towards call and response in the gospel style he turns to which is tinged with R&B and blues inflections.

Table 6.1   Formal structure of '7'

Form	Lyrics/instr. fills	Vocal style and production
Chorus [15]	*All 7 and we'll watch them fall*	High reverbed *a cappella* with full choir effect; a cathedral spatial feel
Interlude [4]	Bass and drums	Evil voices chuckling and cackling away
Chorus [15]	*All 7 and we'll watch them fall*	Vocal production is dry and yet foregrounded in the mix; lyrical delivery clear and emphatic
Interlude [1]	Acoustic gtr. strumming	No vocals
Verse [11]	*And I saw an angel come down unto me*	Prince's voice is alone when beginning this section, chorus backing enters later. Thin vocal timbre, low dynamics, and low register throughout. Sombre tone created
Interlude [1]	Synth piano 3 note figure	No vocals
Verse [11]	*And we lay down on the sand of the sea*	Backing vocal interjections involve higher register than in the last verse. Prince's voice is more live in the mix
Interlude [1]	Synth piano figure	No vocals
Chorus [15]	*All 7 and we'll watch them fall*	More reverb used, with vocals becoming fuller. Prince's voice is multi-tracked and tightly compressed
Interlude [3]	Sitar motif	Vocal fragments flanged in background
Verse [12]	*And we will see a plague and a river of blood*	Prince's voice is foregrounded with fewer effects, with more lively chorus interjections that are reverbed
Verse [12]	*There will be a new city with the streets of gold*	Apart from the final word 'fall' in this verse, with fall chorus, Prince's voice is alone
Chorus [15]	*All 7 and we'll watch them fall*	Full choral backing, with more reverb and compression. Vocal dubbing parts 2 octaves above the main vocal part
Interlude [1]	Pause	Percussion sounds
Coda [12]	Vocals and sitar theme / *Just how old ...*	Broad mix of vocal sounds, sung and non-sung, with the sitar part dominating the mix

So, how does vocal timbre shape the sonic universe of '7', and what techniques does Prince use to bring the song alive and, moreover, make it playful? Throughout the song Prince's main solo voice remains within his mid-register, with the highest note being that which the song starts on (see Example 6.2), 'All 7 and we'll watch them fall'. Not unexpectedly, the melodic line mirrors the text when falling a perfect 4th in this first lyrical phrase. Rounded in its timbre, Prince's voice is confident and assuredly executed, with full backing from the chorusing. At the same time there is more physical exertion in the chorus sections than the verses, directly affecting the timbre in a way that mediate Prince's deepest feelings. His impassioned tone and articulation, with its roots in gospel, is sensitively mixed and staged in the recording, a point of importance when it comes to the overall sound. Moreover, the story Prince narrates is dependent on the most minute fluctuations in vocal timbre. For instance, on the first verse (1:22), 'And I saw an angel come down unto me', a subtle timbre change leads to a more gentle, meek tone, as Prince stresses his reverence. In this instance his timbre is shaped by lower dynamics and a thinner sound, as the acoustic guitar, drums and bass parts are phased up in the mix, often threatening to drown him out. Following this short respite, his vocal line again rises with the support of backing vocals on 'words of compassion, words of peace' (1:32), the timbre becoming more strident. Characteristically, timbral diversity evolves as a dominant feature alongside dynamics and textural thickening as Prince regulates the tension within the melodic phrasing by meticulous attention to inflections, breaths and nuances. On the third verse, 'And we will see a plague and a river of blood' (3:03), which follows directly on from the interlude with sitar motif (see Table 6.1), he elasticizes his words for dramatic effect. Decidedly mournful in tone during this passage, Prince milks every word by stretching out the final pitch of each stanza. During such moments of sustain, he lingers on key words with touches of vibrato, portamento and quasi-spoken inflections. Timbral shifting at this point in the song (the final two verses lasting 24 bars) is an important structuring device that brings us closer to his 'natural voice'. By this we would suggest that something vulnerable emerges from his expressive articulation – the laid-back feel, the deliberate muddying of pitches, the almost sighing quality in his long, hold pitches. Thus, by positioning his solo voice in proximity to the other voices and instruments in the mix, as well as the voices we have just heard, he distils his vocal timbre in the overall audio image. The result is one of great elegance, humility and charm.

When analyzing the features of timbre in '7', it is worth considering the emotional link between timbre and the body. Associations we have with the performer's body are primarily communicated through the sound of the voice, for the intricacies of singing bind us with the performer establishing the basis for identification. Indeed, Prince's corporeality emerges through his recorded voice, arranged and constructed via the aid of technology. Subsequently, in '7' his voice becomes the site for an outpouring of emotions that convey something deeply personal and arguably vulnerable. The rounded, full-throat, mellow vocal timbre Prince turns to in this track channels a spirituality that is linked to the concept of the *Love Symbol* album (originally conceived as a rock soap opera). Through the songs' production, Prince has masterminded most of the material from start to finish, which freely accesses the universe of his sound world. His prominence as a versatile musician is reflected in every detail he performs, while the quality of recording reflects the innovation of technological enterprise during the early 1990s.

Hence, the sonic dimension of '7' raises numerous interesting issues about the relationship between the voice and technology. Perhaps the most compelling aspect of this recorded pop performance is its aesthetic. Prince's voice, as we perceive it in the recording of '7', is highly processed and technologically manipulated to a point that transcends the reality of any live performance. What we are suggesting here is the post-human element brought about in the virtual world of the sound recording. The minute tweaking and airbrushing of a thousand details through digital processing, for example, fetishizes the body through amplification, exaggerating and transforming the performer above the possibilities of human endeavour. In this sense, the arrangement of '7' provides a space for drawing the ear's attention to musical experiences that can never reside in a live performance. Granted, Prince's live performances of '7' will always convince. Yet, the recording is something else, providing an aesthetic challenge to its reconstruction through live performance. Musical editing of the vocal parts in '7', of the intricate timbres and textures, becomes intuitive to the fan; we are referring here to the recognition of the luring quality of vocal tone, its sensibility. We would suggest that this denotes a form of hyperaudibility, granting the listener access to a space where one believes one can hear and feel anything. Of course, Prince knows this tactic well, and his penchant for detail becomes the dominant trait in all his music, forming the materiality of his recorded performances. Prince sculpts his vocal lines immaculately by generating melodic intrigue that is reverbed and ghosted and compressed. Something in his voice alludes attentively to the environment of his reconstruction, where his production style is omnipotent.

Finally, before leaving '7', we might consider the symbolism of the number seven in his musical thinking, not least through the allure of seventh chords (altered and added) in the verse sections. Characteristically, Prince's harmonic ambiguity arises from the subtle interplay between diatonic and modal harmony, and while chunks of the material are grounded in A major, it is his slips into one of his favourite modes, the mixolydian, that transports this song to its heavenly heights. As an earlier study has ascertained, the transition between triadic structures to suspended chords symbolizes significant points of arrival (Hawkins 2000, p. 64). The movement from an A major to A7sus2 chord contributes to the song's flavour, providing Prince recourse to play around with G sharp and G natural. Indeed, in the fifth bar of the verse the reiteration of G natural in the melodic line is so reinforced that one craves permanent resolution. But, alas, Prince slides back to the major towards the end of the phrase, although the bass adheres to a G natural on the 3rd and 4th beats of each bar. Harmonic transitions of this kind are prevalent in all his music, and it is well known that Prince prides himself on a good working knowledge of harmony. In the end, what goes on harmonically has narrative signification. For instance, this shift between A major and the A mixolydian heightens the emotional impact of the biblical references. This happens through referencing a mode that hints in a clichéd manner at the ancient or exotic (Prince has described the mixolydian as sounding Egyptian), which is highlighted further by the twanging and microtonal tendency of the sitar.

[Musical notation with lyrics: "Words of com-pas-sion, words of peace. And in the dis-tance an ar-my's march-ing feet."]

Example 6.3   Lyrical articulation in '7'

Harmonically, '7' is a superb representation of Prince's affinity for the flattened seventh in a mixolydian framework, and the manner with which he toys with the major key of A major and its relative, A mixolydian, exemplifies the deliberate ambiguity of his choice of material. It is as if the uncertainty of the harmonic identity in '7', through the switch points of A and A7 (sus2), matches the introspective nature of a song loaded with religious innuendoes. James E. Perone describes the track as 'a mixture of gospel, alternative, and Quiet Storm that seems somewhat like a 1990s version of Queen's "We Are the Champions"' (Perone 2008, p. 75). While the Queen reference might not be that obvious to all, there is no doubt that the influence of Quiet Storm is relevant.[6] Taking its title from the famous Smokey Robinson 1975 hit, Quiet Storm developed as a late-night radio format that comprised African American stylistic idioms. At any rate, Prince's '7' emulates much of Quiet Storm through features such as its slow-groove, smooth soul feel, soothing vocals (especially in the chorus) and, most of all, the mellow chord progressions. Indeed, the laid back mood of '7' is captured by an attitude of nonchalance. The song's arrangement and mix is tailor-made for relaxed and sober contemplation for, as Perone puts it, 'Prince offers the promise of a brighter future in the heaven that will follow "a plague and a river of blood"' (ibid., p. 75).

Planet Earth

Prince's approach to arranging has immense flair and originality, and this locks into his musical performativity. To exemplify this we have chosen to concentrate on the tracks from his album *Planet Earth*, released in 2007 (just prior to his 21-night engagement in London). That he gave this album away free to readers of Sunday newspapers in the UK (as well as to all ticket holders at his *21 Nights*

---

[6]   Melvin Lindsey from WHUR-FM in Washington, DC, launched Quiet Storm as a late-night music programme dedicated to music rooted in R&B, soul and jazz. By 1979 this had spawned other similar programmes around the US, with San Francisco's KBLX-FM becoming the first to adopt a 24-hour format.

concerts) once again riled the major record labels. In many ways this album epitomizes the solid, industrious nature of Prince's musicianship as much as his tenacity; it is constructed upon a legacy of 30 years in the music industry, and the pleasure of this album lies in the intricacy of detail in each track, the playfulness and the polish. In addition to Purple Rain-like, guitar-based references, there are inevitably countless references to older styles, hits and trends in a mixed bag of songs that are generally crafted with an elegance that boils down to how the pieces are arranged and produced in a vibrant and engaged manner. The first thing that strikes one is the diversity of the material on *Planet Earth*, which is largely due to the cross-flow between genre, style and idiom. Mildly put, this album is designed to encourage multiple hearings. Moreover, it offers Prince a platform for reminiscing and waxing lyrical over the countless styles that he relishes and loves to play. Essentially, the retrospective aspect of his style – a return to what he was doing from the late 1980s to the mid 1990s – is what shapes his stylistic direction and spurs him on in inventing new ideas and techniques.

As a way into identifying proficiency in *Planet Earth*, we have identified the following criteria of compositional and performance working that disclose his creative approach:

1. bass lines
2. layering
3. spatialization
4. jamming
5. figures and riffs
6. tightness and phrasing

Bass Lines

The bass line, a dominant feature in Prince's work, underpins the harmonic structures at the same time as it contributes melodically, and thus contrapuntally.[7] The repetitious nature of his inventive bass lines creates stability as much as added musical interest in a melodic and rhythmic sense. Consistently, Prince has acknowledged the profound influence of Larry Graham on his approach to bass lines. Former member of Sly and the Family Stone, Graham's 'thumpin' and pluckin'' technique revolutionized bass playing and contributed significantly to the development of funk. Moreover, Graham's style and arrangements marked a breakthrough in the bridging of pop melodies and funk grooves, something Prince

---

[7] For a detailed study of electric bass playing in popular music, especially with reference to its profound impact on melodic style and content, see Per Elias Drabløs, 'From Jamerson to Spenner: A Performance Practice of the Melodic Electric Bass', PhD dissertation (NMH, Oslo, 2011).

would inherit and expound upon throughout his career.[8] Mention should also be made of Graham's own band, Graham Central Station, formed after he left Sly and the Family Stone in 1972. Notably, the albums produced by this group stand out for their brilliantly virtuosic slap-happy and thumping bass lines, which also greatly influenced the development of Prince's style.

Planet Earth has much in common with Prince's other albums when it comes to the function of bass lines. Stylistic traits vary from one track to the next, with a deceptive amount of control and melodic accentuation (as much as harmonic and rhythmic interest) being generated by the bass parts. In the title track, 'Planet Earth', a five-string electric bass is used to highlight the rock style of the track in an economical way that allows the material to breathe from the bottom up. In contrast to this track, the next one, 'Guitar', consists of a bass riff that employs consistent quaver notes that fill in the gaps. In addition, glissandi are used to heighten the sense of mobility in the lower range of the song's arrangement. On 'Somewhere Here on Earth', Prince again opts for a spacious feel in the bass part, where in the motive the last five quaver notes drop out. Moments like this prompt response, and in such instances, Prince vocally fills the gaps. Notably, in the bar preceding the verse, the bass player moves up to high pitches to complement Prince's falsetto, which locks into the other instruments within the arrangement at this point (piano, flute, strings and muted trumpet).

A Stanley Clarke-inspired bass line dominates the track, 'The One U Wanna C', working in tandem with the guitar hook, which is played in the low register. This slap bass technique occurs in a more funk-based style in 'Chelsea Rodgers', where the instrumental parts are bass-fixated (Example 6.4). In stark comparison to these two tracks is 'Mr. Goodnight', where the electric bass and a GM-sounding double bass emulated by the keyboards play in unison the Habanera-type groove. Moments of bass fills (2:30) are also used to heighten the musical interest. A standard groove offers respite to the detailed and original performances in the other tracks, for example in 'All the Midnights in the World', where the regulation of the bass line is traditional and regular in its style (Example 6.4). Characteristically, Prince regulates his progression of tracks by the subtleties of instrumental and vocal difference, which is evident in the next track, 'Lion of Judah' where the two-bar syncopated riff steadily builds up during the course of the song (Example 6.4). With occasional slap, the riff is mainly finger played, with fills entering the part towards the middle of the song. In the final track, 'Resolution', the slap bass riff seems an unlikely choice given the song's style. Yet, as the song develops and changes its stylistic direction, the bass leads these twists and turns, steering the arrangement and enhancing the melodic and harmonic ideas.

---

[8] 'Larry Graham: Trunk of the Funk Tree', *Bass Player*, see: http://www.bassplayer.com/article/larry-graham-trunk/apr-07/26994 [accessed: 14 August 2010].

THE PRINCIAN SONIC UNIVERSE   143

'Planet Earth'

'Guitar'

'Somewhere Here on Earth'

'All the Midnights in the World'

'Chelsea Rodgers'

ff raunchy

'Lions of Judah'

Example 6.4   Bass riffs from *Planet Earth*

Layering

Every Prince track is highly layered through the mixing procedures. Polyrhythmic and textural characteristics of each instrumental and vocal track are pronounced with a gradual increase in activity during the course of a song, which adds to the degree of excitement and anticipation. There is a powerful aesthetic rationale for the employment of this technique, which often results in a sense of abandonment at some point in the song, where Prince either solos or gives way to scatting and jamming over a repeated riff. In the initial stages of recording any song, musical material will be built up through the layering of one part over another. And with overlayering the intended textural and timbral material is achieved, with each new line making a difference. Significantly, the editing that goes into layering (especially in terms of erasure and replay) means that the final mix constitutes a permanent rendition of the performance. In this way the recording becomes a historical documentation of an event, and, paradoxically, is prone to becoming outdated as a performer develops and changes direction. In the case of the prolific performer, such as Prince, the matter is arguably different, as change is noted continuously, and seen as representative of a prolific output.

Layering also relates directly to textural shaping, and it is the stacking up of sound sources and musical ideas through multitracking that creates the composite of the arrangement. The density of the texture is therefore contingent on the layering and distribution of musical material in a strictly organized fashion. Finally, it is worth stressing that many of Prince's harmonic ideas are the direct result of the regulation of overlayering and multitracking, creating a richness in vertical and horizontal material.

Spatialization

One of the features we have already touched on is that of the use of spatialization in the mix. How Prince locates his musical ideas spatially in the physical realm of the audio recording is without doubt a principal compositional process that denotes the aesthetics of his tracks. Audio spatialization is virtual, its qualities dramatically controlled and precisely regulated to create the desired effect within the audio setting of the performance environment. Acutely aware of the spatial element in all his productions, Prince excels in creating the sensation of mobility in terms of depth and distance. His arrangement of musical ideas through the audio recording is conceptually determined by the song's message itself.

Purposefully, the Princian aesthetic is about creating new virtual realities within the recording studio context, and his personal style is largely attributable to sonic imaging. The control of the sense of space and the precise cues of sound imaging are a prime determinant of the *polished performance*. Thus, it is the studio production that simulates the 'reality' of a live performance.

Jamming

As we have suggested, the jam session is crucial to understanding Prince's musical stimulus, and it is well documented that much of his output comes from hours of jamming with other musicians. Built into the jam ethos is instrumental proficiency as well as a degree of competitiveness, whereby soloists will contest one another with *ad lib* improvisational or flashy passages. The fad for jam sessions can be traced back to the New York jazz scene during the Second World War, notably at Minton's Playhouse (known today as Uptown Lounge), which musicians such as Ben Webster and Lester Young frequented. Later, the bebop trend involved groundbreaking soloists such as Kenny Clarke, Dizzy Gillespie, Thelonius Monk and Charlie Parker, who established the renowned Minton Jams – their jam sessions would not only challenge but also contest up and coming bands and musicians.

Figures and Riffs

Up to now we have used the term Prince's signature to describe the idiomatic structures in his music that instantly identify him. The variable configurations of shapes, sounds and phrases that distinguish the compositional domain are thus located in figures and riffs. For the purpose of this study, we will define a figure as any musical gesture, while a riff is more a repetitive device, a form of an ostinato that comprises a succession of sounds. A riff does not necessarily entail an exact repetition of notes, and can include a degree of variation. However, its repetition is its defining quality, and riffs are found in bass lines, kit and percussion loops, vocal motifs, instrumental snippets, chord progressions and samples. Commonly, Prince will implement riffs all the way through a track, in ways that are generally unchanged. Compositionally, the use of riffs is a decisive technique that contributes to a sense of organic unity, and single melodic, rhymic and/or chordal motives are employed to structure the arrangement of his songs. A selection of riffs from *Planet Earth* are presented in Example 6.5. It is worth noting that Prince also has a penchant for inserting famous quotes into his music in an original way. In the song, 'Planet Earth' the use of an Earth, Wind and Fire sample (2:41–3:35) is not only a musical tribute, but also a thematic acknowledgment. Cunningly, this sample is woven into a middle section that changes from a pensive and apocalyptic mood to one of full-blown elation. Such a technique, in referencing a band from the 1970s, serves to create a sense of nostalgia that in turn works as a point of familiarity. Musically, this happens through the big band, soul-funk idiom of Earth, Wind and Fire. Following this passage, the mood returns to Prince's preaching-tone, with full gospel backing set against a whining guitar solo reinforcing the moral of the cheeky vocals: 'Do we want to judge one another, lest we be judged too? Careful now … the next one might be you.'

146   PRINCE: THE MAKING OF A POP MUSIC PHENOMENON

'Planet Earth' – piano riff

'Guitar' – guitar riff

'The One U Wanna C' – guitar riff

'Future Baby Mama' – bass riff

'Mr. Goodnight' – bass riff

'Resolution' – voice and rhythm riff

Example 6.5　Selected riffs from *Planet Earth*

Tightness and Phrasing

Being in the moment typifies Prince's groove, and his approach to the tight handling of rhythm is discernible in his strict adherence to metre, often through syncopated figures. The effect of this is one of tightness, where the shaping of his melodic and rhythmic phrases, riffs and figures is conveyed with great clarity. His most striking feature is the enlivening of musical material through performance strategies that control the energy and emphasize the stylistic inflections. On this point, it is important to return to the matter of the *production as performance*; for the engineering and editing behind the mix can smooth out the rough edges of the performance, and more. Production work actually erases human errors, airbrushes the musical lines, and drops in and out vocal and instrumental parts at whatever level deemed appropriate. Take the eighth track from *Planet Earth*, 'Chelsea Rodgers', where the funk referent is entirely dependent on tightness and control. The simplest of harmonic structures, Bbm-Cm-Fm (iv-v-i), albeit with altered notes, is sustained through the groove. The kit, bass and guitar riffs are superimposed with the vocal and synthesizers in rhythmic blocks that respond to

Prince's emotive responses. Much of the 'feel' is down to the performance quality of the production itself. Sculpted around a flurry of brass licks and a catchy bass line, the energy of 'Chelsea Rodgers' is captured by the calculated discipline of the beat. Highly polished, the funk feel is a product of the regulatory energy of the groove, which is built upon a straight four on the beat kick drums, snare, hi-hat and hand-clap syncopation points, and a jerky, slap-bass stomp that provides melodic and rhythmic intensity throughout. In effect, it is the culmination of the pulse, the instrumental stacking and interjections, and the vocal dialogue between Prince and his co-singer on the track, Shelby Johnson, which shapes the contours of the funk idiom. Notably, rhythmic precision is bound up in the phrasing, where blocks of polyphonic density between the two singers contribute to the track's flashy funk-disco aesthetic. Prince mounts the groove with an array of snappy referents to funk: shouts, screeches, shrieks, inflections, nasalized 'ehhh', 'uh', 'ow' and 'a-ha' vocalizations, all of which shape the technical precision of pitch inflection, intervallic rises and falls, tempo changes and snapped-up utterances that vividly complement the instrumental arrangement. Consistently, the build-up in intensity of the track is fashioned by what goes on in the mix as everything culminates in the final jam section (3:48–4:36). This consists of consecutive eight-bar solos (saxophone, trombone and trumpet, respectively), where Prince and Johnson scat as a response to the instrumentalists. Responsorial utterances of this kind typify funk and emulate a live performance situation. The illusion of 'live-ness' is down to the engineering of the track, as much as the tightness of the New Power Generation's performance. In the end, it is the heavily processed control of a rich musical vocabulary that defines the spirit of the production.[9]

Conclusion

Evaluating Prince's music from one album to the next certainly raises questions of value, taste and judgment, not least on the part of the music press.[10] Throughout his career, his work has been ranked with much emphasis falling on what constitutes solid, mediocre or poor material. Albums deemed as top notch are *1999, Purple Rain, Sign o' the Times, Lovesexy, The Hits/The B-Sides* and *Emancipation*, while those rated rock bottom include, *Come, Rave Un2 the Joy Fantastic, Crystal Ball* and *3121*. Meanwhile, *Planet Earth* received mixed reactions at the time of its release, with specific attention paid to the distribution of this album – the free give away CD in the *Daily Mail*, the downloadable version of 'Guitar' by Verizon customers, and the free track 'PFUnk' he posted on the web. Many critics considered the mixed bag

---

[9] For an in-depth analysis of the vocal and groove-based aspects of this track, see Stan Hawkins (2009b).

[10] By music press we are referring specifically to fanzines, magazines, industry reference tools, tabloids, the 'inkies', music trade papers, and weekly and monthly consumer music magazines. See Roy Shuker (2008), chapter 9, pp. 161–72.

of styles on this album to be retrospective, trivial and dull. Perhaps it is inevitable that any artist who can put together well-crafted tracks in virtually any style at such a fast rate is going to be accused of drying up, another regular quip from his critics. Understandably, though, his fanbase seems far more divided when it comes to the qualitative issues of his music. Any glance at blogs on Prince bears this out.

Questions of music criticism thus need to be angled sensitively as value judgments are always a matter of how one owns up to one's own experiences of music. In this respect, measuring *musical creativity* should be part and parcel of any serious evaluation of an artist's music. Why? First, pop music succeeds in contradictory ways: it can be produced brilliantly or sloppily, performed competently or mediocrely, and it can be experienced, say, in terms of attitude, self-indulgent or unpretentious. At the end of the day, all value judgments arise from preferences and how a performance convinces. Second, musical critique, not least from the vantage point of the music researcher, is based upon a technical understanding of what makes the music work, and, at times, what champions originality. Often driven by a curiosity to expose and explain, the music critic situates the music under the microscope within a discursive context, relating the significance of musical sound to an interpretation of its meaning. Of course this possesses its own set of problems when it comes to issues of authenticity, originality and self-fashioning.

Fathoming out Prince's music works entails grasping its assemblage as much as its aesthetics. For all intents and purposes, identifying the features of a recording involves mapping technical codes to the stylistic codes. If, as Franco Fabbri states, it is the semiotic rules affiliated to musical codification that spell out music's rhetoric (Fabbri 1982), how is this then mediated in songwriting and music production? Let us reconsider Prince's employment of an array of techniques and the ways in which these spell out his musical rhetoric. Much of what happens in his musical composition is about *stylistic juxtapositioning* – continuously, stylistic referents are juxtaposed to shape his musical dialect. Accordingly, stylistic codes are manifested through the technological realization of musical intention. The challenge of evaluating an artist's music inescapably involves meticulous listening, which is dependent on the sonic identification of compositional working. As we have debated extensively in this chapter, Prince's musical rhetoric is primarily shaped by what goes on in the recording space, a space where musical ideas are conceived, processed and made to function. It is what happens in the studio that ultimately transfers a specific aesthetic to the live performance setting, and not vice versa. Given that all Prince's musical ideas are conceived in the recording studio environment, it is the detail of their organization in terms of structures, events and processes that lead to the final artefact. Significantly, the formal properties of every arrangement, the sections and sub-sections that harness the choruses, verses, bridges, intros and codas, are defined by a stream of harmonic, melodic, rhythmic detail. It is how this material is treated that directs our attention to Prince's most important compositional tool, recording technology itself. Indisputably, then, the recording studio is the locus of creativity and the domain of musical proficiency. For sure, Prince's personal development as a songwriter and performer is mirrored in the advances of recording practice over the past decades, where his contribution to the field has been profound. To all intents and purposes, his musical rhetoric is encoded by the technological properties of his style. Alone, signal processing impacts on every musical parameter. Consider how sounds are equalized in ways to highlight specific moments, say, by increasing a sense of depth in the mix through panning the sonic image to different positions. For instance, Prince's use of compression helps define his aesthetic, not least when it comes to the gaps, pauses and silences in his arrangements, where every minute regulation of an attack and release can alter the entire mood in a song. On a regular basis, Prince's kit and bass parts are intensified by compressing to the point of 'pumping', a common trait found in rock and electronic-style music. Another common device that we have taken up includes the creative approach to using gates to reduce the sonic signals to utter silence; a technique that accounts for the porous textural quality of his material. Similarly, kit components (kick drum, snares, cymbals, rim-shots) are gated to convey a dramatic shift from high-density dynamic levels to deafening silences! Regularly, Prince will latch instruments to vocal tracks so that he only filters their sound when the vocal part has exceeded its threshold. Such techniques contribute greatly to maintaining clarity in the mix.

To conclude, then, we consider the mix of a song the picture frame within which the sonic image is positioned. The buoyancy of musical ideas within a musical arrangement produces the sensory experiences that steer our listening. This means that working out Prince's music needs to entail accounting for the ways in which musical structures and sound-types evolve temporally through technology. Studio-based pop is compelling because it is produced in countless ways – no production is ever the same. So, back to the tracks on *Planet Earth*: the meticulous attention to the treatment of sound and effects-processing represents a dominant feature in the compositional working of the entire album. When tracing each of the riffs we identified (Examples 6.4 and 6.5), from their inception to their transformation to their culmination, it is the structuring role of technology that becomes a source of great musical appeal. Add to this the intimacy of Prince's voice and its juxtapositioning with all the instruments, and we can begin to comprehend how we experience the richness in dramaturgy of every song's narrative. Perhaps the underlying point being made here has to do with the scrupulous control and organization of sonic events as part of the compositional technique. After all, Prince's realization of musical ideas within the recording space signifies a continuous exploration of new realms of sonic representation. It is this aspect that makes every one of his albums innovative on their own terms – for Prince's treatment of music is about emphasizing the properties of sound in different ways each time. The consequence of this is a steady maintenance of technological proficiency that spells out a sensitivity that acquires signification through the imaginative use of the recording tools associated with designing the mix. Sonic treatment through recording technology therefore defines the Princian aesthetic, disclosing the compositional strategies that are invested into every one of his performances. In the final analysis, then, it is the developments in music technology over four decades that trail the creativity of Prince's tempestuous sonic universe.

Chapter 7

The Live Experience: Performance and Performativity at the O2 Arena

> Even the most perfect reproduction of a work of art is lacking in one element: its presence in time and space, its unique existence at the place where it happens to be.
> (Walter Benjamin 1936, p. 214)

Prince's legendary stage performances and outlandish after-show parties have ensured he is one of the most bootlegged artists of all time. But no recording can recreate the live experience or convey the mastery Prince has over every single moment of his two-hour encounters with his audience. His *21 Nights* residency in London, accompanied by daily media coverage, epitomized why Prince is such a uniquely enduring and fascinating icon after more than three decades as a top international performer. As master and commander of his own hugely successful musical empire, Prince does not need to perform live to fit with any industry routine. This residency was stripped down and free of any clever stage pyrotechnics. Even his talented band seemed eerily peripheral, as if he could have performed the two shows per night alone.

The instant Prince starts performing, everything around him transforms. Generally, he will start his songs at a level he can build up from. In this way, he can transport the crowd, mesmerized by the power of musical expression, to astonishing heights. Every detail of musical gesture is measured and assured. And behind these gestures are rehearsal routines, jam sessions and an exhaustive processing of ideas that give him the courage to enter the live arena of public performance and pull things off. Moulded into Prince's unmistakable signature is a distinct sound, the expressivity of which crosses over effortlessly from voice to instrument. The creative investment of his performance techniques is discernible in the meticulous way he controls volume, dynamics, effects, tuning and amplification. Most of all, his performance skills provide him with the opportunities to explore a vast diversity of musical styles. Hence, his musical creativity is displayed through an extraordinary command of know-how in terms of musicianship. Furthermore, his live performances entail a meticulous process of setting up and monitoring his stage equipment, which serves as a mark of his precision and control.

Prince's live performance shapes our conception and experience not only of his music, but also of the artist himself. Drawing on a range of methodological approaches – ethnographical, cultural and psychoanalytical, to complement the musicological – we show how Prince ultimately achieves his most significant impact on fans by making the live experience feel intimate and authentic. The seemingly unmediated Prince, especially within the intimacy of his much coveted after-show parties, is in fact a meticulously produced experience of the star. Unlike with other stars, for whom the live setting secures their corporeal reality and accessibility, physical proximity to Prince elevates him to an even more unworldly position.

Throughout this chapter we adopt a reflexive position. Both authors have experienced Prince live, together and individually, on countless occasions. We make no apology for drawing on personal experience for that is, we feel, all too often unacknowledged and lacking in formal academic and journalistic criticism of popular music. The production of meaning in live performance has to be understood as a two-way interchange between artist and audience. To this end, we specifically explore the mechanisms by which Prince interacts with his audience through sound, gesture and stagecraft. Therefore we argue that the 'scientific' veracity of musical analysis might in fact be elevated by the admission of subjectivity. It is shown in analyses of practice in disciplines such as art and design how tacit knowledge is a valuable tool for deeper understanding. Polanyi (1967) defined tacit knowledge as 'hunches' or 'informed guesses, information we know and feel without necessarily being able to articulate its foundation. In Polanyi's words, it is how we can 'know more than we can tell' (1967, p. 4). In the context of academic research, Niedderer (2007) questions the compatibility between knowledge of research and practice: 'because of the language-based mode of propositional knowledge, the implicit prioritization of propositional knowledge seems to exclude certain kinds or formats of knowledge associated with practice, which are often called practical, experiential, personal, or tacit knowledge and which evade verbal articulation' (2007, p. 1). We choose to take the view in this chapter, that the tacit knowledge evident in fan experiences of Prince's live events is productive and useful in deepening our understanding of how this extraordinary star 'works' meaningfully on his audience.

The key question for this chapter is what 'live' really means for Prince in the digital age. In a purist sense, 'liveness' is mainly associated with 'authenticity'. But to what extent does Prince's continual touring and showmanship confirm or contradict abiding notions about the role of the live gig, particularly in the context of rock and pop? We will show that for a star like Prince, whose main home is the studio, being in front of a live audience activates a complex network of intersections between star and fan. Essentially, Prince's live and studio work operates dialectically to resonate with fans, and to generate feelings of intimacy and connectedness that transcend the music and, by extension, the underlying capital styles and techniques he deploys. Through analysis of a series of live Princian 'moments', we demonstrate Prince's knowing intervention in the star–fan relationship through gesture and stagecraft. As we emphasized in Chapter 6, it is also important to acknowledge the role that the mass media play in constructing a star's persona and thus mediating Prince to fans both before and after performances. We juxtapose the accounts of media critics with fan responses to demonstrate that any analysis of live music performance must step beyond the boundaries of the musical, and reflect on context.

The 'Aura' of Live Performance

In his 1936 essay, 'The Work of Art in the Age of Mechanical Reproduction', Walter Benjamin wrote of the term 'aura', the magical authenticity of an original artistic work, which he claimed is impossible to replicate through technology. Just as the photograph of a landscape fails to fully mediate the experience of being physically in that open space, an actor on film rather than stage 'feels inexplicable emptiness: his body loses its corporeality, it evaporates, it is deprived of reality, life, voice, and the noises caused by his moving about, in order to be changed into a mute image, flickering an instant on the screen, then vanishing into silence ...' (Benjamin 1936, p. 223).

Benjamin first introduced the notion of artistic 'aura' when he became aware that the modern technologies of reproduction were fundamentally transforming audiences' relationship with original works. For Benjamin, fully appreciating the authenticity of a work lay outside the realm of technical reproduction which, he argued, detached the work from its origins. While Benjamin focused his critique on film and photography, his emphasis on physical proximity to the 'real' work – in effect the 'liveness' of the moment of consumption – ensured his approach could be applied easily to musical performance and reception. A musician must have a history as a live performer to appear 'authentic' in rock terms, 'as someone who has paid their dues and whose current visibility is the result of earlier popularity with a local following' (Auslander 1999, p. 88). Prince's early Minneapolis performances were so outlandish that they have become highly prized by those who attended them, and circulated as bootleg CDs. The shift from local to national and international performance is seen as the true indicator of a star's musical value. Philip Auslander writes that even though The Beatles stopped performing live at the height of their international fame, their credibility and authenticity was ensured by their considerable touring experience. In turn, their musical recordings encouraged the listener to envisage them as a performing unit rather than as an assemblage of produced elements fused into coherent tracks. That so much of Prince's work is valued for the fact that he writes, plays and produces virtually every sound on his records, makes his live appearances even more legendary. The live shows are not so much the authentication of a band's 'realness' in rock terms, but more a different part of the Princian brand. You are no more likely to imagine the New Power Generation recording tracks with Prince in his studio collectively like The Beatles, although you can see them working in harmony live. They are simply two very different Prince 'experiences'.

Benjamin was also worried that new technology was creating mass audiences more attached to the 'inauthentic' reproduction than to the original form, whether through seeing a photograph of a landscape painting or a filmed version of a theatre performance. If the work is in some way mediated to the audience, whether through a lens or a CD recording, there can be no aura, but rather they are 2D simulacra lacking authenticity. But, Benjamin's premise rested on the notion that a CD recording is an imitation of a live experience. This relates to the observation we make about Prince – and potentially of other artists – that the relationship between his recorded self and his on-stage identity is highly nuanced and complex. There is a mutually-reinforcing synergy between the realm of outputs that make up the Princean brand.

We therefore concentrate on Benjamin's counter-assertion, in fact his optimism in the wake of his concerns, that mechanical reproduction might have a liberatory effect, especially when it releases the work of art from its parasitical dependence on ritual. We argue that in all Prince's musical performances, recorded and live, he knowingly creates a dialectic relationship between the 'original' and the 'reproduced' so that one valorizes the other. We intend to show how Prince's live work – with its carefully-crafted sense of spontaneity and innovation '– might have parity with Benjamin's category of authenticity, although in itself it is a technical reproduction.

Prince's live environment is highly influenced by the mechanical reproduction of sound. His music exists in a dual state, developed simultaneously in studio recording and editing techniques and through his frequent live 'enacted' performances. Each informs the other with fluidity. Take, for instance, the 'live' after-show CD that accompanied the *21 Nights* photography book, as it directly questions in which context originality truly resides in his work. Prince's recorded work drove tens of thousands of people to attend his 21 'main' O2 performances. Following some of the shows, Prince performed for a few hundred fans in the more 'intimate' surroundings of the IndigO2 club, within the O2 complex. These after-show parties saw Prince yet again reworking aspects of the main show experience with even greater improvisation, as if the main show was not 'authentic' enough. Highlights of the after-shows were then mixed and distributed in a coveted, limited edition CD. Even this four-stage process problematizes any neat notion of what is live and what is reproduction. An interesting aspect of discussions of authenticity in the live experience is the disagreement over whether live shows confirm auditory authenticity or visual authenticity (Auslander 1999, pp. 90–91). Gracyk argues the live performance and recordings are 'two different media' and continues that 'recording facilitates a certain indifference as to whether the music can be recreated in live performance' (Gracyk 1996, pp. 80, 84). This distinguishes Prince from rock culture where live performance is felt to authenticate the sounds in the recording.

Setting the Princian Stage

While all musical performance is intended for a listener, the success of live performance rests on more than the technical capabilities of the artist. It requires the positive response of a whole audience to create a meaningful atmosphere; artists must set the right scene, ensure the best setlist and rehearse the right stage moves to excite the paying crowd. As Jason Toynbee (2000) argues:

> There is a self-conscious awareness on the part of musicians and the audience of the gap between them, a gap which even the most naturalistic of performers in the most intimate of environments (a pub back room, say) have to confront. From this perspective, creation includes the struggle by musicians to get across to an audience. So, performance mediates creativity and pushes authors into taking account of it. (Toynbee 2000, pp. 53–4)

In a similar vein, Marion Leonard (2007) has written of the critical importance of the stage as a performance site 'as it is from here that musicians are challenged to entertain or overpower an audience, build a fanbase, impress an A&R scout or inspire a journalist to write a favourable review' (2007, p. 99). Leonard's key point is that the feeling of spontaneous, joyous proximity with the star at a live performance is actually contrived and carefully managed both by the star and by the audience to some extent. The artist is able to control the setting, the setlist and the performance, while bearing in mind that the gathered audience are also expecting to have a particular experience and behave in certain ways (ibid.). We will examine how Prince carefully designed his performances, in both the seated main O2 arena and the mainly non-seated IndigO2 after-shows, to elicit the most satisfaction from audiences. We will address how even audience dissatisfaction, such as him not performing at his after-show, was a carefully orchestrated intention to add overall meaning to the experience for the majority of fans. 'While the individual response and behaviour of an audience member cannot be predicted, the "language" of an audience ... can largely be anticipated' (ibid.).

Let us look in detail at one setting. For many who attended Prince's *21 Nights* residency at London's O2 arena in 2007, it still feels like his 'house' years later. The O2 arena is a giant circular tent that was opened in 2000 on a patch of post-industrial wasteland on the south bank of the Thames. Originally known as the Millennium Dome, the arena has a sense of impermanence and liminality, situated as it is on the eastern edge of the city of London with an outer shell of fabric. Furthermore, the A102 Blackwall Tunnel corridor is not the most attractive or welcoming of London's gateways, flanked on either side by warehouses and housing estates.

However, on emerging from North Greenwich station on the Jubilee Line, and glimpsing the arena at twilight, bathed in purple and gold light with twinkly plasma screens bearing his name, it seemed there could be no better location for Prince's captivating epiphany. Compared with central London's vaunted heritage, the psycho-geography of the Docklands area reveals a location with little constancy as it has been continually redrawn over centuries by the activities of its inhabitants, both domestic and commercial. Its architectural remoulding has encompassed evolution and boom, followed by decline and subsequently experimentation and rebuilding as the city limits surge further eastbound. Here the river is edged by buildings of a bewildering range of styles. This is on a par with Prince's own lack of fixity and his continual redrawing of the boundaries of his musical identity. The ebbs and flows of dockland development symbolize London's continued attempts to be a global leader in trade. While Liverpool's port greets all who enter with architectural magnificence, London's eastern-most waterside landscape is notable more for utility and versatility rather than cultural aspiration. Nonetheless, travelling to the O2 by any means of transport – river, road or rail – brings the commuter into close contact with the Canary Wharf district, a dense, tall, steel and glass cathedral to capitalism which was so vaunted by Britain's neo-Conservative government in the mid 1980s that the central pyramid-topped tower is colloquially titled 'Thatcher's Dick'. Iain Sinclair describes Canary Wharf in his much-praised book, *Lights Out for the Territory*:

> The towers of Manhattan rising out of the swampland. Unlimited, on-line credit. A city of electricity. A giant slot machine with clouds in every window. An inverted centre. A conceptual city. A centre that could be anywhere and nowhere. The definitive repudiation of the discredited philosophy of place ... Canary Wharf had the vulgarity to climb off the drawing-board. (Sinclair 1997, p. 221)

Interestingly, it has been estimated that fewer than 10 per cent of the area's affluent workforce reside in the Tower Hamlets housing estates nestling at this formidable tower's hilt.[1] For Prince, whose oeuvre is constantly shifting, ambiguous and on the borders of cultural, gender and ethnic demarcations, this impermanent edifice situated on the most outward facing edge of a cosmopolitan city was a fitting backdrop for him to reflect upon 30 years of working on the edge. Separated from the wealthy business area by the snaking Thames, the arena hopes some of its light and wealth will someday shine upon its neighbouring dereliction.

Just like Prince-the-set-of-shifting-signifiers, the O2 arena's entrance during the residency was littered with a host of contradictions so bizarre that it felt a deliberate act on the artist's part. Just to the right of the main door and into the main reception atrium stood an airport-style X-ray machine. Strangely, subjecting oneself to scrutiny by the machine and its operators was entirely optional. Some fans chose to go through it, perhaps out of deference to Prince, or just for fun and photo opportunities, while thousands of others streamed past. Ticket collectors at the arena entrances politely reminded visitors of the need to keep all cameras and other potential recording devices switched off. But that was it – all the visual trappings of a concerted anti-piracy attempt, but none of the actual substance. Security guards within the O2 intercepted overt attempts to film on mobile phones but most gig-goers were able to leave with a grainy, dry-iced, purple-lit, flickering memento of their favourite song. While some of these clips have made it onto the

---

[1] See http://www.guardian.co.uk/uk/davehillblog/2010/sep/17/tower-hamlets-lutfur-rahman-politics-poverty-faith [accessed: June 29, 2011].

internet, only to be removed days later when intercepted by Prince's lawyers for copyright infringement, thousands have remained as very personal souvenirs on home computers, serving only to trigger sensory memories of an event that is more vividly replayed in the mind's eye. Prince's lip service to artistic security may have been a tongue-in-cheek nod to further heighten the aura and illicit excitement.

Bootlegs are the antithesis of the 'aura' of creativity and uniqueness, democratizing the production and circulation of musical performance. Prince's high-profile, if impossibly ineffective, attempts to prevent any bootlegging of his O2 shows was highly symbolic in his desire to project his live performances as special and highly meaningful. Clinton Heylin (2003) has pointed out that Prince was one of the most bootlegged of all 1980s artists and was unwittingly responsible for probably the best-selling bootleg of all time, the legendary *Black Album*, which remained an underground artefact for a decade until Prince agreed to an official release (Heylin 2003, p. 8).

The layout of the O2 arena for Prince's performances was a significant contributor to the feeling of intimacy in the space. For the basic £31.21 ticket charge, which included a copy of the album *Planet Earth*, it was possible to obtain a good view of the stage from any seat except, ironically, for some of the expensive VIP seats right next to the high stage. 'We don't have a lot of gimmicks or specials – it's really about the man and the music', said Garry Waldie, lighting designer, who described in an interview how much creative input Prince makes to the technical production of his live performances.[2] The show underwent careful choreography, initially designed via a projection of the stage onto a studio floor, to ensure full use of the entire stage by Prince and an unobscured view for all. In common with the theatre-in-the-round, the stage design would be simple with no backdrops. The only embellishment was the illuminated symbol platform with its flickering purple-lit edge. The stage itself became a performer, a constant reminder of the Princian brand. Prince's mode of entry into the arena included a much-anticipated set piece, the subject of gleeful online discussions between fans. Shortly before the performance, the lights dimmed and a large box would be wheeled from the backstage area, through a door under the 'O' end of the main stage, to loud cheers from the crowd. Everyone knew it was Prince being transported to ensure no advance glimpse and maximum impact when he eventually rose onto the stage. The performance would then begin.

Theorizing Performance Gesture

The spectacle of Prince performing is mesmerizing. He engages physically with the instruments he plays in ways that are inextricably linked to his agency. Essentially, it is the ways in which he uses his body when he performs that establishes a sense of meaning within the performance space. Frith has theorized performance

---

[2] http://www.meyersound.com/news/in_media/PrinceLR.pdf [accessed: June 29 2011].

gestures in instrumental playing through the 'material' and the 'purpose' of body movements (Frith 1996, p. 219). Mastering a musical instrument (and by this we include the voice) entails goal-oriented intentionality, and differences in gesture from one body to the next are based on an artist's character. Physical posturing and playing positions map out the artist's behaviour and encode the stylistic nuances that we encounter when viewing a performance. In this respect, it seems appropriate to draw on the idea of the social experience and how this is distilled in musical performance. Analysing the social experience of music needs to make reception a key area of focus (Mowitt 1987, pp. 176–7).

As the electronic production of musical sounds have disembodied the performer from the audience, so have musicologists become more interested in the relation between the player's body and reception. In his book *The Sight of Sound: Music, Representation, and the History of the Body*, Richard Leppert argues that the visual experience of music is vital to performers and audiences for understanding how music communicates: 'Music, despite its phenomenological sonoric ethereality, is an embodied practice, like dance and the theatre' (Leppert 1993, pp. xx–xxi). Recent studies in non-verbal behaviour have also used the musical concert as their laboratory. Increased eye contact between musician and audience leads the latter to better appreciate the music performed by the former (Antionetti et al. 2009)

Gesture in musical performance can be defined as a movement by a performer that embodies meaning. It is more than a simple shift of the body to undertake a mechanical action in music playing, such as pushing a button or pedal; it is a signifying bodily statement. Rather than producing the sound, it accompanies the sound and provides visual signification. Gesture performs a fundamental role in the creation of meaning in music performed live or on video, yet has received limited attention in the area of pop music scholarship. One reason for this is that pop music has tended to be associated with recorded music. The creation of technologies to reproduce and mediate musical sounds meant that the reception of music has undergone a significant cultural shift. When the gramophone was invented in the 1890s there was 'a vital shift in the experience of listening to music; the replacement of an audio-visual event with the primarily audio one, sound without vision' (Laing 1991, pp. 7–8). Composition and performance became instead the means to promote recorded music sales, rather than the other way round.

Visual aspects of performance signal three different effects. Firstly, they ensure that the performer is not merely the producer of a sound but, like the audience, also a listener who elevates the moment of reception to a shared cultural experience. A simple interactive technique, such as instructing the crowd to clap or sing, ensured that the 16,000 fans at the O2 each felt connected to Prince. Secondly, the performer can indicate emotion through facial and physical gestures that can engage the spectator to identify with feelings in the lyrics and sounds. Thirdly, visual gestures can bring to life the persona of the artist by seemingly allowing the audience access to their 'real' personality. Prince uses contorted facial expressions to suggest complex technical effort in playing certain guitar solos, which in reality he probably finds very easy. Similarly, he conveys humour and particularly winks of irony to ensure his audience's satisfaction on being 'in' on his joke.

Social psychologists studying person perception often focus on the face as the main locus for encoding and decoding emotions. Ekman, Hagar and Friesen (1981), among others, have shown that there are recurring features across cultures in the emotional meaning of certain expressions, which they labelled emblems, illustrators, regulators and affect displays. Emblems are body movements understood by the group or culture effecting them, and which are used instead of speech. An example is John Lennon's use of the 'peace' sign or Paul McCartney's 'thumbs up'. Illustrators are gestures that are used to illustrate spoken words. Their major function is to help the audience decode a message or meaning more easily, for example, by pointing or using the fingers to draw a shape or words in space. Regulators support the interaction and communication between sender and recipient, and may come in the form of movements or posture such as affirmative nodding or head shaking. Affect displays are used a lot in the playing of instruments, for example facial expressions that reflect the intensity of an emotion. They may be reinforced with postural stances. A further category is called 'adaptors', but as these are not used intentionally to communicate, we will focus on the first four terms. This approach has been tested out in popular music already, in the work of Kurosawa and Davidson (2005), to explore the expressions and physical gestures of The Corrs. While we have observed some of Prince's movements are essential for the playing of certain instruments, or to sing clearly and audibly, others function to draw the audience's attention towards specific interpretations and allegiances, creating a strong sense of intimacy even in a huge space.

Prince's mastery of signification has been demonstrated throughout his career through the creation of unique emblems, but it was apparent that Prince is using fewer now than he once did. Prior to the 2002 *One Nite Alone* tour, when Prince had converted to the Jehovah's Witness faith, he made frequent use of sexual emblems to allude to cunnilingus, as if to lend a feminine balance to the occasional phallocentricism of his guitar playing. Other emblems that Prince continues to use, and that were utilized at the O2, are his complex 'doves' hand movements, which date back to the *Purple Rain* tour in 1985. They take little practice, so were most enthusiastically relayed by the die-hard fans bringing them into closer alignment with the star than their less familiar neighbours.

Prince uses fewer illustrators now than he once did. The sheer theatricality of Prince's earlier performances involved a great number of enactments of lyrical content, such as pointing to the heavens to connote God. Instead, as we noted, his primary gestural means of relating to his audience was through regulators and affect displays closely tied into his playing and singing. A major feature of his O2 performances was audience sing-alongs to familiar hits. Whereas in 2002, Prince barely acknowledged his back catalogue, in 2007 he playfully toyed with audience memories of his biggest hits. For significant sections of each track, he would stop singing (or playing) and would instead point his microphone at the crowd beckoning the joyful crowd to fill the long gaps. His most frequent regulator was to put his hand behind his ear. This magical synergy between Prince and his enlivened, rapturous audience helped bring him closer to those sitting even in the farthest seats from him at the O2. One of us attended seven performances in seats ranging from the seventh row on the ground floor to near the back row of the top tier. Audience participation was enthusiastic in all parts of the auditorium.

One cannot underestimate the intensity with which Prince conveys delight and induces excitement in his audience. When he smiles, he beams widely at the audience, arms out at the side. Rather than adopting the Jesus like stance of Cliff Richard, as mentioned in Chapter 2, Prince's hands are held low to diffuse any sense of him having power, and rather to open up his body – and correspondingly his self – to the gleeful crowd. His over-the-top camp arrival at each of the performances at the O2 was followed by his exultant and self-exposing entrance on stage, all of which connoted playfulness and pleasure, with him promising the audience an honest and authentic encounter rather than a contrived approach designed to conceal.

Prince's major attention was directed to affect displays, which had the effect of portraying him as spiritually rapt and transported by the sounds he was creating for his audience, uniting them in a shared emotional response. Whether playing his guitar or keyboard, he would close his eyes, bite his lower lip and slowly shake his head as if in equal measures of pain and ecstasy. Through every cuff flick, Prince embellishes his instrumentalism with great campness, adding impact and flourish, as if the very act of witnessing his technical mastery is akin to theatre. This is his most powerful gesture – to create a sense of unity and empathy between himself and the public through the reification of his own music. Prince would look back, revelling in his old hits with as much celebration as his fans, beckoning us to sing and dance in time with him so that he appeared little more than a showman and conductor while he often stood alone on the stage. In fact, the slight singular figure became our puppet-master, pulling our limbs and heartstrings as tightly as he controlled his own performance. The understanding of his stagecraft is highly sophisticated and clearly well-researched. Turning to mime, and referencing a host of bygone artists, including the expressiveness of Chaplin, he conducts his band with perfect control, this also becoming an affect display. Without a doubt, Prince's live direction of his musicians is akin to that of James Brown who employed such stagecraft to enhance the sense of liveness, of spontaneity, even though each event had been heavily rehearsed and planned.

The 'Feel Good' Factor: Drawing the Crowd In

One man and his synthesizer: that was all it took to secure the pop star Prince's position as probably the most original, intimate and authentic contemporary artist of his generation. An hour into his thirteenth sell-out show at the O2, his backing band disappeared down a staircase near the back of his symbol-shaped stage. The only lighting in the darkened auditorium was a spotlight on Prince, alone, with his electric piano. For 45 minutes, Prince singularly performed the highlights of his back catalogue by pressing just one computer-driven button on his neatly disguised digital musical database. What looked like an elegant white piano was in fact a portal to instrumental versions of the biggest hits of his 30-year career, booming out a studio-produced backing for the most live moment of his concert. Whether or not the irony was deliberate on Prince's part, the 16,000-strong audience responded with sheer adulation. They cheered and danced with delight at the first few bars of a much-loved track, only for the grinning Prince to abruptly flick a switch to another song. Over and over again, he directed not only the show, but also every audience member's response to him as his sound and ego filled every recess in that huge circular auditorium.

While this account might help to articulate some of the means by which Prince creates a tremendous live atmosphere and rapport, Leonard points out that we should not look at just the performance of set pieces but also at inter-song banter and exchanges between artists and audiences. As Berger also states, 'most bands try to involve the audience with devices such as between-song banter, sing-along sections, eye contact and a vocabulary of flashy stage antics' (Berger 1999, p. 43). The Elvis 1968 comeback special is memorable not only for the stunning performances, but also for the jokey banter between Presley and his co-stars and the asides to the audience. At the other end of the emotional spectrum, Lady Gaga reportedly broke down in tears on stage in London in May 2010 after revealing that her grandfather was fighting for his life in hospital. Undoubtedly, Prince's sheer playfulness is key to his intimacy. Whether he was beckoning audience members on stage for impromptu dancing contests, or revealing to the throng that he used to be sent out to buy his mother's tampons, the abiding memory of a night with Prince is sheer fun. No wonder many, one the present authors included, prolonged the experience for many hours at the dead-of-night aftershow parties.

But how authentic was the interface between Prince and his audience? Is the live Prince expressing a persona rather than himself? This is Auslander's take, which he illustrates through Suzi Quatro (2009, p. 308). But in Frith's view, pop stars are 'involved in a process of double enactment: they enact both a star personality (their image) and a song personality, the role that each lyric requires, and the pop star's art is to keep both acts in play at once' (Frith 1996, p. 212).

Prince turns to an array of musical devices to draw in his crowd through live performance, which includes different forms of participatory involvement, such as shouting, singing, chanting and clapping. In addition to these sonic markers are the visual responses of arm swaying, dance motions and the crowd rising from their seats. The spectacle of crowd participation is one of the most critical factors in experiencing Prince live, and there are very few artists who manage to exert such control over their audiences.

The central role of the groove in Prince's music contributes significantly to the 'feel good' factor in the live context. In the footsteps of James Brown, Prince knows how to trigger that start of a groove with a click of the finger, a short yell, a downward stroke on the guitar, a bass drum kick or a simple piano riff. Invariably, as a groove starts up, Prince will command his audience to respond, and, as we have already indicated, this occurs in many different guises. Rhythm is the primary musical element of a groove, and how this is organized through beat patterns, repetition, variation, pauses, cuts, silences and timbral enhancement determines its reception. The success of a song working in the live context is ultimately down to getting the audience emerged in the groove, and experiencing it as pleasurable.

'Feeling good' is no doubt one of the most central aspects of the Prince live experience, and this is related to being satisfied by the events of a performance and how they unfold musically. The matter of 'feeling' in a live performance, in Danielsen's words, is 'about cultivating the right swaying motion; about accurate timing; about being in place, in time; about precision and relaxation at once' (Danielsen 2006, p. 198). To this we would add the 'feel good factor', which is derived from recognizing a song one already knows and experiencing a profound sense of familiarity with the person performing live in front of you; in the end, it is Prince's well worn standards that bring the house down every time. This is because when they are performed, they are true to their form. Responding with conviction on the part of the artist and the crowd, therefore, demands being in the state of a groove that really grooves. A sloppy or half-hearted performance will instantly fail. Any musician knows this only too well!

One of his most played songs, with the highest of 'feel good' factors, is the synth-driven hit '1999' (from 1982, and analysed in Chapter 4) – this defining song in Prince's career contributed directly to his rise to superstar status. Ideally suited to the rock stadium setting, a synthesizer fanfare with close-positioned chords, F and Gm, opens this song. Nailed down by a C pedal in true church organ style, the majestic gesture of this opening is elegantly drawn out by a moderate 120 bpm, with a live, splashy cymbal crash on the first beat. Following this eight-bar, introductory, deafening fanfare the groove kicks in with the C pedal shifting to an F pedal at the onset of the verse, but this time in successive crotchet beats, four to the bar. Something massively erotic characterizes the groove as it grinds towards the chorus. Indeed, the funk-pop idiom of the song captures a Family Stone sensibility, both in the phrasing of the chorus and the hook, 'they say two thousand, zero, zero, party over, oops, out of time'. It is at this point that the groove rises in fervour to its most intense state. The musical details that determine this are located in the bassline that now starts its movement from the subdominant to the tonic (Bb-D-F-Bb-D-F), and the drum patterns. The melodic phrasing, instrumentation and vocals also have a big impact. Close inspection also reveals a number of other qualities that afford the groove its intensity, and although this analysis refers to the recorded version of '1999', these elements play an equally important role in the live performance of the song.

The weighted gesture of accenting pitches, beats, wah-wah guitar strokes, anticipatory pauses and clearly articulated words generate immense excitement in Prince's grooves. Underpinning the compositional aspects of every groove are intricate variations and cross-rhythmic figures, all of which serve to syncopate and reinforce the basic crotchet pulse. Melodic phrasing and vocal chorusing, for example, constitute a counter-rhythm to the four-on-the-beat crotchet notes in the bass line and clean, funky, James Brown-type rhythm guitar parts. Remarkably, the melodic rhythm in '1999' is almost identical to 'Manic Monday', which Prince wrote two years later, performed by The Bangles.[3] Another crucial element that contributes to the 'feel good' factor in every live performance of this song is the exaggerated presence of 'gaps' in the material. These occur not only in the clipped and precise cut off points in the rhythmic material, but also in the spaces between the melodic phrasing, which always end abruptly only to be cheekily continued by the syncopated two-bar riff that opens the song (F-Gm/F). In a sense, the sung parts function dialogically with the metrical constituents of the bass, kit and guitar strokes. The overall riff, then, comprises closely interlinked parts that create a polyphonic fabric that is rhythmically charged and full of tension and release. The main purpose of groove in funk-pop is to unite everyone and to take things to a higher plane. The case with Prince's grooves is that they are tightly controlled, obeying the inner mechanisms of beat regulation and propensity. Moreover, they succeed to thrill in any live performance because they adhere to standardized formulae that are open to playful manipulation. It is how Prince renders these basic structures appealing that leads to pleasurable response and participation.

Another way to consider the impact of Prince's groove is through the technicalities of layering in a live performance context. His grooves can be considered a hybrid of various layers that not only function materially, but also culturally meaningfully. Built into this notion is the idea of stylistic referents and idioms that are engrained within our culture. Take the collective approach to musicking that has its roots in the aesthetic qualities of African American popular styles. The historical backdrop to Prince's musical mannerisms, when it comes to grooving, are entrenched in the cultural and historical process of defining black identity in the US. This impinges directly on its reception amongst white and black audiences. The meeting of Prince with European audiences, who are still predominantly white, affirms the presence of many similarities and differences. Significantly, all the concerts we have attended have been in Europe, and as Europeans we are acutely aware of the predispositions that have historically shaped our responses to black music. The source of appeal in black music certainly lies in the not unproblematic construction of otherness and the formidable force of an African American musical aesthetic. This aspect directs our attention again to the groove, and how in Prince's signature this is mapped against an approach to music as a vibrant social activity. The spontaneity of his phrasing when he grooves, his improvisatory gestures when he jams, and the structures behind his dialogue with his band and audience are most relevant when experiencing him live. His performance strategy ultimately lies in a combination of gestures that are charged by his groove-oriented songs. And even when he slows down, for numbers like 'Purple Rain', 'Nothing Compares 2 U', 'Anna Stesia' or 'If I Was

---

[3] Gratitude to Per Elias Drabløs for pointing out this as well as various other features in '1999'.

Ur Girlfriend', the groove is always there, albeit gentle, undulating and irresistibly complementary. In this sense, Prince's musical material always makes room for the actualization of rhythmic feel that is ensured by the confidence of a style of performance that is exhibitionist by nature.

Both the production and the arrangements behind his songs in live concerts contribute significantly to bringing them alive (often in the aftermath of audiences being well versed with the recorded version). All of us know this can be one of the most contentious areas of disappointment when attending live concerts of favourite artists. To pull this off in a new acoustic surrounding, with a completely different aura in place, is one of the most challenging tasks facing any musician. Impeccably, Prince comes up with new arrangements of his songs at every live event; after all, we would argue, this is the nature of playing live and being a 'real musician', however contestable such a claim may be. In any case, this means that his grooves are modified to suit the theme and mood of a concert, which involves, say, tempi changes from what we are used to in his recordings, new solo passages, modulations, extra verses, extended jam sections and so on. Moreover, the temporal conditions of a song's performance in a live context are contingent on the visual aspects of the artist's performance. How Prince visually follows the contours of his guitar playing through expansive movements draws our attention to the signification of the gestures we see and hear; hence, the relation between sound and performance on stage, established through a wealth of gestures, has everything to do with the mannerisms of the instrumental and vocal performance. That said, dancing is just as important, and, as we have discussed earlier, this also forms a vital part of Prince's spectacle.

Finally, the large-scale relationship between artist and crowd means the complex musical production behind a single song needs to be multi-dimensional. The implications of gesture, musically, are about creating and heightening the feelings of the closely-knit crowd, and, to this end, communicating playfulness is part and parcel of showing an audience that one is sincere.

Sincerity and the Critic's Response

> ... (S)incerity is the quality most highly valued in ... rock and roll aesthetic, from punk to mainstream folk-rock. Its presence guarantees the validity of a musical style and, by extension, of a way of life. Its importance is enhanced by, and in turn enhances, the intimate emotional connections between musicians and their fans. (Shank 1994, p. 153)

One of the ways in which musicians' sincerity is relayed and reinforced is through critical media reception. A star's public persona is influenced as much by the mass media as it is by his or her own self-representation or musical style (Frith 1996). Music critics will often highlight an artist's adherence to their ascribed generic aesthetic as an indicator of the sincerity of their musical expression. Our analysis of newspaper coverage of Prince's live shows reveal, in Feigenbaum's terms, 'points of anxiety and contraction' within the discursive conventions of criticism itself (Feigenbaum 2005, p. 39). During this study we have examined a cross-section of reviews of Prince's live performances in the UK over a wide span of years. Specifically, we have selected coverage of his 1986 *Parade* shows at London's Wembley Arena, his 2002 so-called 'comeback' concerts at London's Hammersmith Carling Apollo, and his *21 Nights* residency at the O2. These specific events were chosen because one or both of us attended the concerts, fan responses as well as formal journalistic reviews were available to us, and each event served as a key moment in Prince's reception by the mass media in the UK. Our examination focuses on how the critics 'construct' Prince's persona over time, specifically through references to generic or musical influences. We were also curious to see to what extent 'official' reviews tallied with the responses of audience members. As Mark Fenster points out, critics' discursive positions 'are both as audience members who are presumably similar to their readers, and as speakers from a position of expertise and authority that differentiates them from their readers' (Fenster 2002, pp. 83–4). It was interesting to see the extent to which Prince's physical proximity to fans in a live event beckoned a more rapturous response. This gave insights into how 'liveness' may work on a deeper, more meaningful level for fans as opposed to it serving as an evaluation of the star's musical proficiency. In this way, we identified distinct markers between the rock critics' and fans' discourses about reception, which, to return to our point in Chapter 6, suggests that the media's representation of Prince and his output is potentially unrepresentative of the way he is generally viewed and received by his audiences.

A dominant ideology of rock criticism valorizes authenticity and originality; musicians are presented both as authentic spokespeople for their generation and as romantic artists (Frith 1983, p. 176). This vision of popular music as authentic creativity was particularly strong in the US. Frith's claim that 'American rock writers are mythologists' (Frith 1983, p. 10) suggests that critics take American history as their starting-point, with its accounts of individualism, independence and breaking through new frontiers. McLeod's (2001) analysis of US album reviews over the period 1971–99 finds that throughout this period the writing 'valorises serious masculine "authentic" rock and dismisses trivial, feminine "prefabricated" pop music' (McLeod 2001, p. 47). McLeod argues that the semantic markers of rock criticism are the masculine ('aggressive intensity', 'violence', 'rawness', 'authenticity', 'seriousness') versus the feminine ('softness', 'blandness', 'vapidity', 'sweet sentimentalism'). This leaning is reinforced by Feigenbaum's (2005) study of press coverage, which found that masculine markers typically denote excellence in musicianship and musical influence. In contrast, female markers refer to the voice and body of the performer.

We made a number of observations concerning the style of reviewing and the characteristics of Prince that critics have chosen to emphasize over time. At the height of Prince's popular success in the mid 1980s, critics writing for the quality and specialist media were keen to focus on his black musical influences as if borne of a desire to neatly categorize him, as if unable to grasp the bi-racial thrust of his oeuvre. Meanwhile, the tabloid media concentrated on his physical sexuality to the exclusion of virtually all other facets of his work in order to play down the theatrical androgyny and emotional drives in his performance.

Parade, Wembley Arena, London 1986

Critics use artist comparisons to familiarize readers with the characteristics of artists, and in Prince's case it has been almost entirely comparisons with earlier black musicians. His overt referencing of white or other ethnic musicians is rarely if ever noted unless he performs a cover version or collaborates. Prince's live shows are usually marked by his slippage from genre to genre, segueing seamless through rock anthems by Led Zeppelin, Red Hot Chili Peppers or Foo Fighters as often as he might channel James Brown. His guitar solos, which will as often be performed on a Hohner as a Les Paul Jnr, are as likely to summon the memory of Jeff Beck as Jimi Hendrix. Prince is only really ever compared with other male artists, and rarely, if ever, female influences, such as Joni Mitchell or Betty Davis.

A review by *NME*'s Gavin Martin starts by citing typical black references in order to situate Prince against a musical heritage of showmen, specifically Louis Jordan, Little Richard and Sly Stone.

> And it's true he's unlikely to unleash the tension and angst that his forebear Sly Stone did in 'There's a Riot Goin On'. But once you've seen the show, none of that matters. Prince contrives a lavish celebration and tribute to black culture, to those who dared break and cross barriers to explicit beauty and sensuality and to his own career, which has used all those traits. (Gavin Martin, 'The Flesh and the Soul', *NME*, 23 August 1986, p. 43)

He is not felt to match his forebears' status but nonetheless shares their authenticity and, it is assumed, their revolutionary zeal.

The Guardian's Adam Sweeting anchors Prince's summoning of black musical influences to his focus on the body:

> There's no question that Prince knows his rock 'n' roll but there's a tough R&B bedrock to everything he does – even when he's playing his Beatles-and-acid tricks, there's plenty of Sly Stone and Jimi Hendrix in there to keep the wandering mind anchored firmly to the body and its explicit needs. (Adam Sweeting, 'The Crowd Prince of Pop', *The Guardian*, 14 August 1986)

By contrast, the focus of the tabloids was entirely on his physicality. The *Daily Star* framed his upcoming shows a week ahead by concentrating on his sexually-charged performance on tour in the US, with no mention of his music.

His sexy swivelling, his crazy costumes and his sizzling X-rated lyrics are a far cry from the quiet, polite church-going schoolboy whose nickname was 'Skipper'. (Terry Willows, 'Prince of Fun', *Daily Star*, 9 August 1986, p. 9)

A few days later, the same paper centred on the star's 'wild man' image, despite the fact he was fully dressed for most of the show:

> Prince the Purple Poser sends his fans wild. Wearing figure-hugging black pants and high-heeled boots he explodes into action, gyrating and pulsating across the Wembley stage and thrusting his hips at the sell-out crowd. (Kerry Allott and Barry Gardner, 'Naked Frenzy', *Daily Star*, 13 August 1986, pp. 2–3)

At the actual show, Prince did remove his top for a fairly short period of time when performing 'Kiss' in a style that replicated the dance-based promotional video. For a far greater part of the performance, Prince wore a quintessential marker of acceptable mainstream masculinity – a suit and tie, albeit in canary yellow. His hair was short, neat and slicked back, and in no way 'wild', as the animalistic innuendos in the media reports would suggest. As such, the reviews seemed universally to disassociate Prince's performance and dance from his voice and from his emotional enunciations. The overt sexualization of Prince, coupled with the emphasis on his blackness, disregards the more political or subversive elements of his music.

Just as the broadsheets latched onto Prince's black influences as a marker of his musical integrity and sincerity from a fairly 'male' perspective, the tabloid press utilized 'female' markers to situate him primarily as pop entertainment – an exciting event but largely a transient and disposable spectacle. Notably, a discussion amongst fans on the prince.org site makes little if any reference to Prince's physicality, though his physical presence is meaningful and special to posters:

> I was in the 13th row, but in the scramble when everyone rushed forward, I ended up right in front of Prince against the camera man boarding. It was wierd because I was so close I could smell him! Because he had been taking a hammering in the british press, even when Around the World In A Day started, I wasn't convince he would actually be on stage. Then the courtain opened at 'I Think I wanna Dance!' and I though, wow, he's tiny!!!!! I went all three nights (12th,13th,14th) in the expensive seats (£12.50, as opposed to £10.00). This left me broke for a month as I was only just turned 16. My highlights: HEAD! The best rendition of When Doves Cry yet, 17 Days, Paisley Park, Sting coming on stage to join him!

> I also was there on August 14th. It was my first concert, not just of Prince, but of anyone. I'd wanted to go to LiveAid but my parents had forbidden it as I was too young (15), but nothing was going to stop me seeing Prince. Before the concert I was scared that it'd be an anticlimax and I'd get disillusioned, everyone knew

me as the Prince kid. Man he tore it up. The crowd was electric, every time there was a flutter in the curtain the place erupted. I was up the side and we got twice as close to the stage in the rush when ATWIAD started. Awesome night, like the pyramids and the Taj Mahal you're blown away when you actually get there.
http://prince.org/msg/7/227447 (accessed: June 29, 2011)

This next fan directly notes the contrast between media coverage and the real experience:

> 14th august 1986, wembley arena. incredible.i think it was at these shows that the british music press realised that behind the tabloid rubbish, here was a talent that only comes along once in a generation, and to their credit for the next few years he was worshipped by the likes of NME and Melody Maker. he got ron wood and sting on stage for 'miss you' the rolling stones track, while he did his mick jagger impersination ! (sting and ron looked completely lost onstage!). the revolution were sooo tight as a band.the horn section of eric leeds and atlanta bliss gave it that jazz review feel that is still with him now.
> http://prince.org/msg/7/227447 (accessed: June 29, 2011)

2002, One Nite Alone

The build up to Prince's *One Nite Alone in Europe* tour was curiously categorized as Prince making a 'comeback', when in fact he had never gone away. Accordingly, critics veered towards comparisons with his 'heyday' *Purple Rain* era rather than charting his gradual evolution and longstanding melding of jazz, funk, blues and pop in his stage shows. As Gavin Martin commented in his review in *The Independent* on 5 October 2002:

> Many music business commentators maintain that Prince lost the plot around the time he painted the word Slave on his face and began plotting his escape from the industry. Last night's performance suggested something quite the opposite

> In many ways this review confirms the writer's own critique, by sounding surprised that Prince 'looks great' and concluding, almost reflexively, that: 'it has never been wise to write the [sic] Prince off, all the evidence is that's as true now as it ever was'.

By 2002, the emphasis is on Prince as an instrumentalist and on his rapport with his audience. References to his musical influences were all but absent, the emphasis being on Prince as a singular phenomenon.

Kitty Empire wrote in *The Observer* on Sunday 6 October 2002, as if to rebuke some of the stereotyping of him, and to celebrate his multi-genre approach:

Well before he became the reclusive eccentric, Prince was a multi-instrumentalist funk prodigy. Tonight reminds you of that. It's as though he is simply made of music, whipping his band through a (lengthy) jazz-funk set which becomes a priapic rock show, which later becomes a good-natured singalong of 'Nothing Compares 2 U'. There's a stunning interlude where he turns electric bluesman and segues into Led Zeppelin's 'Whole Lotta Love', which sees men of a certain age actually quaking with awe.[4]

Similarly, David Sinclair in *The Times* wrote on 5 October that 'The man makes up his own rules', at his surprise that Prince could deliver such a successful concert while ignoring his core repertoire.[5]

While there's a general acceptance on the part of critics that Prince transcends categorization, there is still no accurate reflection of how he makes his audience actually feel.

We compared these reviews with a collection of audience responses to the London shows. Prince's NPG music club website was transformed into a user-generated content posting board for fan reviews. Whereas the critics retain distance from the event, fans effuse about the rapport they felt with the star himself through his audience interaction.

'AIDY', who had managed to see multiple shows and after-shows reported: 'Prince made us laugh, sing and dance. As for the few brave enough to go up on stage and solo with him, big respect!'[6] Many reported close encounters with Prince himself, who had allowed them into the sound check and invited them to go on stage during his performances. The cool, distant superstar is portrayed in a very different light by his audience. Keita wrote: 'Prince was so relaxed and friendly. He allowed non-NPG fans to go to just in front of the stage'.[7] 'Nige' went to the sound check: 'We picked up our tickets and laminate, and proceeded into the sound check. I never expected you to just walk on, sit there and just jam with us. Playing some bits, and even doing a karaoke spot with some members (which has to be said were pretty good!)'.[8]

Most fans focused primarily on their emotional reaction and their sense of rapport with the star, before praising his musicality and showmanship. The songs the fans highlight as memorable also differ from the critics' choices. An effusive 'Gavin, London' surmised: 'So I'll tell you: every second of tonight was a joy. It's 2 late 2 go into detail. But this was the best prince gig I've been 2 by a long way. The

---

[4] See http://www.observer.co.uk/review/story/0,6903,805269,00.html [accessed: June 29, 2011].

[5] See http://www.timesonline.co.uk/printFriendly/0,1-245-436450,00.html [accessed: June 29, 2011].

[6] See http://www.npgmusicclub.com/npgmc/newz/tour2002/100402.html [accessed: October 31, 2010].

[7] Ibid.

[8] Ibid.

band brought the Rainbow Children 2 life. Prince was divine. The Horns 2 die 4. Drums thumping. A bass and a bass player and keyboards like U never hear ... The concert – that is truth.'[9]

21 Nights, O2 Arena, 2007

Feigenbaum (2005) has analysed how language employed in rock criticism frequently functions as a marker of gender difference. She focuses on the use of *inter-* and *intra-*gender artist comparisons, adjectival gender markers and metaphorical gender markers in artist background information, lyrical and musical analysis and descriptions of fans. Liz Evans had already lamented the dominance of established male rock critics: 'A tightly woven old-boy network still exists throughout music journalism, especially at the roots of supposedly more liberal, right-on and cutting edge papers' (1997, p. xvi).

While it might be rather essentialist and sweeping to assert a gender-based division in reviewing, it was in evidence in the critic's reviews of the *21 Nights* event. For example, while *The Telegraph*'s Neil McCormick (2 August 2007) refers, somewhat offensively, to Prince as a 'priapic midget, who has concocted some kind of personal mythology equating sex and spirituality ...', before drawing attention to Prince's 'sexy dancers', Kitty Empire's long review of the opening night for *The Observer* on 5 August 2007, pays tribute to his 'compact, dapper form'. One of the least traditional previews to the residency came from Liz Jones in *The Guardian* on 10 May 2007, when Prince first announced the shows. Jones, a Prince biographer and self-confessed superfan, provided an uncensored inner monologue unconstrained by journalistic conventions of distance, as she described her fevered attempts to gain his attention in the front row, and how she licked a drop of his sweat that splashed on her. She would reflect: 'I have always found that he stirred something deep and naughty inside me. I loved the fact that he was painfully shy, and that he loved women with not a hint of misogyny. He wanted to be our girlfriend, to dress us and hear our problems.' Perhaps her most 'unjournalistic' revelation is that she once saw him on '17 consecutive nights at Wembley Arena'. Clearly her emotions got the better of her: in actuality, he played 16 nights in total, seven being the most he played consecutively. But it does not matter a bit, because fans know exactly what Jones means and identify with how she feels. If it was a deliberate ploy – which it most likely was, for Jones' undoubted fandom brings with it immaculate memories and attention to detail – it was a very clever and touching one.

Kwame Kwei-Armah also took a refreshing fan's viewpoint in the *Telegraph*, which had guest reviewers at each concert: 'I love looking at audiences at a live performance, for it is there that one sees the true power great artists have over us mere mortals. But seldom have I seen power of this magnitude displayed. Initial smiles and shouts grew into wild tears of joy.' One of the most satisfying observations was

---

[9] Ibid.

how people reacted to songs they knew with emotion before they could verbalize the title to their companion. These types of raw, subjective and gut responses served as a far more effective record of this startling and magical residency.

The proliferation of recorded music has made the live event a significant opportunity for fans to share physical proximity with their favourite artists (Thornton 1995, p. 27). Attending gigs is also seen as something of an endorsement of true fandom, especially if the fan has attended several concerts and watched the star's development over time. In the case of Prince, his fansites revealed that while attention was given to the number of main gigs attended, special cachet was endowed to those who obtained coveted after-show tickets.

A special frisson (some would say frustration) surrounded Prince's after-show parties at the IndigO2, the 2,400-capacity nightclub within the O2 complex. Soon after the *21 Nights* main show tickets sold out, the artist announced he would now offer tickets for far smaller, 'intimate' after-shows to several hundred paying guests. There was a disclaimer that while the after-shows would have a distinctly Princian air, there was no guarantee that he would personally perform. On some evenings the crowd was entertained either by a DJ or, at best, members of the New Power Generation *sans* the headline artist, causing some public disquiet.[10] The overall effect, however, was to make the after-shows the talking point of the concert series and to lend added aura to them when he did play. One of us attended two of the after-shows, both very different sets, moods and performances, with Prince playing for several hours at both.

The most acute difference was the proximity to Prince's physicality. Witnessing Prince walk out onto the small stage, with minimal lighting and pomp, brought his actual bodily presence into sharper relief for the first time after seeing him on countless occasions at larger live performances since 1986. The backlit, cosmeticized, majestic superstar of the symbol-shaped stage was now transformed into a shy, translucent-skinned man in a woolly jumper carrying his guitar. The fabrics draping his delicate frame were so fine, his knee joints could be picked out with each guitar lick. Walter Benjamin would claim: 'The authenticity of a thing is the essence of all that is transmissible from its beginning, raging from its substantive duration to its testimony to the history which it has experienced' (1936, p. 215)

While Benjamin's treatise lamented technical reproduction of original works of art and, as such, might be read as being averse to all contemporary sound recordings and videos within popular culture, his words are acutely apt in describing the use value of Prince's after-shows. They are the authentic distillation of the entire Princian mastery of studio sound, of stagecraft and the authorship of visual signification. Through meticulous self-creation, Prince has ensured that the utterance of his name connotes signifiers of music virtuosity, performative magnificence and global business dominance. But in the very same thought process, we envision the man, his very real knees and his guitar interacting

---

[10] http://news.bbc.co.uk/1/hi/entertainment/6942963.stm [accessed: June 29, 2011].

with very ordinary fans, lucky enough to acquire £31.21 tickets. In harnessing the income generating primacy of the live experience, ensuring he is one of the biggest grossing live performers on earth, Prince guarantees that he is ultimately known among his millions of fans as a profoundly accessible and identifiable character. He is matchless as a global superstar in knowing that eventual success and durability is dependent upon maintaining his close relationship to his fans, be that in person or through sonic or visual signifiers in his studio and promotional work. The 'aura' of Prince resides not necessarily in him being present at an aftershow, but rather in just knowing that he actually still performs these legendary, exclusive events before very ordinary, everyday fans. Or, as Benjamin writes, that he can 'meet the beholder or listener in his own particular situation' (1936, p. 215).

Conclusion

At the time of writing, Prince has just announced a series of concerts in New York city in December 2010, and has just completed a mini-tour of Scandinavia, which was described by some commentators as his best performances to date. More than 30 years have passed since he signed his first recording contract and he continues to bedazzle tens of thousands of followers each year with his live performances. For Prince, as with so many other artists, the internet has not only transformed the way we receive his music but also drastically destabilized the primacy of his pop recordings as income generation. But as we have attempted to demonstrate, Prince's identity has always been founded on his seeking a close rapport with his audience and, in the words of one of his most famous songs, 'nothing compares to' experiencing him live.

Through these seven chapters, we have shown that a close interdisciplinary critical reading of an individual icon has merit, particularly when we consider that star in context. In this way, we envision Prince-the-star at the nexus of a host of factors that synthesize at any given moment to create meaning. To experience Prince, we must locate him in the context of his emergence amidst dynamic socio-cultural and socio-political upheaval during the 1980s. In Chapter 1, we examined how Prince's own background, living on the borders of social, cultural and political boundaries, became inflected in his output to mediate an original and authentic pop identity for the MTV generation. His complex relationship with his own family has been channelled into his self-creation as a new form of pop subject, in full control of his sound, image and brand. Prince quickly attracted a global following of fans drawn to his ambiguity, refusing to be situated within any one music genre, ethnic identity or sexual preference. He offered a safe and unique space for anyone to play out their own complex subjectivities in uncertain times, regardless of sex, colour or creed. While highly marketable, Prince's ludic evocations had little in common with the postmodern 'queering' of rival stars such as Madonna. Whereas Madonna and Michael Jackson continually remodelled and reinvented themselves, Prince was wholly consistent with a stable identity. From his earliest days of performing, Prince has generated a distinctive sonic signature and secure brand while others have waxed and waned.

In Chapter 2 we delved deeper into the Princian politicking by examining how the star has utilized his dandified approach to styling as a confrontational gesture, both in ethnic and gender terms. While he is undoubtedly a highly successful musical star in the first instance, Prince operates on the visual plane almost as powerfully, so that his image intersects with his sonic signification at any given moment. In this chapter, we explored Prince's attraction to the rich cultural and contestational heritage of the dandy movement to show how he uniquely enunciates his relationship with his ethnic origins and gender. Moreover, we examined how the sonic and the visual intersect at the moment of reception to forge fascinating areas for contemplation. His playful, unthreatening disavowal of fixity was nonetheless impassioned in its evocation of a humanist philosophy founded on freedom of expression and choice. This was communicated most powerfully and rather more controversially in his messages about sex.

By juxtaposing the holy and the profane, Prince was following a troubled path trodden by his musical predecessors. We explored in Chapter 3 how a struggle between good and evil had characterized both the content of African American music and also the duality of its marketing over time, sometimes in exploitative ways. Prince's attitude to his spirituality and his sexuality is one of the most reflexive aspects of his work. Our close analysis of his lyrics, musicality and performances demonstrated a star who was using his mind and body to explore rather than to proselytize, unlike several of his named contemporaries. It is this very reflexivity in so many aspects of his work that ultimately points to his normality. How strange it is that such an unusual, distinctive and massive star could be able to communicate his very ordinary, often confused humanity to a global audience. Therein lies one of so many points of identification with this remarkable figure.

Much of Prince's success as an artist is due to his perfectionist approach to recording and production. In Chapter 4 we considered the sonic processing of the recorded voice, and how it is staged as an object of desire. In this part of our study we found that that recording techniques not only accentuate musical accuracy, but also play a major role in determining empathy. Prince's voice can be interpreted as an idealized representation of an image that is virtual yet so real. We pointed to the virtual domain of the recording, where Prince's presence is felt through technological realization in a way that often evokes erotic desire. Our findings concluded that the fetishization of his produced voice was so explicit in Prince's songs that this served to foreground the gendered traits of his masculinity and femininity.

Prince's relationship with his female fans, and women in general, is particularly acute, and we devoted Chapter 5 to close scrutiny of the star in the context of gender identification. Whereas in other chapters, we have explored a range of different texts to illustrate various points, here we focused on just one in quite an unusual way for the study of popular music and cultural studies. We selected his feature film *Purple Rain* because it has been heavily criticized as sexist, and it is possible to see how those concerns arise on a formal level. But, reading the film both intertextually in light of Prince's overall relation to gender, and by employing female-centred models of identification espoused by Melanie Klein, a different possibility emerges. If nothing else, we argued that models of spectatorship other than dominant Freudian-Lacanian approaches can be useful in 'reading' popular cultural texts and explaining how this star ultimately might reflexively expose troubling aspects of patriarchal heteronormativity.

Throughout this book we have suggested the close correlation between issues of spectatorship and musical performance, and in Chapter 6 we focused on the range of instrumental techniques Prince employs to articulate notions of subjectivity. Consistently, we have pointed to the African American music tradition Prince emanates from that is moulded with styles such as white mainstream rock. We discussed how his style intersects with a range of performance and songwriting practices that are manifested in the format of standardized song form. Our music analysis also found that his improvisatory and jamming skills are integral to a compositional process that encapsulates the virtuosity of a unique pop style. Prince's virtuosity is about stylistic versatility and cross-over. At the end of the day, it is the intricacies of his profound musicianship that make him the pop icon he is.

As the authors of this book, our own richly rewarding and combined effort inspired a critical journey through Prince's unrivalled career and influence that began at London's 02 arena in September 2007. It seemed fitting to close this book with a rapturous and highly personal analysis of the live experience. We make no apology for slipping into personal conjecture towards the end of the chapter as it is clear from our own research and reading that much more work is needed to develop a critical vocabulary to describe the power and aura of live performance. There is a rich literature on performance that successfully and evocatively analyses the gestural and performative features from the stage, to which we are greatly indebted. It is works such as these and the array of interdisciplinary works on popular music to which we owe much gratitude for permitting this attempt at a serious examination of a cultural icon. Without these groundbreaking studies and their authors, there would be no place for this examination of the likes of Prince or so many other of his contemporaries.

But we are left with a gap in knowledge, a way to articulate, successfully and atmospherically, the moment of identification, that rare intersection between the star and the individual audience member at a given moment. In one of his final papers, 'Encore' (1972–73), Lacan tried to step outside the patriarchal parameters of language. He attempted to explain this by using the metaphor of romantic love as something that defies description in words. Lacan was trying to describe the indescribable, to find new words and concepts and in doing so he identified the margins of analysis and the slipperiness of its edges. We completed our readings of Prince with the example of speechless rapture experienced at a small after-show party, but instances of ecstasy such as this have occurred a million times for us as authors and fans at random moments, ranging from the first hearing of a new album or the first sight of a new promotional image. There is no doubt in our minds that we have countless more such moments ahead of us thanks to the phenomenon of Prince.

Selected Discography/Filmography

Albums

1999, Prince, Warner Bros. Records, 1982
20Ten, Prince, NPG Records, 2010
3121, Prince, Universal/NPG Records, 2006
Around the World in a Day, Prince and The Revolution, Warner Bros. Records, 1985
Black Album, Prince, Warner Bros. Records, 1994
Chaos and Disorder, Prince, Warner Bros. Records, 1996
Come, Prince, Warner Bros. Records, 1994
Control, Janet Jackson, A&M, 1986
Controversy, Prince, Warner Bros. Records, 1981
Crystal Ball, Prince, NPG Records, 1998
Diamonds and Pearls, Prince and the New Power Generation, Warner Bros. Records, 1991
Dirty Mind, Prince, Warner Bros. Records, 1980
Emancipation, Prince, NPG Records, 1996
For You, Prince, Warner Bros. Records, 1978
Girl 6, Prince, Warner Bros. Records, 1996
Graffiti Bridge, Prince, Paisley Park Records, 1990
Like a Prayer, Madonna, Sire/Warner Bros. Records, 1989
Love Symbol, Prince and the New Power Generation, Warner Bros. Records, 1992
Lovesexy, Prince, Warner Bros. Records, 1988
Musicology, Prince, Columbia/NPG Records, 2004
Night Moves, Bob Seger and the Silver Bullet Band, Capitol, 1976
Off the Wall, Michael Jackson, Epic, 1979
Once Upon a Time, Donna Summer, Casablanca, 1977
Parade, Prince and The Revolution, Warner Bros. Records, 1986
Planet Earth, Prince, Columbia/NPG Records, 2007
Prince, Prince, Warner Bros. Records, 1979
Purple Rain, Prince and The Revolution, Warner Bros. Records, 1984
RaveUn2 the Joy Fantastic, Prince, Arista/NPG Records, 1999
Sign o' the Times, Prince, Warner Bros. Records, 1987
The Hits 1, Prince, Paisley Park Records, 1993
The Hits/The B-Sides, Prince, Paisley Park Records, 1993

Tracks

'1999', *1999*, Prince, Warner Bros. Records, 1982
'7', *Love Symbol*, Prince and the New Power Generation, Warner Bros. Records, 1992
'3121', *3121*, Prince, Universal/NPG Records, 2006
'Act of God', *20Ten*, Prince, NPG Records, 2010
'All the Midnights in the World', *Planet Earth*, Prince, Columbia/NPG Records, 2007
'Anna Stesia', *Lovesexy*, Prince, Warner Bros. Records, 1988
'Annie Christian', *Controversy*, Prince, Warner Bros Records, 1981
'Automatic', *1999*, Prince, Warner Bros. Records, 1982
'Baby, I'm a Star', *Purple Rain*, Prince and The Revolution, Warner Bros. Records, 1984
'Bang a Gong (Get It On)', *Electric Warrior*, T. Rex, Reprise, 1971
'Beginning Endlessly', *20Ten*, Prince, NPG Records, 2010
'Chelsea Rodgers', *Planet Earth*, Prince, Columbia/NPG Records, 2007
'Controversy', *Controversy*, Prince, Warner Bros. Records, 1981
'Dirty Mind', *Dirty Mind*, Prince, Warner Bros. Records, 1980
'Earth Song', *HIStory: Past Present and Future, Book 1*, Michael Jackson, Epic, 1995
'Everybody Loves Me', *20Ten*, Prince, NPG Records, 2010
'Eye No', *Lovesexy*, Prince, Warner Bros. Records, 1988
'Face Down', *Emancipation*, Prince, NPG Records, 1996
'Future Soul Song', *20Ten*, Prince, NPG Records, 2010
'Gett Off', *Diamonds and Pearls*, Prince and the New Power Generation, Warner Bros. Records, 1991
'Guitar', *Planet Earth*, Prince, Columbia/NPG Records, 2007
'Human', *Crash*, The Human League, A&M, 1986
'I Wanna Be Your Lover', *Prince*, Prince, Warner Bros. Records, 1979
'If I Was Your Girlfriend', *Sign o' the Times*, Prince, Warner Bros. Records, 1987
'Jam of the Year', *Emancipation*, Prince, NPG Records, 1996
'Just Be Good to Me', *On The Rise*, SOS Band, Tabu, 1983
'Justify My Love', *The Immaculate Collection*, Madonna, Sire/Warner Bros. Records, 1990
'Kiss', *Parade*, Prince and The Revolution, Warner Bros. Records, 1986
'Lavaux', *20Ten*, Prince, NPG Records, 2010
'Let's Go Crazy', *Purple Rain*, Prince and The Revolution, Warner Bros. Records, 1984
'Lion of Judah', *Planet Earth*, Prince, Columbia/NPG Records, 2007
'Love Song', *Like a Prayer*, Madonna, Sire/Warner Bros. Records, 1989
'Manic Monday', *Different Light*, The Bangles, Columbia Records, 1986
'Material Girl', *Like a Virgin*, Madonna, Sire/Warner Bros. Records, 1984
'Mother Popcorn', *It's a Mother*, James Brown, King, 1969

'Mountains', *Parade*, Prince and The Revolution, Warner Bros. Records, 1986
'Mr Goodnight', *Planet Earth*, Prince, Columbia/NPG Records, 2007
'My Name Is Prince', *Love Symbol*, Prince and the New Power Generation, Warner Bros. Records, 1992
'Nothing Compares 2 U', *The Family*, The Family, Paisley Park Records, 1985
'Paisley Park', *Around the World in a Day*, Prince and The Revolution, Warner Bros. Records, 1985
'Partyup', *Dirty Mind*, Prince, Warner Bros. Records, 1980
'People Get Ready', *People Get Ready*, The Impressions, Paramount, Universal, MCA, Kent, 1965
'Pray', *Everything Changes*, Take That, BMG, 1993
'Purple Haze', *Are You Experienced*, The Jimi Hendrix Experience, Polydor, 1967
'Purple Rain', *Purple Rain*, Prince and The Revolution, Warner Bros. Records, 1984
'Raspberry Beret', *Around the World in a Day*, Prince and The Revolution, Warner Bros. Records, 1985
'Resolution', *Planet Earth*, Prince, Columbia/NPG Records, 2007
'Sea of Everything', *20Ten*, Prince, NPG Records, 2010
'Sex Shooter', *Apollonia 6*, Apollonia 6, Warner Bros. Records, 1984
'Sexy MF', *Love Symbol*, Prince and the New Power Generation, Warner Bros. Records, 1992
'Sgt. Pepper's Lonely Hearts Club Band', *Sgt. Pepper's Lonely Hearts Club Band*, The Beatles, Parlophone, Capitol, EMI, 1967
'Sign o' the Times', *Sign o' the Times*, Prince, Warner Bros. Records, 1987
'Slave', *Emancipation*, Prince, NPG Records, 1996
'Soft and Wet', *For You*, Prince, Warner Bros. Records, 1978
'Somewhere Here on Earth', *Planet Earth*, Prince, Columbia/NPG Records, 2007
'Sticky Like Glue', *20Ten*, Prince, NPG Records, 2010
'Take Me with You', *Purple Rain*, Prince and The Revolution, Warner Bros. Records, 1984
'The Cross', *Sign o' the Times*, Prince, Warner Bros. Records, 1987
'The Holy River', *Emancipation*, Prince, NPG Records, 1996
'The Ladder', *Around the World in a Day*, Prince and The Revolution, Warner Bros. Records, 1985
'The One U Wanna C', *Planet Earth*, Prince, Columbia/NPG Records, 2007
'Thieves in the Temple', *Graffiti Bridge*, Prince, Paisley Park Records, 1990
'Thunder', *Diamonds and Pearls*, Prince and the New Power Generation, Warner Bros. Records, 1991
'Tramp', *King and Queen*, Otis Redding and Carla Thomas, Stax/Atlantic Records, 1967
'U Got the Look', *Sign o' the Times*, Prince, Warner Bros. Records, 1987
'Ventura Highway', *Homecoming*, America, Warner Bros. Records, 1972
'When Doves Cry', *Purple Rain*, Prince and The Revolution, Warner Bros. Records, 1984
'Whole Lotta Love', *Led Zeppelin II*, Led Zeppelin, Atlantic Records, 1969

Films/Videos

A Nightmare on Elm Street (1984, dir. Wes Craven)
Cream (1991, dir. Rebecca Blake)
Godspell (1973, dir. David Greene)
Grease (1978, dir. Randal Kleiser)
Halloween (1978, dir. John Carpenter)
Jesus Christ Superstar (1973, dir. Norman Jewison)
Last House on the Left (1972, dir. Wes Craven)
Mutiny on the Bounty (1962, dir. Lewis Milestone)
Pretty Woman (1990, dir. Garry Marshall)
Privilege (1967, dir. Peter Watkins)
Purple Rain (1984, dir. Albert Magnoli)
Saturday Night Fever (1977, dir. John Badham)
Shanghai Surprise (1986, dir. Jim Goddard)
Sign o' the Times (1987, dir. Prince)
Stardust (1974, dir. Michael Apted)
Under the Cherry Moon (1986, dir. Prince)
Wall Street (1987, dir. Oliver Stone)

Bibliography

Ang, I. (1986), *Watching Dallas: Soap Opera and the Melodramatic Imagination* (London: Methuen).
Antonietti, A., Cocmazzi, D. and Iannello, P. (2009), 'Looking at the Audience Improves Musical Appreciation', *Journal of Nonverbal Behaviour*, 33/2 (June), pp. 89–106.
Auslander, Philip (1999) *Liveness: Performance in a Mediatized Culture* (London and New York: Routledge).
Auslander, Phillip (2009), 'Musical Persona: The Physical Performance of Popular Music' in Derek B. Scott, *The Ashgate Research Companion to Popular Musicology* (London: Ashgate), pp. 303–16.
Balaji, Murali (2009), 'Why Do Good Girls Have to Be Bad? The Cultural Industry's Production of the Other and the Complexities of Agency', *Popular Communication*, 7/4 (October), pp. 225–36.
Barthes, Roland (1975) *The Pleasure of the Text*. (New York: Hill and Wang).
Barthes, Roland (1977) 'The Rhetoric of the Image' in *Image-Music-Text* (London: Wm. Collins Sons and Co.), pp. 32–51.
Baudrillard, Jean (1994), *Simulacra and Simulation* (Ann Arbor, MI: University of Michigan Press).
Becker, Ernest (1997) *The Denial of Death* (London: Simon and Schuster).
Benjamin, Walter (1936), 'The Work of Art in the Age of Mechanical Reproduction' in *Illuminations* (1992) (London: Fontana), pp. 211–44.
Benvenuto, Bice and Kennedy, Roger (1986) *The Works of Jacques Lacan: An Introduction* (London: Free Association Books).
Berger, H.M. (1999), *Metal, Rock and Jazz: Perception and the Phenomenology of Musical Experience* (Hanover, CT: Wesleyan University Press).
Biddle, Ian (2009), 'Caught in the Silken Throat: Modernist Investments in the Male Vocal Flesh' in I. Biddle and K. Gibson (eds), *Masculinity and Western Musical Practice* (Farnham: Ashgate), pp. 259–77.
Biddle, Ian and Gibson, Kirsten (eds) (2009), *Masculinity and Western Musical Practice* (Farnham: Ashgate).
Booth, M. (1983), *Camp* (New York: Quartet).
Bordwell, David and Thompson, Kenneth (1997), *Film Art: An Introduction*, 5th edition (New York: McGraw-Hill).
Botting, Fred (1996) *Gothic* (London: Routledge).
Bourdieu, P. (1983), *Distinction: A Social Critique of the Judgment of Taste* (London: Routledge).

Brackett, David (2000), 'James Brown's "Superbad" and the Double-Voiced Utterance' in R. Middleton (ed.), *Reading Pop* (Oxford: Oxford University Press), pp. 122–40.
Brown, Geoff (1995), *The Complete Guide to the Music of Prince* (London: Omnibus Press).
Butler, Judith (1999), *Gender Trouble: Feminism and the Subversion of Identity* (New York and London: Routledge).
Camilleri, Lelio (2010), 'Shaping Sounds, Shaping Spaces', *Popular Music*, 29/2, pp. 199–211.
Carcieri, Matthew (2004), *Prince: A Life in Music* (New York: Universe).
Cashmore, Ellis (1997), *The Black Culture Industry* (London: Routledge).
Cleto, F. (ed.) (1999), *Camp: Queer Aesthetics and the Performing Subject: A Reader* (Detroit, MI: University of Michigan Press).
Clifford, James (1988), *The Predicament of Culture: Twentieth Century Ethnography, Literature, and Art* (Cambridge, MA: Harvard University Press).
Collins, Patricia Hill (2005), *Black Sexual Politics: African Americans, Gender, and the New Racism* (London: Routledge).
Croft, Michael J. (1994), *Market Segmentation: A Step-By-Step Guide to Profitable New Business* (London: Routledge).
Cubitt, Sean (2000), '"Maybellene": Meaning and the Listening Subject' in R. Middleton (ed.), *Reading Pop* (Oxford: Oxford University Press), pp. 141–59.
Danielsen, Anne (1998), 'His Name was Prince: A Study of *Diamonds and Pearls*', *Popular Music*, 16/3, pp. 275–91.
Danielsen, Anne (2006), *Presence and Pleasure: The Funk Grooves of James Brown and Parliament* (Middletown, CT: Wesleyan University Press).
Dawe, Kevin (2010), *The New Guitarscape in Critical Theory, Cultural Practice and Musical Performance* (Farnham: Ashgate).
Decker, Ernest (1997), *The Denial of Death* (London: Simon and Schuster).
Dick, Bernard F. (2002), *The Anatomy of Film* (New York and Boston: Bedford/St. Martin's).
Didron, M. and Millingston, E.J. (1851), *Christian Iconography* (London: John G. Bohn).
Drane, D. (2001), *Fashion and Its Social Agendas: Class, Gender and Identity in Clothing* (Chicago, IL: Chicago University Press).
Eidsheim, Nina (2008), *Voice as a Technology of Selfhood: Towards an Analysis of Racialized Timbre and Vocal Performance* (University of California, San Diego, PhD dissertation).
Ekman, P., Hager, J.C. and Friesen, W.V. (1981), 'The Symmetry of Emotional and Deliberate Actions', *Psychophysiology*, 18, pp. 101–6.
Evans, L. (1997), *Girls Will Be Boys: Women Report on Rock* (London: Pandora).
Fabbri, Franco (1982), 'A Theory of Musical Genres: Two Applications', D. Horn and P. Tagg (eds), *Popular Music Perspectives* (Göteborg and London: IASPM).
Fairclough, Norman (1995), *Media Discourse* (London: Hodder Education).

Fast, Susan (2001), *In the Houses of the Holy: Led Zeppelin and the Power of Rock Music* (New York: Oxford University Press).
Feigenbaum, A. (2005), '"Some Guy Designed This Room I'm Standing In": Marking Gender in Press Coverage of Ani DiFranco', *Popular Music*, 24, pp. 37–56.
Fenster, M. (2002), 'Consumers' Guide', in S. Jones (ed.), *Pop Music and the Press* (Philadelphia: Temple University Press) pp. 81–92.
Ferguson, George (1977), *Signs and Symbols in Christian Art* (New York: Oxford University Press).
Fitzgerald, Jon (2007), 'Black Pop Songwriting 1963–1966: An Analysis of U.S. Top Forty Hits by Cooke, Mayfield, Stevenson, Robinson, and Holland Dozier-Holland', *Black Music Research Journal*, 27/2 (Fall), pp. 97–140.
Foucault, Michel (1998), *The Will to Knowledge: The History of Sexuality Volume 1*, trans. R. Hurley (London: Penguin Books).
Frith, Simon (1983) *Sound Effects: Youth, Leisure, and the Politics of Rock 'n' Roll* (London: Constable).
Frith, Simon (1988), *Music for Pleasure* (Cambridge: Polity Press).
Frith, Simon (1996), *Performing Rites: Evaluating Popular Music* (Oxford: Oxford University Press).
Frith, Simon and McRobbie, A (1978) 'Rock and Sexuality' in *Screen Education*, 29, pp. 3–19.
Frith, Simon and McRobbie, A. (1990), 'Rock and Sexuality' in S. Frith and A. Goodwin (eds), *On Record: Rock Pop and the Written Word* (London: Routledge), pp. 317–32.
Geertz, Clifford (1973), *The Interpretation of Cultures* (New York: Basic Books).
Gilmour, Michael J. (ed.) (2005), *Call Me the Seeker: Listening to Religion and Popular Music* (London: Continuum).
Goodwin, Andrew (1988), 'Sample and Hold: Pop Music in the Digital Age of Reproduction', *Critical Quarterly*, 30/3, pp. 34–49.
Gracyck, Theodore (1996), *Rhythm and Noise: An Aesthetics of Rock* (London: I.B.Tauris).
Gramsci, A. (1971), *Selections from the Prison Notebooks of Antonio Gramsci* (London: Lawrence and Wishart).
Green, Adam (2007), 'Queer Theory and Sociology: Locating the Subject and the Self in Sexuality Studies', *Sociological Theory*, 25/1, pp. 26–45.
Grossberg, L. (1992), *We Gotta Get Out of This Place* (London: Routledge).
Hall, Manly P. (1952) *The Secret Teachings of All Ages*. (Los Angeles: The Philosophical Research Society, Inc.).
Hall, Stuart (1992), 'What Is This "Black" in Black Popular Culture?' in Gina Dent (ed.), *Black Popular Culture* (Seattle, WA: Bay Press), pp. 21–33.
Hall, S. and Jefferson, T. (eds) (1976), *Resistance through Rituals: Youth Subcultures in Post-War Britain* (London: Hutchinson in association with the Centre for Contemporary Cultural Studies, University of Birmingham).
Halloran, J.D. (ed.) (1970), *The Effects of Television* (London: Panther Books).

Harper, Phillip Brian (1989), 'Synesthesia, "Crossover," and Blacks in Popular Music', *Social Text*, 23 (Autumn–Winter), pp. 102–21.
Hawkins, Stan (1992a), 'Prince: Harmonic Analysis of "Anna Stesia"', *Popular Music*, 11/3, pp. 325–36.
Hawkins, Stan (1992b), 'Stylistic Diversification in Prince of the Nineties: An Analysis of "Diamonds and Pearls"', *Skriftserie*, 4 (Oslo: Institutt for musikkvitenskap og teater).
Hawkins, Stan (1997), '"I'll Never Be an Angel": Stories of Deception in Madonna's Music', *Critical Musicology Journal* (Leeds), [online] available at: http://www.leeds.ac.uk/music/Info/critmus/ [accessed: 5 August 2010].
Hawkins, Stan (2000), 'Prince: Harmonic Analysis of 'Anna Stesia' in *Reading Pop: Approaches to Textual Analysis in Popular Music*, ed. R. Middleton (Oxford: Oxford University Press), pp. 58–70.
Hawkins, Stan (2002), *Settling the Pop Score: Pop Texts and Identity Politics* (Aldershot: Ashgate).
Hawkins, Stan (2004), 'Dragging out Camp: Narrative Agendas in Madonna's Musical production' in S. Fouz-Hernández and F. Jarman-Ivens (eds), *Madonna's Drowned Worlds* (Aldershot: Ashgate), pp. 3–21.
Hawkins, Stan (2007a), 'Aphex Twin: Monstrous Hermaphrodites, Madness and the Strain of Independent Dance Music' in J. Richardson and S. Hawkins (eds), *Essays on Sound and Vision* (Helsinki: Helsinki University Press), pp. 27–53.
Hawkins, Stan (2007b), '[Un]Justified: Gestures of Straight-Talk in Justin Timberlake's Dongs' in F. Jarman-Ivens, *Oh Boy! Masculinities and Popular Music* (London: Routledge), pp. 197–212.
Hawkins, Stan (2009a), *The British Pop Dandy: Masculinity, Popular Music and Culture* (Farnham: Ashgate).
Hawkins, Stan (2009b), '"Chelsea Rodgers" was a Model: Vocality in Prince of the Twenty-first Century' in D. Scott (ed.), *The Ashgate Research Companion to Popular Musicology* (Farnham: Ashgate), pp. 335–48.
Hawkins, Stan (ed.) (2011), *Pop Music and Easy Listening: The Library of Essays on Popular Music* (Farnham: Ashgate).
Hennion, Antoine (1983), 'An Anti-Musicology of the Pop Song', *Popular Music*, 3, Producers and Markets, pp. 159–93.
Heylin, C. (2003), *Bob Dylan: Behind the Shades Revisited* (London: HarperCollins).
Hill, D. (1989), *Prince: A Pop Life* (London: Faber and Faber).
Hoggart, Richard (1958), *The Uses of Literacy: Aspects of Working-Class Life with Special Reference to Publications and Entertainments* (Harmondsworth: Penguin).
hooks, bell (1992), *Black Looks: Race and Representation* (London: South End Press).
hooks, bell (2004), *We Real Cool: Black Men and Masculinity* (London: Routledge).
Hoskyns, Barney (1988), *Prince: Imp of the Perverse* (London: Virgin).
Jancovich, Mark (1992), *Horror* (London: Batsford).

Johnson, Mark (1987), *The Body in the Mind: The Bodily Basis of Meaning, Imagination and Reason* (Chicago, IL: University of Chicago Press).
Jones, Liz (1997), *Slave to the Rhythm* (London: Little Brown).
Jones, Steve (2002), *Popular Music and the Press* (Philadelphia, PA: Temple University Press).
Kant, Immanuel (1965), *Observations on the Feeling of the Beautiful and Sublime* (Berkeley and Los Angeles, CA: University of California Press).
Kaplan, E.A. (1987), *Rocking around the Clock: Music Television, Postmodernism and Consumer Culture* (London: Methuen).
Karlen, Neal (1985), 'Prince Talks', *Rolling Stone* (Spring).
Kellner, Douglas (1995), *Media Culture: Cultural Studies, Identity and Politics between the Modern and the Postmodern* (London and New York: Routledge).
Kress, Gunter and Van Leeuwen, Theo (1996), *Reading Images: The Grammar of Visual Design* (London: Routledge).
Kress, Gunter and Van Leeuwen, Theo (2001), *Multimodal Discourse: The Modes and Media of Contemporary Communication* (London: Hodder Education).
Kurosawa, K. and Davidson, J.W. (2005), 'Non-verbal Interaction in Popular Performance: The Corrs', *Musicae Scientiae*, 9/1, pp. 111–36.
Lacan, Jacques (1972–3) '*The Seminar XX, Encore: On Feminine Sexuality, the Limits of Love and Knowledge,*' ed. by Jacques-Alain Miller, transl. by Bruce Fink, (1998) (New York: W.W. Norton & Co.).
Lacan, Jacques (1977), *The Four Fundamental Concepts of Psychoanalysis* (London: Hogarth Press and the Institute of Psychoanalysis).
Lacasse, Serge (2000), 'Intertextuality and Hypertextuality in Recorded Popular Music' in M. Talbot (ed.), *The Musical Work: Reality or Invention* (Liverpool: Liverpool University Press), pp. 35–58.
Laing, Dave (1991). 'A Voice without a Face: Popular Music and the Phonograph in the 1890s', *Popular Music*, 10(1), pp. 1–9.
Laing, D. (2006), 'Anglo-American Music Journalism: Texts and Contexts', in A. Bennett, B. Shank and J. Toynbee (eds), *The Popular Music Studies Reader* (London: Routledge), pp. 333–9.
Laver, J. (1968), *Dandies* (London: Weidenfield and Nicolson).
Leavis, F.R. (1930), *Mass Civilisation and Minority Culture* (London: Minority Press).
Leonard, M. (2007), *Gender in the Music Industry: Rock, Discourse and Girl Power* (London: Ashgate).
Leppert, R. (1993), *The Sight of Sound: Music, Representation, and the History of the Body* (Berkeley, CA: University of California Press).
Lewis, Jon (1985), 'Purple Rain', *Jump Cut*, 30 (March), pp. 1, 22, 43.
Lobert, Anja (2008), 'Cliff Richard's Self-presentation as a Redeemer', *Popular Music*, 27/1, pp. 77–97.
Lyotard, Jean-Francois (1994), *Lessons on the Analytic of the Sublime, trans. Elizabeth Rottenberg* (Stanford, CA: Stanford University Press).

McClary, Susan (1989), 'Terminal Prestige: The Case of Avant-Garde Music Composition', *Cultural Critique* 12, pp. 57–81.
McClary, Susn (1991), *Feminine Endings: Music, Gender, and Sexuality* (Minneapolis: University of Minnesota Press).
McClary, Susan (2000), *Conventional Wisdom: The Content of Musical Form* (London: University of California Press).
McLeod, Kembrew (2001) '*1/2: A critique of rock criticism in North America' *Popular Music* (2001) Volume 20/1. pp. 47–60.
McDowell, Colin (1997), *The Man of Fashion: Peacock Males and Perfect Gentlemen* (London: Thames and Hudson).
McGuigan, J. (1992), *Cultural Populism* (London: Routledge).
McLeod, K. (2002), 'Between Rock and a Hard Place: Gender and Rock Criticism' in S. Jones (ed.), *Pop Music and the Press* (Philadelphia, PA: Temple University Press), pp. 93–113.
McRobbie, A. and Garber, J. (1991), 'Girls and Subcultures' in K. Gelder (ed.) (1997) *The Subcultures Reader* (New York: Routledge), pp. 112–20.
Machin, David (2010), *Analysing Popular Music: Image, Sound and Text* (London: Sage).
Maultsby, Portia (2009), 'Dayton Street Funk: The Layering of Multiple Identities' in D. Scott (ed.), *The Ashgate Research Companion to Popular Musicology* (Farnham: Ashgate), pp. 259–82.
Middleton, Richard (1990), *Studying Popular Music* (Milton Keynes: Open University Press).
Middleton, Richard (2006), *Voicing the Popular: On the Subjects of Popular Music* (London: Routledge).
Mitchell, Juliet (ed.) (1986), *The Selected Melanie Klein* (London: Penguin).
Mitchell, Juliet and Rose, Jacqueline (eds) (1985), *Feminine Sexuality: Jacques Lacan and the école freudienne* (London and New York: W.W. Norton).
Modleski, T. (1982), *Loving with a Vengeance: Mass Produced Fantasies for Women* (London and New York: Methuen).
Moore, Allan F. (2001), Rock: The Primary Text – Developing a Musicology of Rock (Aldershot: Ashgate).
Moore, Allan F. (2002), 'Authenticity as Authentication', *Popular Music*, 21/2, pp. 209–23.
Moore, Suzanne (1988), 'Getting a Bit of the Other: The Pimps of Postmodernism' in R. Chapman and J. Rutherford (eds), *Male Order: Unwrapping Masculinity* (London: Lawrence and Wishart), pp. 165–92.
Mowitt, J. (1987), 'The Sound of Music in the Era of Its Electronic Reproduction' in R. Leppert and S. McClary (ed.), *Music and Society: The Politics of Composition, Performance and Reception* (Cambridge: Cambridge University Press), pp. 173–97.
Mulvey, L. (1975), 'Visual Pleasure and Narrative Cinema', *Screen*, 16/3 (Autumn), pp. 6–18.

Neal, Mark Anthony (1999), *What the Music Said: Black Popular Culture and Black Public Culture* (New York: Routledge).
Negus, Keith (1996) *Popular Music Theory* (Cambridge: Polity Press).
Negus, Keith (1997), 'Sinead O'Connor: Musical Mother' in S. Whiteley (ed.), *Sexing the Groove* (London: Routledge), pp. 178–90.
Niblock, Sarah (2005), 'Prince: Negotiating the Meanings of Femininity in the Mid-1980s' (PhD diss., Middlesex University).
Niedderer, Kristina (2007), 'Mapping the Meaning of Experiential Knowledge in Research', *Design Research Quarterly*, 2/2, pp. 1 and 5–13.
Nilsen, Per (1999) *DanceMusicSexRomance: Prince: The First Decade* (London: Omnibus Press).
O'Brien, L. (1995), *She Bop: The Definitive History of Women in Rock, Pop and Soul* (Harmondsworth: Penguin).
Paulik, Laurie (1998) 'Twang is Not a Colour: Where are African-Americans in Today's Country Music?' http://www.carlray.com/twang.htm (accessed June 27, 2011).
Paytress, Mark (2003), *Siouxie and the Banshees: The Authorised Biography* (London: Sanctuary).
Perone, James E. (2008), *The Words and Music of Prince* (Westport, CT: Praeger).
Polanyi, Michael (1967), *The Tacit Dimension* (London: Routledge and Kegan Paul).
Radano, Ronald and Bohlman, Philip (eds) (2000), *Music and the Racial Imagination* (Chicago, IL: University of Chicago Press).
Radway, J. (1987), *Reading the Romance: Women, Patriarchy and Popular Literature* (London: Verso).
Rank, Otto (1929), *The Trauma of Birth* (repr. London: Routledge, 1999).
Redhead, S. (ed.) (1993), *Rave Off: Politics and Deviance in Contemporary Youth Culture* (Aldershot: Avebury).
Reed, Teresa L. (2003), *The Holy Profane: Religion in Black Popular Music* (Lexington, KY: The University Press of Kentucky).
Riviere, Joan (1929), 'Womanliness as a Masquerade', International Journal of Psycho-Analysis, 10, pp. 303–13.
Robertson, Pamela (1996) *Guilty Pleasures* (Durham, NC: Duke University Press).
Rojek, Chris (2007), 'Celebrity and Religion' in Sean Redmond and Su Holmes (eds), *Stardom and Celebrity: A Reader* (London: Sage), pp. 171–80.
Rose, Jacqueline (1996), *Sexuality in the Field of Vision* (London: Verso).
Ross, Andrew (1989), 'Uses of Camp' in Andrew Ross (ed.), *No Respect: Intellectuals and Popular Culture* (New York: Routledge), pp. 135–70.
Sadler, M. (1931), *Bulwer: A Panorama* (London: Constable).
Savage, J. (1997), *Time Travel: From the Sex Pistols to Nirvana; Pop, Media and Sexuality* (London: Vintage).
Schwichtenberg, Cathy (1993), 'Madonna's Postmodern Feminism: Bringing Margins to the Center' in *The Madonna Connection: Representational Politics,*

Subcultural Identities, and Cultural Theory (Boulder, CO: Westview Press), pp. 129–45.
Scott, Derek (2003), *From the Erotic to the Demonic: On Critical Musicology* (Oxford: Oxford University Press).
Scott, Derek (2009), 'Introduction' in D. Scott (ed.), *The Ashgate Research Companion to Popular Musicology* (Farnham: Ashgate), pp. 1–21.
Scott, Derek (ed.) (2009), *The Ashgate Research Companion to Popular Musicology* (Farnham: Ashgate).
Segal, Hannah (1955), 'Notes on Symbol Formation' in E. Bott Spillius (ed.) (1988), *Melanie Klein Today, Volume 1: Mainly Theory. Developments in Theory and Practice* (London: Routledge), pp. 156–73.
Shank, B. (1994), *Dissononant Identities: Rock 'n' Roll Scene in Austin, Texas* (Hanover, CT: Wesleyan University Press).
Shaw, Arnold (1986) *Black Popular Music in America: From The Spirituals, Minstrels And Ragtime To Soul, Disco And Hip-Hop* (New York: Macmillan).
Shuker, Roy (1994), *Understanding Popular Music*, 1st edition (London: Routledge).
Shuker, Roy (2008), *Understanding Popular Music*, 3rd edition (London: Routledge).
Sinclair, Iain (1997), *Lights Out for the Territory: Nine Excursions in the Secret History of London* (London: Granta).
Small, Christopher (1998), *Musicking: The Meanings of Performing and Listening* (Hanover, CT: Wesleyan University Press).
Sontag, Susan (1964), 'Notes on Camp' in Susan Sontag (2009), *Against Interpretation and Other Essays* (London: Penguin), pp. 275–92.
Southern, E. (1997), *The Music of Black Americans: A History* (London: W.W. Norton).
Stacey, Jackie (1994), *Stargazing: Hollywood Cinema and Female Spectatorship* (London: Routledge).
Steven, Peter (1980), 'Saturday Night Fever: Just Dancing', *Jump Cut*, 23 (October), pp. 13–16.
Stewart, Earl L. (1998), *African American Music: An Introduction*, 3rd edition (London: Wadsworth).
Strinati, D. (1995), *An Introduction to Theories of Popular Culture* (London: Routledge).
Stuart, Andrea (1990), 'Feminism: Dead or Alive' in Jonathan Rutherford (ed.), *Identity: Community, Culture, Difference* (London: Lawrence and Wishart), pp. 28–42.
Sullivan, Mark (1987), ''More Popular Than Jesus'': The Beatles and the Religious Far Right', *Popular Music*, 6/3, pp. 313–26.
Tagg, Philip (1989). Open letter: Black music, Afro-American and European music. *Popular Music*, 8/3: 285–298.
Taylor, Timothy D. (1997), *Global Pop: World Music, World Markets* (London: Routledge).

Théberge, Paul (1997), *Any Sound You Can Imagine: Making Music/Consuming Technology* (Hanover, CT: Wesleyan University Press).
Thornton, S. (1995), *Club Cultures: Music, Media and Subcultural Capital* (London: Polity).
Tomlinson, Gary (1992), 'Cultural Dialogics and Jazz: A White Historian Signifies' in K. Bergeron and P.V. Bohlman (eds), *Disciplining Music: Musicology and Its Canons* (London: University of Chicago Press), pp. 64–94.
Toynbee, Jason (2000), *Making Popular Music: Musician, Aesthetics and the Manufacture of Popular Music* (London: Hodder).
Toynbee, Jason (2007), *Bob Marley: Herald of the Postcolonial World* (London: Polity).
Vincent, Rickey (1996), *Funk: The Music, the People, and the Rhythm of the One* (New York: St. Martin's Griffin).
Waksman, Steve (2001), *Instruments of Desire: The Electric Guitar and the Shaping of Musical Experience* (Cambridge, Mass.: Harvard University Press).
Walden, George and Barbey, Jules (2002) *Who's a Dandy: Dandyism and George Brummell* (London: Gibson Square Books).
Walser, Robert (1993), *Running with the Devil: Power, Gender and Madness in Heavy Metal Music* (Hanover, NH: Wesleyan University Press).
Walser, Robert (1994), 'Prince as Queer Poststructuralist', *Popular Music and Society*, 18/2, pp. 79–89.
Warner, Timothy (2003), *Pop Music – Technology and Creativity: Trevor Horn and the Digital Revolution* (Aldershot: Ashgate).
Weber, Max (1947), *The Theory of Social and Economic Organisation* (London, Edinburgh and Glasgow: William Hodge).
Wicke, Peter (2009), 'The Art of Phonography: Sound, Technology and Music' in D. Scott (ed.), *The Ashgate Research Companion to Popular Musicology* (Farnham: Ashgate), pp. 147–168.
Wilmer, Val (1989), *Mama Said There'd Be Days Like This: My Life in the Jazz World* (London: Routledge).
Winship, J. (1986), *Inside Women's Magazines* (London: Pandora).
Zagorski-Thomas, Simon (2010), 'The Stadium in Your Bedroom: Functional Staging, Authenticity and the Audience-Led Aesthetic in Record Production', *Popular Music*, 29/2, pp. 251–66.

Index

References to music examples are in **bold**

Abba, 'The Visitors' 83
albums
   20Ten 33
   1999 45, 86
   Around the World in a Day 7, 49, 63, 83
   The Black Album 66, 157
   Chaos and Disorder 31
   Come, cover art 69
   Controversy 45, 55
   Crystal Ball 32
   Diamonds and Pearls 23, 31, 56, 64
   Dirty Mind 5, 20, 25, 66, 67
   Emancipation 8, 31, 56
   For You 20, 39, 40, 68, 82
   Girl 6: 31
   Graffiti Bridge 131
   The Hits I 134
   Love Symbol 31, 134, 138
   LoveSexy 56, 63, 66
   Musicology 32
   Prince 20, 39
   Purple Rain 11, 15, 45, 54
   Sign o' the Times 66, 68, 69, 127
   see also *Planet Earth*
America, 'Ventura Highway' 78
Anderson, Andre 25
Apted, Michael, *Stardust* 99
Arkestra 58
audio technology 7–8
aura, Benjamin on 153
Auslander, Philip 153, 161
authenticity
   acoustic guitar 20
   as commodity 17
   concept 15–16, 32
   and live performance 153, 154
   Moore on 17
   and music 22

Prince 16, 17, 19, 33
   and rock criticism 165

Baker, Susan 66
Balaji, Murali 37
Bangles, 'Manic Monday' 163
Barthes, Roland 27, 70
Bassey, Shirley 49
Baudelaire, Charles 45
Baudrillard, Jean 17
Beatles, 'Norwegian Wood' 83
Benjamin, Walter 171, 172
   on aura 153
Berger, H.M. 161
Biddle, Ian 86
Blind Lemon Jefferson 56, 57
Blinn, William 98
blues, origins 56–7
Bohlman, Philip 19
Bolan, Mark 23, 24
   see also T. Rex
bootlegging 157
Bordwell, David 102
Bowie, David 23, 42, 53
Boy George 48, 51
Brackett, David 80
Brown, James 160
   'Mother Popcorn' 31
Brummell, 'Beau' (George) 45
Butler, Judith, *Gender Trouble* 28

Camilleri, Lelio 124
campness 48–9
   see also dandyism
Carcieri, Matthew 82
Civil Rights Movement 58
Cleto, Fabio 48
Clifford, James 67
Clinton, George 42, 58
Cocker, Jarvis 71

Collins, Joan 49
commodification 37
   of authenticity 17
concerts
   21 Nights residency *see* O2 concerts
   One Nite Alone in Europe concerts (2002) 165
      reviews 168–70
   Parade shows, Wembley Arena (1986) 165
      reviews 166–8
Cooke, Sam 57
country music, black artists 37–8
Cubitt, Sean 75

dance music, black 58–9
dandyism 45
   Prince 11, 24, 26, 43–4, 46, 53, 173
   see also campness
Danielsen, Anne 58–9, 87, 162
Davis, Miles 132
   jazz-rock fusion 4
Dawe, Kevin 126
discography 175
Duran Duran 25
Dylan, Bob 58

Earth, Wind and Fire 40, 58, 90
Easton, Sheena 30, 97, 127
Ed Sullivan Show 39
Eidsheim, Nina 136
Empire, Kitty 168–9, 170
Essex, David 99
ethos, meaning 59–60
Evans, Liz 170

Fabbri, Franco 149
Fairclough, Norman 36
faith
   Prince 11, 55–6, 67
   and sexuality 59
Feigenbaum, A. 165, 170
female spectator 96
   Purple Rain film 100, 107
female subjectivity 101
femininity, self-fashioning 51
feminism 23
Fenster, Mark 165

films
   list 175, 178
   Under the Cherry Moon 56, 70–71, 122
   see also Purple Rain
Foucault, Michel, *History of Sexuality* 73
Frankie Goes to Hollywood 48
Franklin, Aretha 58
Frith, Simon 2, 26, 40, 51, 157–8, 161, 165
funk music 4–5, 58

Gaines, Rosie 24
Galliano, John 95
Garcia, Mayte 64
Gaye, Marvin 39, 57
gaze, Lacan's theory 100, 101
Geertz, Clifford 59–60
George, Nelson 38
Gordy, Berry 38
Gore, Tipper 66
Gracyk, Theodore 154
Graham Central Station 142
Graham, Larry 141
   Graham Central Station 2000 61
Grateful Dead, 'Dark Star' 83
Green, Adam 29
Greene, David, *Godspell* 99
Grossberg, Lawrence 18
guitar, electric, influence 126
guitar playing
   Hendrix 125–6
   Prince 123–4, 127, 128
   'Purple Haze' 78, 81
   'U Got the Look' 128
guitarscape concept, and the body 126
Gundersen, Edna 73

Hall, Manly P. 60
Hall, Stuart 40
Halloran, James D. 21
Harper, Phillip Brian 38, 39
Hawks, Howard, *His Girl Friday* 24
Hendrix, Jimi
   guitar playing 125–6
   'Purple Haze' 78, 81
Heylin, Clinton 157
Hill, Dave 26, 97
hooks, bell 9
hyperreality 17

identity
    construction of 22
    masculine, Prince 32–3, 35
ideology, meaning 60

Jackson, Janet
    Control 30
    'Someone to Call My Lover' 78
Jackson, Michael 5, 9, 25, 39, 40, 56, 73, 119
    'Earth Song' 68, 71
    Off The Wall 39–40
Jagger, Mick 42
Jam, Jimmy 30
jazz, canonization 4
jazz-rock fusion, Davis 4
Jehovah's Witness
    beliefs 61
    Prince 55, 61, 159
Jewison, Norman, *Jesus Christ Superstar* 99
Joan Collins Fan Club, The 48
Johnson, Mark 40
Johnson, Robert 38, 56
Johnson, Shelby 148
Jonas Brothers 73
Jones, Liz 170
Jones, Paul 99
Jones, Steve 30
Joplin, Scott 41
jouissance 112

Kaplan, E. Ann 50
Klein, Melanie 12, 95
    analysis, application problems 121–2
    child, identification with mother 104
    depressive position 101, 102
    external reality 102
    female subjectivity 101
    mother object 101
    Oedipus conflict 115
    paranoid-schizoid position 102–3
    and the spectator 103, 174
    see also under Purple Rain (film)
Kleiser, Randal, *Grease* 99
knowledge, tacit 152
Kwei-Armah, Kwame 170

Lacan, Jacques 46, 112, 174
    theory of

castration complex 114
    the gaze 100, 101
Lacasse, Serge 133–4
lace, signification 46
Lady Gaga 161
Laver, J. 45
Leavis, F.R. 21
Led Zeppelin, 'Whole Lotta Love' 15, 169
Lennon, John 55
Lennox, Annie 51
Leonard, Marion 155, 161
Leppert, Richard, *The Sight of Sound* 158
Lewis, Jon 96, 97, 110, 111
Lewis, Terry 30
LinnDrum machine 88
    '1999' 90
Little Richard 42
live performance
    and authenticity 153, 154
    prerequisites 154–5
    Prince 151–2, 153
Lobert, Anja 68, 69, 71

Macaronis 46
McClary, Susan 42, 132
McCormick, Neil 170
McDowell, Colin 47
    The Man of Fashion 46
Machin, David 36
McLeod, Kembrew 165
McRobbie, Angela 26
Madonna 22
    creative control 29
    gender disruption 28
    'Justify My Love' 28–9
    Like a Prayer 28
    Prince, comparison 28–9
    Sex (book) 28
    Shanghai Surprise (film) 70
Magnoli, Albert 98
Malcolm X 9
Marilyn 51
market segmentation 38
Marley, Bob 59
Martin, Gavin 166, 168
masculinity
    black 9
    and musical conventions 42

Prince 32–3, 35
Maultsby, Portia 4–5
Mayfield, Curtis 58
message songs 58
Middleton, Richard 19
Minneapolis Sound 83
　elements 5, 30
Minnelli, Liza 26, 49
mixolydian mode, songs 83, 139
Moon, Christopher 82
Moore, Allan 20, 77
　on authenticity 17
Mosley, Tony 31
Mötley Crüe 50
Motown 38
MTV 5, 42, 172
Mulvey, Laura 26
music
　and authenticity 22
　and the body 158
　critical discourse analysis 36
　and subjectivity 8
music criticism 149
　see also rock criticism

Negus, Keith 37
'New Power Generation' 19, 25, 31, 134, 148
New Romantic movement 22, 44
New York Dolls 23
Niedderer, Kristina 152

O2 arena 155
　entrance security 156–7
O2 concerts (*21 Nights* residency) 1, 13, 151, 170–72
　after-show performances 154, 171–2
　crowd participation 161–2
　dancing 164
　fan responses 165, 170–71
　'feel good' factor 162
　reviews 170
　solo performance 160–61
　staging 157
Other, gaze of 24
Otherness
　musical fashioning 52–3
　Prince 35, 40, 47

Paisley Park 7, 30
　Records 83
Palmer, Robert, 'Addicted to Love' 24
Parents Resource Music Center 55
　anti-Prince criticism 66
Paris Fashion Week 95
Paulik, Laurie 37, 38
Paytress, Mark 29
Pendergrass, Teddy 39
performance
　affect displays 159, 160
　facial expressions 159
　gestures 158–9, 174
　and recording, blurring 36
performativity, Prince 35, 151, 157
Perone, James E. 23, 140
Perry, Katy 95
persona production, and recording studio 2
Pet Shop Boys 48, 49
phallus, the, and female identity 114
Planet Earth 33, 140–48
　aesthetic 144
　bass lines 141–2, **143**
　figures and riffs 145, **146–7**, 150
　jamming 145
　layering 144
　reception 148–9
　spatialization 144
　tightness 147–8
pleasure principle 20–22
　in cultural studies 21
Polanyi, Michael 152
pop, rock, distinction 18
pop score 6
power-dressing 45
Presley, Elvis, 1968 comeback special 161
Prince
　album covers 39–40
　　see also albums
　ambiguity 18, 19, 22
　androgyny 96fn2
　artist collaborators 30
　asexuality 73
　auteurship 16
　authenticity 16, 17, 19, 33
　black church roots 9
　brand 30–32
　celibacy, declaration of 73

charisma 61–2
compression, use of 132–3, 150
control 83, 130
crucifixion pose 67–8
as dandy 11, 24, 26, 43–4, 46, 53, 173
early life 18
earnings 30
ethnicity 9, 20, 37
faith 11, 55–6, 67
and female fans 26–7, 95, 173
and the feminine 12, 95
gating, use of 132, 150
gender role 2, 5–6, 26
glam rock persona 23–4
guitar playing 123–4, 127, 128
halo effect 68–9
heterosexuality, destabilizing of 41–2
humour 3
image creation 39, 67–73
incorruptible body 71–2
influences on 166
irony 3
jamming 8, 91, 145, 174
Jehovah's Witness 55, 61, 159
Madonna, comparison 28–9
masculine identity 32–3, 35
mission 67
music industry, attitude to 16–17
musical
    rhetoric 149
    spirituality 62–4
    sublimity 78–9, 93
musicians, referencing of 166
musicianship 4
name change 69
Otherness 35, 40, 47
Parents Resource Music Center,
    criticism by 66
performance
    audience participation 159–60
    live 151–2, 153
performativity 35, 151
physical stature 20
queerness 47–8, 54
on Rolling Stones tour 25, 38
sexual/spiritual blending 55, 173
songwriting 124–5
superhuman elevation 69–71
tabloid images 27
technology, engagement with 130, 149–50
tracks, list 176–7
    see also tracks
uniqueness 2–3
visual signification 25–6
vocal
    style 6, 11–12, 75–6, 89, 93, 94, 173
    timbre 136, 137–8
    zoot suit style 47
producer, power of 5
purple, connotations 78
Purple Rain (film) 12, 15, 19, 28, 70
    cinematic genres 99
    dancing 118–19
    depressive position 110, 118–20
    domestic violence 108
    and female spectator 100, 107
    gender disruption 103, 105, 111, 120
    Gothic genre 100
    identity issues 111, 119–20
    Kleinian reading of 103–22, 174
    misogyny 103–4, 110
    monstrous in 121
    objects in conscious/unconscious 107
    paranoid-schizoid position 103, 104, 106, 109
    portrayal of women 96–7
    projective identification 113–14
    'Purple Rain' 118
    rite of passage 99
    story 97, 98
    subjectivity 98, 118, 119

Quatro, Suzi 161

Radano, Ronald 19
recording, and performance, blurring 36
recording studio, and persona production 2
Redding, Otis 57
    and Carla Thomas, 'Tramp' 135
Reed, Teresa L. 56, 57
religion, in black popular music 56
Richard, Cliff 56, 67, 69, 71–2, 73, 160
rock, pop, distinction 18
rock criticism
    and authenticity 165
    gendered language 165, 170

Rolling Stones, 'Satisfaction' 83
Rose, Jacqueline 111–12, 114
Ross, Andrew, 'Uses of Camp' 49
Ross, Diana 39
Rotten, Johnny 29

Sadler, Michael, *Bulwer: A Panorama* 45–6
Saturday Night Fever 68
Savage, Jon 22
Scott, Derek 82
Segal, Hannah, symbol substitution 110
Seger, Bob, 'Night Moves' 78
Seventh Day Adventists 60–61
sexuality, and faith 59
Shaw, Arnold 38
Shuker, Roy 18
sincerity 164–5
Sinclair, David 169
Sinclair, Iain, *Lights Out for the Territory* 156
singles *see* tracks
Siouxie Sioux 29
Sly and the Family Stone 61, 141, 142
   see also Stone, Sly
Small, Christopher 89
Smash Hits 25
songs
   message 58
   mixolydian mode 83, 139
songwriting, process 76
Sontag, Susan 48
Springfield, Dusty 49
Springsteen, Bruce 44
Stacey, Jackie 51
Staple Singers 58
Staples, Mavis 30, 49, 97
Steven, Peter 99
Stone, Oliver, *Wall Street* 45
Stone, Sly 119
   see also Sly and the Family Stone
Stubbes, Philip 46
subjectivity
   female 101
   and music 8
Sullivan, Mark 65–6
Summer, Donna, *Once Upon a Time* 39
Sun Ra 58
Supremes, The 39

Sweeting, Adam 166

T. Rex, 'Bang a Gong (Get It On)' 23
   see also Bolan, Mark
Take That, 'Pray' 68
Théberge, Paul 35, 130
Thompson, Kenneth 102
Tomlinson, Gary 4
Toynbee, Jason 155
Toynbee, Jayson 59
tracks
   '7' 134–5
      a capella 135
      aesthetic 138–9
      chord structure 139
      chorus 135, **135**
      formal structure 137
      harmony 139, 140
      lyrical articulation **140**
      mixolydian mode 139, 140
      pause, use of 136
      Queen reference 140
      'Tramp' bass line **135**
      vocal timbre 137–8
   '1999'
      analysis 162–3
      'feel good' factor 162
      four-chord riff 90, **91**
      gaps 163
      groove 163
      instruments 90
      jamming 91
      LinnDrum use 90
      'party' groove 91–2, **92**
      themes 89–90
      vocal style 92–3
      vocals 91
   '3121': 73
   'Act of God' 33
   'All the Midnights in the World' 142
   'Anna Stesia' 56, 63–4
   'Automatic' 86
   'Baby, I'm a Star' 119
   'Beginning Endlessly' 33
   'Chelsea Rodgers' 142, 147–8
   'Computer Blue' 116
   'Cream' 23–5
   'Darling Nikki' 66, 116

INDEX

'Dead On It' 66
'Everybody Loves Me' 33
'Eye No' 66
'Face Down' 32
'Future Soul Song' 33
'God' 62–3
'Guitar' 142, 148
'I Would Die for You' 118
'Jam of the Year' 8
'Kiss' 28, 167
    Hendrix reference 78
'Lavaux' 33
'Letitgo' 69
'Let's Go Crazy' 99, 105
'Lion of Judah' 142
'Love Song' 28
'Mountains' 71
'Mr Goodnight' 142
'My Name is Prince' 31
'Nothing Compares 2 U' 169
'Paisley Park' 7
'PFUnk' 148
'Planet Earth' 142
    Earth, Wind and Fire reference 145
'Purple Rain' 62
    guitar solo 81, 82
    harmony 79
    melodic hook 79–80, **80**
    musical references 78
    performativity 80–81
    in *Purple Rain* film 118
    speech forms **79**
    structure 77–8
'Raspberry Beret' 49
    harmonic shifts 83–4
    mixolydian mode 83
    non-verbal sounds 84–5
    riffs 83, 84, **84**
'Resolution' 142
'Sea of Everything' 33
'Sexy Motherfucker' 31
'Sign o' the Times' 67
'Slave' 32
'Soft and Wet' 82
'Somewhere on Earth' 142
'Sticky Like Glue' 33
'Take Me with You' 109
'The Beautiful Ones' 111

'The Holy River' 56, 64–5
'The Ladder' 63
'The One U Wanna C' 142
'Thieves in the Temple' 131
    compression 132–3
    'erotic gaps' 132
    gating 132
    quotation 133
'Thunder' 56, 64
'U Got the Look' 68, 127
    backing vocals 129
    groove 128–9
    guitar playing 128
    recording process 129
'When Doves Cry'
    groove 88, **88**
    LinnDrum use 88
    melodic rhythm 87
    non-bass 85–6, 86
    non-verbal sounds 86–7
    production 89
    Purple Rain film 116
    scatting 88
    vocalizations 86
transculturation 5

videos
    'Cream' 24
    'Raspberry Beret' 49–51, 52

Waksman, Steve 125
Walser, Robert 26, 35
Warner Bros. 17, 19, 30–31, 82
Watkins, Peter, *Privilege* 99
Weber, Max 61
White, Maurice 58
Wicke, Peter 7–8
Wilmer, Val 51
Wonder, Stevie 38, 39
writings, *21 Nights* 1

Yellow 49

Zagorski-Thomas, Simon 129–30
Zazous 43, 47
Zoom 9030 128
Zoot Suiters 46–7